I0030413

Let Them Finish
Stories from the Trenches

Authors:

Melody Zacharias
Kellyn Pot'vin-Gorman
Rie Irish
Randolph West
Sage Franch
Lori Lalonde
Susan Ibach
Elizabeth Hosang
Angela Tidwell
Tracy Boggiano
Brian Carrig
Leighton and Kerrine Nelson

PUBLISHED BY

Melody Zacharias
http://www.SQLMelody.com

Copyright © 2018 by Melody Zacharias
All rights reserved. No part of this book may be reproduced or transmitted in any form or by any means without the prior written permission of the publisher.
ISBN: 978-1-9994310-0-6

Warning and Disclaimer:
Every effort has been made to make this book as complete and as accurate as possible, but no warranty of fitness is implied. The information provided is on an "as is" basis. The authors and the publisher shall have neither liability nor responsibility to any person or entity with respect to any loss or damages arising from the information contained in this book.

Feedback Information

We'd like to hear from you! If you have any comments about how we could improve the quality of this book, please don't hesitate to contact us by visiting www.SQLMelody.com or sending an email to SQLMelody@gmail.com.

Foreword

By: John Morehouse

We all come from different walks of life. Some of us are male, some are female, some are Caucasian, some are People of Color, some are gay, some are straight, some are from foreign lands, some are born here in the United States, and we all probably have varying religious beliefs or perhaps none at all. That which makes someone different from another could go on for pages. None of these characteristics make one individual more important than another. Yet, we often find ourselves aligning to those individuals that share our traits and our own characteristics as that makes us more comfortable. Discussions around difficult topics with other people who share our own values is much easier. These conversations however create boundaries within ourselves and our cultures. These boundaries prevent the exploration of new ideas, new thoughts and desires and cause us to be stagnant.

Diversity, however, helps to break down these boundaries, plain and simple. Inclusion of different people from different walks of life help to bring a unique set of viewpoints into conversations. These varying opinions hopefully force us to think outside of ourselves, to examine our own thoughts and beliefs and reach beyond our boundaries. Diversity should be an element that which binds us together in humanity and allows us to move forward.

Unfortunately, that isn't always the case. Diversity is difficult at times. This is just a simple truth. It will make your blood boil one day and be the cause for joyous celebration the next. Diversity will make you question the sanity of others.

Here's the trick. Hard is just that, hard. Hard is not objective. Hard is subjective. What is hard for one individual is not necessarily hard for another. Plain and simple. Hard, however, does not give way to impossible. Very little in this life is impossible (ok, time travel is probably impossible) with the right knowledge, desire, and willingness to challenge our boundaries.

Even though it is hard, we should heed caution. A stone thrown into a body of water can cause downstream ripples with unforeseen problems. Diversity can also cause ripples in the water. This is not to say that you can be too diverse; rather that diversity can lead groups of people who think they are diverse to exclude others in the name of diversity. Conversations in which other individuals are not heard because they happen to be male, or female, or white, or black, or well, really pick any characteristic only defeats the purpose of diversity.

As you read the forthcoming chapters in this book, I urge you to keep in mind that hard is just hard. Yes, some individuals have it easier than you. Some have it harder than you. Neither of those two negate that an individual's experiences are less or more valuable or valid than your own. Each of these authors have shared their unique stories to help bring their own diversity to light. It isn't a competition of who has it harder; it's just hard.

Also, make sure that you aren't throwing a stone into the water. The ripples of change can be a good thing when done correctly; however, it can be devastating if done incorrectly. Tread carefully. Ask questions, listen, talk softly and have compassion. Diversity is meant to help ease the impacts of the ripples.

Finally, open your mind. Listen to these stories. As you read them, challenge your own thoughts and beliefs. Reach beyond your own boundaries. After all, this is life and let's face it, none of us will be getting out alive. Let us all strive to have more compassion, patience, and understanding for the those that have a different walk of life. Doing so will only make humanity stronger.

Acknowledgements

The writing of this book was a collaborative effort taken up by many very talented IT professionals. All too often, books like this get derailed due to some, but usually most of the authors getting bogged down by work, life, family, health, or some other unexpected ordeal. So, it needs to be acknowledged that these authors can be relied upon to complete the things they commit to. You all possess a rare and valuable talent.

IDERA has been invaluable by providing the support and encouragement needed. They provided the light at the end of the tunnel that gives us all hope that the many hours spent after work (and family), is not all in vain. The avenues for distribution that they are providing was necessary for all of us to justify our efforts. This support shows their leadership and should make talented people want to work for and with IDERA.

I give a very sincere "thank you" to all of you for your contributions to this book. I hope you all feel as I do, that the effort to bring the messages in this book to light was worthwhile.

Melody Zacharias

Editors

Meagan Longoria – MVP: Data Platform

Meagan Longoria is a Solution Architect with BlueGranite who lives in Denver, Colorado. She is a Microsoft Data Platform MVP who spends a lot of time thinking about how to use Biml, DAX, and data visualization techniques to make data useful for people. Meagan has over ten years of experience with business intelligence, data warehousing, and reporting. She has presented at PASS Summit, IT/Dev Connections, the Kansas City Developer Conference, and many SQL Saturdays and user group meetings across North America. Meagan is a board member of the Denver SQL Server User Group and an active member of the Mile Hi Power BI User Group.

You can visit her blog at DataSavvy.me or follow her on Twitter at @MMarie.

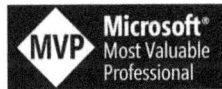

Teresa Ouellette

Teresa Ouellette currently resides in Victoria BC and has lived in or visited most of the provinces and territories of Canada. She has worked and volunteered in many capacities including Library Technician, Health and Safety Officer, Office Manager, Administrative Assistant, Computer Operator, Technical Services Coordinator, various positions in a women's shelter and girls group home, on a crisis line and is currently employed as a Business Consultant. All of this variety has provided a wealth of experience for this mother of 2 young adults and new grandmother. She enjoys all aspects of the great outdoors and is in her happy place on a new hiking trail, exploring a new neck of the woods or curled up with a cup of coffee and a good book.

Melody Zacharias – MVP: Data Platform

If you read about me in the Author section, it was mentioned that I wear many hats. This is an excellent example of what that means. In this book, you will find my name under the Author banner, the Editor banner, and the Publisher banner. The publisher also let me write the synopsis on the back cover as well as the Acknowledgements.

Data is my passion, but coffee is a very close friend.

You can follow my blog at: SQLMelody.com

You can learn more about the IT services my company provides at Clearsight-Solutions.ca

You can follow my infrequent Twitter posts at: @SQLMelody

Contents

CHAPTER 1

Let Her Finish: Supporting Women's Voices in IT

By: Rie Irish - Microsoft MVP Data Platform

There is an interesting anecdote about Bill Gates giving a lecture in Saudi Arabia. He had been invited to give a speech and found himself facing a segregated audience. The vast majority of the audience was made up of men, with a small contingent of women segregated on the side and separated from the men by a partition. All the women were wearing a niqab with a veil. During the question and answer session, one man stood up and asked if it was realistic for Saudi Arabia to become one of the top ten countries in the world in technology. Mr. Gates responded with, "… [I]f you're not fully utilizing half the talent in your country, you're not going to get too close to the top ten."

There is some argument as to whether the events in the anecdote actually occurred, but unless you are stuck in the 1950's, the sentiment should ring true.

Next time you attend a meeting, watch what happens when women at the table offer ideas. If your office is like most in America, you'll notice women are interrupted almost three times as often as men. Some interruptions are intended to offer support & be helpful. Other times, the interruption is an attempt to assert dominance. Regardless of why it's happening, the results are the same: Women are being pushed out of the conversation. When our voices aren't heard, we can't be part of the decision-making process, we can't display our talents, and we don't catch the eye of those in upper management that could bring promotions.

Headlines these days are full of examples of how IT can be a hostile place for women. It's harder to be successful with a lack of effective mentors, a "Brogammer" culture, and women constantly having to fight to have our voices heard. The consequences are real. Being heard & included translates directly to performance come review time. The wage gap isn't closing as fast as it should. Women are leaving tech at 2.5 times the rate of men, and 47% of women in tech are considering a career change in the next year.

This chapter will argue that these are real issues. We'll cover positive solutions that help women's voices be heard. We'll talk about how your culture and company can help women thrive. Women need to learn to say "Let me finish.", "Stop interrupting me." and "I just said that." Men can be, and HAVE to be, part of the solution. They can help women become part of the conversation. This topic is important for men and women in IT because a rising tide lifts all boats. We need men to be our allies at work. Women can't solve this on our own. Learn how you can help make your team work better together, create better solutions to problems and without conflict to get there.

Speaking While Female

An American workplace study in 2015 found that men not only interrupted twice as often as women, they were 3 times as likely to interrupt a woman. This same study found that women almost never interrupt men. An Australian study from the same year found that women don't speak as much without interruption as men. When they looked at a series of speaking engagements like city council meetings, presentations, board meetings, court cases, etc. the results were revealing.

Of the 311 interruptions questioning a speaker's authority and credibility, 213 were directed towards women. Female witnesses were called emotional, unreasonable, or words to similar effect 163 times. Of those gendered comments, 120 were made by men. Additionally, women were more likely to be punished for their interruptions than their male peers by the chair during public hearings.

In early 2017, the US Senate held hearings to determine if Jeff Sessions (R-Alabama) should be confirmed as the US Attorney General after being appointed to the office by the 45th President of the United States. During these hearings, **Senator Elizabeth Warren** (D-Massachusetts) attempted to read a letter into the Congressional record on the Senate floor. The 30 year-old letter, authored by Coretta Scott King, directly addressed the topic at hand – the ability of Jeff Sessions to protect the civil rights of all Americans. Just as importantly, the letter was already part of Senate history. In 1986, it had been read by Ted Kennedy (D-Massachusetts) during Senate hearings regarding Senator Sessions' nomination to be a federal judge.

Do you think it's an example of politics and not sexism? What if I told you that over the next 24 hours, 4 other senators were allowed to read the letter in part or in full, without interruption or admonishment. Their names are Tom Udall, Jeff Merkley, Sherrod Brown and Bernie Sanders. I'm sure you can easily tell what they have in common. They're men. Men who were allowed to speak.

During a September 2016 US Presidential debate, Donald Trump interrupted Hillary Clinton a total of 51 times. She interrupted him only 17 times. If we're going to count all the times Secretary Clinton was interrupted by the debate moderator, that number jumps to 70 times. During the same campaign, Matt Lauer was widely criticized for the disproportionate number of times he interrupted Hilary Clinton during an interview. Women across America collectively shrugged. They knew what it was like, this wasn't new or shocking. Just another day that ends in "y".

Even When She's a Professional Equal

South By SouthWest (SXSW) is an annual conglomerate of film, interactive media, and music festivals and conferences located in Austin, TX. Each year, there are 7 days of music and art, but also discussion panels, keynotes, and other offerings to professionals from around the world to share ideas. During a 2015 gender & diversity panel, Google's Executive Chair Eric Schmidt and Steve Jobs biographer Walter Isaacson repeatedly interrupted U.S. Chief Technology Officer Megan Smith, the sole female panelist on stage during the talk. Finally, during the Q&A portion of the panel, he was reprimanded by an audience member. This woman, Judith Williams, also happened to be Google's global diversity manager. "Given that unconscious bias research tells us that women are interrupted a lot more than men, I'm wondering if you are aware that you have interrupted Megan many more times?" Williams asked, to uproarious applause and approval from the audience.

It would seem that few women can escape being interrupted or spoken over. Even when you're a justice on the US Supreme court. The male justices on the court spent a lot of time interrupting the two youngest female justices, Elena Kagan and Sonia Sotomayor. In recent sessions, Justice Sotomayor was interrupted 57 times during arguments, while Kagan got cut off 50 times. Justices Breyer, Roberts, Kennedy, and Alito are interrupted at half that rate, anywhere from 24 to 27 times. The only female justice who isn't interrupted at increased rates is Justice Ruth Bader Ginsberg. The prevailing theory as to why this is the case gives credit to her petite stature, quiet voice and the profoundness of her words are when she finally does speak. It is impossible to interrupt the Notorious RBG without coming across as aggressive and being very aware of it.

YEARS ago, while producing the hit TV series "The Shield," Glen Mazzara noticed that two young female writers were quiet during story meetings. Knowing he wanted to hear their ideas and wanted them to contribute, he pulled them aside and encouraged them to speak up more.

Watch what happens when we do, they replied.

Almost every time they started to speak, they were interrupted or shot down before finishing their pitch. When one had a good idea, a male writer would jump in and run with it before she could complete her thought. Mazzara found a clever way to change the dynamics that were holding those two female employees back. He announced to the writers that he was instituting a no-interruption rule while anyone — male or female — was pitching. It worked, and he later observed that it made the entire team more effective.

Amplification

During the 2ⁿᵈ term of the Obama Administration, he had assembled the most diverse cabinet of any president before him. This wasn't quite the case during his first term, but as those initial appointees graduated from the administration, they were replaced by women and persons of color. But these women identified a problem. They weren't getting invited to the meetings where decisions were being made. And when they did, they weren't being heard. So they came up with a two part plan. First, once they did make it into the meeting, they invited another woman from the team. Second, when a woman in a meeting presented an idea or made a key point, they repeated it and gave her credit for it. Doing this simple thing, which seems so obvious now, forced the men in the room to recognize the contribution — and denied them the chance to claim the idea as their own. They called this technique "Amplification". I've tried it and can attest that it works beautifully.

Dealing with the Interruption

So what's a working woman to do? We've established that she's going to get interrupted frequently. How can we limit the impact? Let's talk about some techniques you can use to foil the interrupter's plans.

Let it go, but follow up with a question instead of disengaging. Stop speaking & wait for a break in what they're saying. Then re-engage them, pull yourself back into the discussion by asking a question about their contribution to the conversation.

Another, more indirect approach, is to simply let the person interrupt, *then repeat again exactly what you started saying*, in a polite, respectful tone. Wait until there's a break in their statement and start over. Say everything you said in your sentence up until that point and then continue.

When you want them to stop speaking over you, add in a hand gesture as you continue speaking. The idea is to ever so slightly raise your hand with your palm facing slightly above parallel to the ground. You might even lift you index finger slightly apart from the rest. Accompany this with the facial expression that's part patient nod & part "give me a moment".

Lightly touch the interrupter & say that you'd like to finish. If they're sitting near you in the meeting, lightly touch their hand or arm & repeat the gesture from above. They'll pause in their comments & you'll be allowed to continue.

Just keep talking. This is probably the hardest one to do. Just continue talking in your normal voice as if the person hasn't interrupted you. Women are taught to be polite from childhood. Be nice, be quiet, know your place. We have a lower threshold for what's considered rude behavior. Even though this person has interrupted us, we are hesitant to be perceived as rude ourselves. My advice: Be rude. Just a little. Okay, maybe a lot. Make sure your ideas are heard.

10 Words Every Woman Should Learn

They're small phrases but very powerful. You should take them for a test drive today. Teach yourself to own your half of the conversation and not let it get stolen from you.

"I just said that. Let me finish. Stop interrupting me."

Just as important are 10 words every man should learn. Let's face it, we can't solve the gender in tech crisis by ourselves. If we could, our mother's generation would have handled it and we'd all be on the patio sipping sangria, enjoying a good laugh. We need the good men out there to stand up and be our allies. We need good men to have our backs in these meetings. We need them to pay attention when this kind of thing happens and say "She just said that. Let her finish. Stop interrupting her."

The Feminized Society Myth

Do you think women are represented equally in movies, TV, and news? Do you think they get an equitable amount of screen or speaking time? Think of a TV show or a news program that you frequently watch. If your answer is yes, then I hate to be the one to tell you that you're probably wrong.

Each year, The Center for the Study of Women in Television and Film examines on-screen representations of female characters in the top 100 grossing films every year. Its findings in 2014 were less than ideal. Men made up 75% of protagonists or the character from whose perspective the narrative is told, while 13% were male/female ensembles. This leaves women with a very disappointing 12% of the storytelling market share. Females comprised 29% of major characters. Females accounted for only 30% of all speaking characters. If you wanted ethnic or racial diversity in your movie experience, then 2014 was not the year for you. 74% of all female characters were White, 11% were Black, 4% were Latina, 4% were Asian, and 3% were female "aliens".

In a study published in 2015, two linguists, Carmen Fought and Karen Eisenhauer, examined every Disney movie since *Snow White* first debuted in 1937. They were measuring female representation from screen time to speaking parts. The trend used to be that female characters dominated speaking time: *Sleeping Beauty* and *Cinderella* garnered 71% and 60% respectively. In the modern era, only Brave, Inside Out, Tangled and Maleficent have females speaking the majority of the time. Take, for example, the movie *Frozen*. Two Strong, independent female leads. Sisters. Heroines. This film has to be heavy in female speaking time, right? Hardly. The main characters, Elsa and Anna, are responsible for only 41% of the speaking time, while the male secondary characters make up almost 60% of speaking time. In the ten years between 1989 and 1999, a serious shift in the balance occurred. In *Aladdin*, Jasmine & other female characters speak for only 10% of the film. In *Pocohontas*, the title character manages a mere 24% of talk time. In Mulan, the movie about a girl warrior that SAVES ALL OF CHINA, female characters speak only 23% of the time.

I'm willing to bet those numbers surprised you. So how have we never noticed this before? These are female targeted films so surely female characters dominate the story. It's called the Gender Disparity Gap, and it's real. Just like a fish doesn't know it's in water, our brains have learned to accept what we're presented as the norm. The Geena Davis Institute for Gender in Media did an analysis across a broad spectrum of media, compiling talk & screen time for men & women. Then they followed up by asking both men and women to judge when the two genders reached parity or equal screen/talk time.

Men perceive 50-50 gender parity if women make up a mere 17% of screen/speaking time. When that number reaches a staggering 33% for women, men perceive women are getting the majority of screen-time. There is a pervasive myth that we live in a feminized society, that women get their way, that they run things, that we control anything, that we talk all the time and have a voice. But it is a myth. One study found that women had to make up 60-80% of attendees in a meeting to occupy equal time in conversation. When asked about importance, 80% of women in business think gender parity should be a priority compared to only 48% of men.

What is Gender Bias?

Bias (noun)- Any tendency which prevents unprejudiced consideration of a question or behavior. Gender bias occurs because individuals' stereotypes and prejudices about gender become implicitly, unknowingly, but systematically implemented into every-day life.

Simply put, it's an unfair difference in the way men and women are perceived. It comes in many forms. Even gender is a cultural term. The very definition involves culturally constructed roles and expectations for men and women and for girls and boys. Women are expected to act in a way defined as feminine: quiet, kind, subservient, etc. Men are expected to act masculine: loud, aggressive, powerful, etc. People quite often use the terms Gender Bias and Sexism interchangeably, but they aren't the same. Gender Bias includes both prejudice and discrimination.

Where Does all of this Come From?

Where does bias come from? We go out into the world & make decisions every moment of every day. We possess an instinct that tells us if a person, place or object is safe or not. This is what guides our "fight or flight" response. We're hard wired this way. When we see something or someone that *feels* dangerous, we have already launched into action subconsciously before we have even started thinking. Our sense of comfort or discomfort has already been engaged.

Our minds have grown accustomed over the years to seeing male leaders and women working in the home. Television bombards us with images of what we should be, what we should like, and how we should behave. Society has cultivated an image over the years of what it means to be a woman and what it means to be a man. Our culture is so awash in gender bias for both men and women, it's become the very definition & fabric of our everyday lives. Bias can be like an iceberg. You're only aware of about 10% of it. It's unconscious, learned behavior. And so begins the source of bias…

"If you asked me to name the greatest discoveries of the past 50 years, alongside things like the internet and the Higgs particle, I would include the discovery of unconscious biases…"

Prof. Nancy Hopkins MIT Professor of Biology, Boston University Graduation 5/18/2014

Gender Bias in Hiring

In the 1970's there were virtually no women in the more prestigious professional orchestras. In the 1980's, that number was less than 10%. When asked why this was the case, conductors & adjudicators gave reasons like "The more women, the poorer the sound." "Women are more temperamental than men and more likely to demand special attention." "I just don't think women should be in an orchestra." This is despite a graduation rate for women at Juilliard of 45%. Having the disparity pointed out to the them, the industry decided to make some changes. They instituted blind auditions. Adjudicators and musicians were separated by a curtain. The floor was muffled. They didn't exchange any conversation. The results were immediate. Women quickly made up almost 45% of orchestra musicians.

In a 1999 study, Steinpreis, Anders, & Ritzke set out to examine the impact of gender on our decision making in resume review & hiring. Search teams made up of university professors were asked to evaluate candidates for a tenure-track assistant professor position for a psychology department. Resumes were sent out that were identical with one exception. They contained different, gender-specific names: Karen Miller and Brian Miller. Both men and women overwhelmingly chose to hire the male candidate. Search committees preferred Brian to Karen with a 2:1 ratio. When evaluating their experience, search teams expressed reservations for Karen 4 times more often than they did for Brian. Karen was described as less competent and less hirable. On Karen's resumes with more experience but less education, they would indicate they were looking for more schooling. On her resumes with more education but less experience, as you can probably guess, they wanted a longer work history. The female candidate was often recommended a lower salary... up to 40% lower.

In fact, they frequently called into question the validity & honesty of her credentials with judgement without teaching evaluations. And my personal favorite, "I would need to see evidence that she had gotten the grants and publications on her own."

Why Does it Matter?

In a piece for the New York Times, Sheryl Sandberg and Adam Grant talked about the balancing act that women are faced with. "When a woman speaks in a professional setting, she walks a tightrope," they write. "Either she's barely heard or she's judged as too aggressive." Women are told to not be bossy while getting dinged on a review for not being aggressive enough.

- Male executives who speak more often than their peers are rewarded with 10% higher ratings of competence. When female executives speak more than their peers, they're punished with 14 percent lower ratings. This translates directly into money when it comes time to hand out raises.
- In 2015, a University of Texas study showed that when a woman challenged an existing process and suggested a new one, she was considered to be disloyal. Even when they were told she possessed unique knowledge on the topic, her ideas were discounted. The same did not apply for men.
- When women's voices aren't heard, they aren't assigned "stretch projects" that get them noticed, get them promoted and get them assigned to the next big thing. In short, guys get to work on the cool stuff while women are stuck doing the technical house work.
- Women are far more likely to receive personality criticism during a performance review. Men receive comments like:
  "Take time to slow down and listen. You would achieve even more."
- *Women are far more likely to be told:*
  "You can come across as abrasive sometimes. I know you don't mean to, but you need to pay attention to your tone."
- *The not-so-constructive feedback for women includes things like:*
  "watch your tone" and "be nice"

In an article published in Forbes in 2014, Kieran Snyder found that personality criticism showed up only twice in 83 critical male reviews but showed up an astonishing 71 out of 94 reviews of women.

Why Women Are Leaving Tech

It's no longer just a pipeline issue. Not anymore. Women are leaving tech at an alarming rate. Currently the rate for women leaving tech is more than twice the rate as men (41% vs 17%). High school boys & girls participate in STEM at about the same rate, and many elite colleges report 50% of Intro to Computer Science classes are women. Yet men are employed in STEM occupations at twice the rate of women. At larger tech companies, men outnumber women 4 to 1. Of women in technology fields, 27% reported feeling stalled (48% of AA women) and 32% reported they are likely to quit within the next year

- **Lack of helpful mentorship:** When women received mentorship, it's advice on *how they should change*. With men, it's concrete steps for career moves. Reviews of women are far more likely to contain personality criticism while men are praised for the same behaviors.

- **Organizational Climate:** Women often describe feeling like an outsider in what they describe as mildly discriminatory environment. It's that "Brogrammer" culture. Recruiters even pursue developers with promises of foosball tables & kegs in the office instead of highlighting collaborative, flexible working environments. Tech companies hire so few females that it is common to be the only women in a company's IT department. It's very isolating and uncomfortable. You'd like to be treated no differently, just "one of the guys", but can't if that involves strip clubs or talking about the weekend's conquests.

- **Unclear Evaluation Criteria:** Women are frequently given vague, unactionable feedback. Be nice. Watch your tone. Try not to be so bossy. Men with a highly visible leadership style are described positively, while women are described as "abrasive" or "running over people"

- **Company & HR policies** that make it harder for women to stay employed. Women often cite a lack of or short maternity leave and not enough flexibility. In our culture, women are still the de facto care taker when you have children. So when winter rolls around & kids start coming home from school with a cough, it's the Mom that would most benefit from a flexible schedule. The wage gap is real, and it starts when a woman sends HR her resume. Women candidates are undervalued & research shows they're offered less money based solely on their gender.

- **Not having their voices heard.** Women cite a lack of visibility on "stretch assignments", having to prove themselves over and over, lack of advancement opportunities, and having their ideas appropriated by men.

- **Untrained Managers:** technical women often rank their managers lowest on communication skills, receptiveness to ideas, availability & feedback compared to technical men. Think about how it works in IT. Someone is a great developer, so he gets promoted to team lead. He's a great team lead so he gets promoted to manager. Nowhere along the way has the company offered him any management training. He's winging it. In many cases, these developers turned bosses have a management style that is more like old friends than supervisor/employee. So when presented with a new developer that he has less in common with, who doesn't go out for beer with the guys after work, was in a sorority rather than a fraternity, doesn't hike or bike…. He doesn't have the skill set he needs to be her boss.

Solutions to Keep Women in Tech

- Start with your human resources department. Hold recruiters and hiring managers accountable if ever candidate they pursue looks the same. Explain how unconscious bias works and how we're all prone to fall victim to bad instincts. Make sure men and women with equivalent credentials start out at equal levels and the rate is competitive with the industry. Your company should routinely evaluate the pay ranges of their staff to insure they aren't falling short of the law.

- Engage and empower senior male and female executives to "sponsor" up & coming women. Sponsorship is more than advice or mentoring. This involves using influence with senior executives to get female employees invited to the meeting and to make sure their ideas are heard. A sponsor can be instrumental in helping someone get assigned to a stretch project. With a sponsor, women are 70% more likely to see their ideas implemented.

- Make performance standards crystal clear with granular detail & actionable advice focused on performance instead of vague advice. Stop the "be nice" or "watch your tone" comments in reviews. Include items that give someone an actual path to improvement or promotion. Concrete steps they can take with regards to projects or assignments that will get them noticed by upper management.

- Train managers on providing actionable feedback performance reviews and then hold them accountable. Train your managers on how to be a good boss to everyone on their team. Make sure they understand that diversity within a team leads to better solutions & product breakthroughs because of the wide range of experiences on the team

- Finally, Institute HR policies that don't penalize women & encourage flexibility. Make sure your maternity leave policy is industry standards. Allow employees to work flexible schedules that fit the needs of their family while still giving them a chance to be successful at work.

CHAPTER 2

You don't look Gay

By: Randolph West - Microsoft MVP Data Platform

Content warning: this chapter might make some people feel uncomfortable because it discusses sex. I encourage you to read it all the same. Sex is nothing to be ashamed of.

When we contemplate what it means to be human, expression of self is the most sacred of all things. How you see yourself, and how you want the world to see you, is the single most important driving force of humanity today.

But first a bit of background. This will necessitate a look at human history as well, for context. While I can't promise to keep it short, I'll do my best to make it interesting. I like history. It's a special interest of mine.

Queer Soup

When you were born, you were assigned a sex at birth by a doctor or midwife. This sex classification would have been male or female, based on your physical genitalia. That's all there is to it. Our entire lives are dictated by some soft tissue between our legs when we are born which we don't even take seriously for the next ten to fifteen years.

Before very long, we are assigned traditional roles based on that single physical characteristic. We are dressed in traditional clothing made up from traditional colours. We are encouraged to play sports that everyone else with the same sex assignment plays. If you somehow feel like you want to go against that assignment for any reason, societal norms say that it's wrong. There's no reason for it, it's just wrong.

This is what heteronormativity is: the socially preferred ("normal") view that we can divide everything into two sides, and that we are expected to fit neatly into that binary system.

Unfortunately, this neat convenience is just that: convenient. How can a physical characteristic assigned at birth by someone else possibly account for your own feelings, desires, and self-expression? That's where gender identity comes into it.

I learned more about gender and sex identity in three months on Tumblr than I did in the previous 35 years of traditional education. And what I discovered is that gender is whatever you want it to mean. However, because sex and gender are conflated in Western society, this is as good a place as any to talk about alphabet soup. Every June in North America it seems like there are more letters to memorize for Pride Month.

Unless you've been living off the grid, you will have seen some variation of these letters to describe people who do not fit into the heteronormative sex or gender binary. This is what those letters mean. Some are overloaded with two or more meanings, and some are region-specific.

L - lesbian (women who have romantic or sexual attraction to other women)

G - gay (men who have romantic or sexual attraction to other men)

B - bisexual (men and women who have romantic or sexual attraction to other men and women)

T - trans (gender identity or expression that is different to their assigned sex)

Q - queer / questioning (this can also include gender-fluid or gender-queer people)

I - intersex (physical sex characteristics are ambiguous)

A - asexual / agender / aromantic (the "a-" prefix means "not")

2 - two-spirit (Native American only: a third gender not defined by identity or sexual attraction)

The A is not for "Ally".

You may see these letters written out as (for example) LGBTQ, LGBTQIA, LGBTQ2, and in some cases followed by plus signs (LGBTQ+), because humans are bad at labels and inclusivity. While there has been discussion over the years to find one word for this group of people, there is no consensus. And anyway, what's the point? If we ignore individual definitions of identity and expression, we silence and erase the people who use them. It's like some Americans of Irish descent calling themselves "Irish". Who am I to judge?

Other words that don't have a letter to describe them include pansexual (sexual attraction to any gender or sexual identity), demisexual (sexual attraction only after you get to know someone, irrespective of sex or gender), and allosexual (the opposite of asexual).

Humans love labels, and for some reason we love them more if they are scientific. Homo sapiens. Brassica oleracea. Heterosexual. Cisgender. These are just words to describe things. Cisgender describes a person whose gender matches the sex they were assigned at birth: AMAB stands for "assigned male at birth", while AFAB stands for "assigned female at birth". Most people who read this are cisgender. It's not an insult used by "liberals" or "SJWs" (social justice warriors); it's a literal description of most of the 100 billion people who have lived and died on Planet Earth. If you feel offended by this label, maybe you need to look at the other letters and see if something fits.

I know this is a lot to take in, and who has time for it? Surely, it's just better if we pick one or two words and stick with it? Right? Here's the thing, though. Words have power. Words are used to oppress and suppress. What if I asked you to stick with a label you had no say in. It's like identifying by the nickname you were called at school.

Through the years of human civilization, humans have considered themselves superior to other species, including animals, by divine right. And because that's how humans think, we've extended definitions of our superiority to make it "scientific" that people themselves are different in some way or another. Foreigners. Women. Slaves. Melatonin-rich people in general. There's a good chance I'll be accused of saying that the Bible made us racist white misogynists, but there's an element of truth to it.

A Look Back

By definition we call everything before recorded history "pre-history", and that just refers to a pre-historic time. It doesn't specifically mean the time of cave people, though in terms of human pre-history, the cave people are somewhere right near the beginning of that story.

Humans that first looked like us developed around 200,000 years ago. Humans that behaved like us (abstract thought, art, and technology including hunting implements) developed around 50,000 years ago. It took another 10,000 years for modern humans to leave Southern Africa and spread across the world.

The Neolithic period (neo means "new", lithic means "stone") started around 12,000 years ago (10,000 BCE). That's when we figured out agriculture, which in turn caused us to change from a nomadic lifestyle (moving around all the time to find food) to forming settlements. And that is when we started rapidly developing as a species.

Recorded human history goes back to around 5,000 years ago. That's the time of the Sumerians and Ancient Egyptians, and coincidentally (but importantly), the earliest forms of writing. The Sumerians figured out a way to write on clay tablets, which means a lot of their cuneiform script has survived. Two thousand years before they developed writing (around 5000 BCE), the Sumerians moved to an agricultural lifestyle. They developed mathematics a thousand years after that.

I don't want to downplay the Sumerian influence on modern humanity. They were one of three civilizations that invented wheeled vehicles (the wheel itself was discovered earlier). They also invented arithmetic, developed writing at the same time as the Ancient Egyptians, came up with a legal system, developed irrigation, and invented new hunting implements and military weapons. As with all human culture, they had a mythology.

To summarise, we had more than 40,000 years of abstract thought until the Bronze Age came along around 6,000 years ago. I don't know about you, but it's mind-boggling to me that we have no knowledge of nearly 90% of human history. Except that we do.

Those 40,000 years without writing or staying in one place would have required the sharing of language, ideas, concepts, dangerous plants and animals to avoid, bedtime stories, and history lessons. In other words, mythology developed in different cultures over those years, and with agriculture eventually ushering in the Bronze Age, we had the beginning of the stories that became Sumerian and Egyptian mythology, which in turn influenced European traditions. In fact, a lot of the Bronze Age civilizations are referred to by name in the Hebrew Bible (commonly known as the Old Testament).

Many cultures borrowed from Sumerian mythology in the same way that West Side Story is pretty much the same plot as Romeo and Juliet. It is only in more recent years, relatively speaking, that we consider original ideas to have higher value than copying others. You can thank the printing press for that.

Before writing, there was oral tradition, meaning that a culture's history, moral code, ethics and knowledge were passed down through word of mouth to younger generations. Some more abstract concepts might be taught through parables or fables, not because it was less intellectual, but because it was easier to remember. Think of the stories your own parents or caregivers taught you. A mythology containing stories of natural spirits and gods might be have started as warnings of dangerous plants and animals, that through human creativity became more colourful over the generations.

With the development of writing, the oral traditions of many pre-historic cultures could be recorded, and those writings could be handed down alongside or instead of the mythology. We have examples of that today. You will teach your children to read and write, but you'll also tell them jokes and stories you learned from family and friends that have no copies in writing.

But to my original point, writing hasn't been around all that long, and before that we were only just figuring out agriculture and counting to ten. As it happens, it takes around 10,000 years for human skin colour to change based on where we live relative to the equator. A 2015 study led by Dr Iain Mathieson out of Harvard University discovered that "white people" only developed around 8,000 years ago.

In the history of humankind, being white is so insignificant as to be meaningless. If you're a white supremacist, you are not only descended from black people anyway, but these ancestors were black because of the sun.

How does this relate to gender? There is a prevailing myth (and as we've already established, mythology is very powerful, having been around ten times longer than writing) that there are only two genders. What's happened at some point is that we conflated sex and gender.

As I mentioned earlier in this chapter, our physical sex organs are used to define how we are named and raised, when in fact the only relevance they have is how we procreate. It just so happens that we enjoy the act of smushing these sex organs together in several ways that don't result in procreation. Add to this a Bronze Age mythology that guilts us into thinking it's bad to feel good, because 6,000 years ago, humans needed to focus on not getting killed a lot more than they do now.

I get it. Old habits die hard. We've been learning for thousands of years about binary systems. If a culture is imposing a mythology on their people in order to grow their civilization, it is understandable why the act of sex is restricted to making more babies that can be taught the traditions of that civilization. But at some point, we took over the planet and conquered nature with indoor plumbing and diesel-powered SUVs. We also have the Internet which connects billions of humans across the planet and allows us to share our stories and create new ones. This is where Tumblr comes in.

Gender and Sex Identity

We are part of a species that has been identifiably abstract and artistic for 50,000 years. We only really started talking about gender being the same as sex in the last few hundred years. Think about that for a moment. What we know now is that gender is not the same as your biological sex organs. We've only spent one percent of our time on earth as smart humans talking about gender as a thing, and how it is a part of your personal identity.

But speaking of one percent, here's something that might blow your mind. Between 1 and 2% of all (yes, all) humans have red hair. There are over 7 billion people alive today, so that's between 70 and 140 million people with red hair, or as much as one third of the population of the United States.

Did you know that the percentage of Intersex people could be as high as 1.7%? As mentioned in the earlier list, Intersex people have ambiguous physical sex characteristics. It is prevalent enough that medical professionals have developed visual classifications for genitalia that decide whether a baby is "male" or "female". One of these is the Quigley scale, which defines seven classes between "fully masculine" and "fully feminine" genitalia. Seven does not go into two, so for cultural and social reasons, doctors may perform surgery to make the ambiguity less evident. Parents might be ashamed and not tell their children. And those are just the sex organs you can see at birth. Other people may only discover that they are Intersex when they hit puberty. This doesn't even cover genetic factors, including people who have more X chromosomes than the average (known as Klinefelter syndrome).

Put simply, there are tens of millions of people alive today who are born with sex characteristics that do not fit the socially acceptable binary of male and female. Just as you know someone with red hair, and irrespective of how you feel about male and female, someone you know was born Intersex.

Gender is a social construct. We are coded to behave in certain ways, prefer certain colours, play certain sports, and take interest in certain things based solely on the genitalia we are born with. Assuming for the moment that these smushy bits are on the left or right side of the Quigley scale, it is nothing more than a cultural habit to define what someone should like or do based on external characteristics. It is the same as saying that a child with red hair should learn the piano.

Interestingly, cultural habits can change, and they do change. Before 1900, pink was considered a masculine colour and blue a feminine colour. This changed in the 1930s and 1940s. As recently as 1953, Americans began associating pink with being feminine. How quickly we forget.

Pink is just a colour, folks. Skin colour literally changed from black to white less than 10,000 years ago. It only took 70 to turn pink into a colour for girls. Children don't care what genitalia they have. They don't care what colour you dress them in. They don't care what the colour of their skin is. Why do you care so much about it?

Diversity, the theme of this book, is not just a word bandied about by people on social media. Humans are a mix of different cultures, colours, genders, sexual orientations, who have likes and dislikes including TV shows and films, food, books, and so on. Some people like the same things, and you might choose to be friends with them. Some people might like different things, exposing you to ways of thinking that you can use to create completely new ideas. You could use parts of Sumerian mythology to come up with a story about a saviour who comes to earth to cleanse the sins of your ancestors. You could use parts of Japanese mythology to come up with a story about a boy from a desert planet who saves a galaxy from a tyrant with the help of a green space wizard.

Diversity is a human thing, which means it's a messy thing, and labels chosen by other people aren't helping. If you meet someone who doesn't conform to gender norms, respect their choice. If we can memorise the name of our favourite Starbucks drink, so too can we accept personal pronouns.

And for goodness sake, let people use the toilets they want to. Every toilet on a plane, on a bus, or in your own home, is gender-neutral. If you're looking at other people's sex organs while they're eliminating, maybe you're the problem.

Gay

Gender is many things, but one thing it is not, is the basis of sexual orientation. How I identify myself (a choice) has no bearing on who I am romantically or sexually attracted to (not a choice). We can dress it up in terms like "man crush", but it's increasingly evident that sexual attraction is not linked to body parts.

This confuses people. It confused me for the longest time. The simple fact is that people are people. If someone identifies as a woman, they are a woman. If they identify as a man, they are a man. Surgery and outward physical appearance don't define gender, nor should they.

I am sexually attracted to people who identify as men. I am also attracted to really smart people, which has made things awkward once or twice in my 20s after I came out at 19 as "not straight". As for gender identity, my best label so far is "Randolph", and if I'm questioned further, "go fuck yourself".

I dress, walk and talk like a man. For convenience (there's that word again) I call myself gay. I have the privilege to do so, and I live in a country that accepts this label. People are comfortable with the idea of men living together now, and adding "guilt-free warlock unicorn" isn't helping anyone outside of my subculture.

I'm the luckiest person I know. Lucky to be alive. Lucky to have all my limbs. Lucky to have almost full control of my mental faculties. Lucky to get paid from time to time to do interesting things. As lucky as I have been in my life, there are millions of people in the world who are less fortunate. As I write this in June 2018, there are still 28 states in the United States of America where it possible to fire someone for the simple fact that they are a part of the LGBTQ community.

Even worse, some countries carry the death penalty for the way someone is born.

So yes, I have privilege. I grew up white during the tail end of Apartheid in South Africa. I was in grade 12 the year Nelson Mandela came to power, so it took a while for the sea change to take effect, and the only challengers for jobs I took were other white people. That's the very definition of white privilege, when your competition is only 10% of the population. Heck, my second and third jobs were offered to me by friends. Sure, I had to do interviews, but they were tilted in my favour.

The change that came over the country from 1994 was profound. Hardliners expected, perhaps hoped, for a bloody civil war. Somehow, Nelson Mandela and F.W. de Klerk managed to broker a mostly peaceful transition to fully democratic rule and were awarded a shared Nobel Peace Prize. The country's nuclear arsenal was dismantled. South Africa drew up a new constitution with a Bill of Rights that is still one of the best in the world, including protections for gender and sexual orientation. This may seem trivial in 2018 as I write this, but in 1993 when the interim constitution was drawn up it was a big deal, especially on a continent known for its history of human rights abuses.

Given all that, it's hilarious that a significant percentage of white people are still upset that they are no longer in charge, no longer special, having to compete with ten times the population than before for the same work. And, despite employment equity legislation that tries to improve opportunities for previously disadvantaged people, white people still control a large percentage of the country's economy. Equality is a noble pursuit, but it requires buy-in from everyone.

I knew I was different growing up. It felt like I was from another planet. I didn't understand a lot of what was going on at primary school, or the point of it all. I just wanted to read books. When I did participate, I finished the work easily. However, I was bored and easily distracted. I used big words and was made fun of. I was also bullied because I was one of the youngest kids in my class, and small for my age. Kids called me names, some of them unprintable. Teachers would call me bright but lazy. I was labelled as a gifted child and attended pointless gifted child classes after school for a while. My father bragged about my high IQ to his friends.

Up to then I had interpreted "gifted" to mean that I would never have to work hard to achieve success. As it turns out, that was definitely not the case.

My father died a month after Nelson Mandela came to power and my world imploded. After finishing high school and not getting into the universities I was provisionally accepted at due to poor performance, I took a detour into journalism school, but my heart really wasn't in it. I spent most of my time in the student radio station. Unfortunately, that's where my interest in my major started and ended.

It was at journalism school where I finally realized at the age of 19 that I was attracted to men, despite knowing since I was ten. University was a rough experience when that information was made available to the people around me. When I came out, I was called a liar by omission, and then threatened to have my heart ripped out, that sort of thing. Masculinity is so fragile.

Here's a fun fact. South Africa decriminalized homosexuality in 1997. It required a challenge in the Constitutional Court once the constitution was signed into law in 1996. But decriminalizing it doesn't automatically stop people from hating you. It doesn't protect you from being murdered for wearing a Pride t-shirt, which happened to the son of a person I knew. In many parts of South Africa, as in the rest of Africa, being perceived as gay is an invitation for violence and a possible death sentence.

I came home from journalism school halfway through 1996, recently outed, and later that month my grandmother died. Eight days later, my second grandmother died. Those were interesting times.

It turns out that I'm on the Autism Spectrum. I was diagnosed as an adult with High Functioning Autism. When I got that diagnosis, it was a revelation. It explains a whole lot, but importantly it explains that I don't like change, and when I lost two of the most important figures in my life within eight days, I had the first of several meltdowns. My best friend at the time was witness to his friend losing touch with reality and breaking down. I contemplated suicide several times that year. Each time it came back to what it would do to my mother, brother and sister.

This is not a cry for sympathy. This is not a request for solace. I have grieved the loss of family members just as I'm sure you have in your own life. We are not immune to death. I'm writing all of this to explain what happened next.

I'm white. I present as male. I'm autistic. I'm attracted to men. On the one hand, I have the world at my doorstep. On the other, I might be killed because I'm attracted to men, and I guess heterosexual men feel threatened. Is that the basis for all the hate in the world today, men feeling threatened?

Throughout my younger life I tried to fit in better, which was sometimes tough. When I changed high schools, I stopped performing in choir. I became the class clown in order to deflect attention. If someone was laughing at me, they weren't punching me. I realized that school was a game and figured out how to do the least amount of work for the most recognition.

But after the year of death in 1996, I grew angry. I figured the world owed me something. Then again, if the comment section of the Internet (Twitter) is any indication, anger is a thing that affects many a privileged white kid, so I wasn't unique. I wasn't special. It didn't feel that way at the time. I developed a bite to my humour. One of my friends would say "Be careful you don't cut yourself on that tongue."

Through the lens of 41 years, I can see how petulant and entitled I was. Even now I can regress into that frame of mind, and it's frighteningly easy for me. It takes hard work to be a decent human being. It requires considered thoughtfulness to be kind to others. Most importantly, it requires sheer force of will to apologize for something. Entitlement is an illusion that I was buying wholesale.

Then the best thing happened. I encountered diversity in my own little community. But first, a story.

In 2000, I attended Johannesburg Pride. I didn't actually march in the parade, mind you. Even so, I went with friends to the event, which was a month later than usual, and it rained. A lot of entitled gay white males (GWM) were unhappy with the planning because maybe the beer tent was too busy or they got a little bit wet during the parade. I don't remember why I was upset. Entitled as I was, I figured I could do a better job. After all I was a software developer with a small web hosting company on the side. How hard could it be? ("How hard could it be?" is the rallying cry of average white men the world over.)

In late 2000 I joined a committee that eventually organized the 2001 Johannesburg Pride Parade and Mardi Gras, extending Pride to a week-long series of events including a lot of activities that recognized people and contributions outside of the standard GWM mentality of "party, drugs, party, drink, party, sex, party". I met a lot of people that I normally would never have interacted with. The co-chairs were a black Jamaican lesbian woman and a brown Muslim gay man. For the first time in my life I met militant lesbians complete with short bleach blonde hair and boots, and invited them into my home several times for meetings. It was intense.

Prior to that, my experience of lesbians were mullets who drank beer and played pool at the local gay bars while the "boys" drank cocktails, took ecstasy, and danced to electronic dance music (EDM). And then I joined this committee thinking how I could do a better job and was given a lesson in history and humility.

I learned that the first Pride March in South Africa took place in 1990 (as late as 1990!) and was organized by Simon Nkoli. There were very few attendees because homosexuality was a criminal offence at the time. South Africa had a law that was known colloquially as "two men at a party". If you had more than two men at a party and not enough women, when the police raided you could be arrested for homosexuality and thrown in prison (or "disappeared").

South African members of the LGBT community (as it was known at the time) created their own slang called Gayle. Similar in principle to Polari in the UK, women's names were used as code words. Dora meant "drink". Beulah meant "beautiful". Priscilla meant "police".

This wasn't the big lesson for me, though. I learned that people of all races participated in the first Pride March, and they wore paper bags over their heads so that they wouldn't be recognized.

People of all races. Not just white gays from the suburbs looking for a drink and a good time. I learned about Simon Nkoli, who argued that race and sexual orientation were "inextricably linked" and that he couldn't be free as a black man in South Africa if he wasn't free as a gay man.

I learned about how women argued and won the right to have the G and L swapped around so that we were LGBT and not GLBT. Men already had everything else, even in our community. I met and spoke with some of the original members of the gay rights movement in South Africa. I got into long arguments (from my place of privilege) with community members who were tired of arguing with young white gays but did so anyway.

I learned about what happened during Apartheid to people who didn't look and speak like me, who were murdered or "disappeared".

I realized that I was a small part of a bigger community. I remember discussing the need to hire buses to bring in members of our diverse community to the parade, members who couldn't afford to pay for transport, members who were not white and privileged. And through it all, it was the militant lesbians who showed the most compassion.

As with all committees, the usual attrition took place. People who were fired up at the start were dropping out due to stress, time constraints, and politics. Every committee is political, and you have to deal with keeping the gays with money happy so that the party (which generates all the revenue to pay for Pride) goes ahead, while still being representative of the entire community. There was a Black Pride contingent that we negotiated with to participate in the parade. There was a long argument about the route the parade would take that was safe to walk through (downtown Johannesburg is considered one of the most dangerous cities in the world), and not too far from the centre of the city which was easy to get to.

A few weeks before the parade was due to go ahead, the non-profit that owned the rights to the Pride name and constitution was dissolved for financial reasons. We suspended the Pride constitution in an emergency meeting, and through sheer force of will managed to keep the event running. Two weeks beforehand we still weren't sure if it would go ahead, especially with the new Pride Week concept.

I swore after that experience that I would never serve on a committee again, but thankfully that promise didn't stick. I was given the opportunity to serve on a committee with a shared living history of the LGBTQIA movement in South Africa and Jamaica, and my payoff was leading the 2001 Pride Parade through Johannesburg as a flag bearer (we had a section of the original Pride rainbow flag).

Failing Upwards

I am the luckiest person I know. In my first three jobs, I worked for women. Personality conflicts aside (because remember I was an angry person back then), I credit these bosses for being balanced and fair. When I didn't have a driver's licence, the second boss appealed to my sensibilities to help me get one and become more independent. One time I screwed up with a major client by leaving a profanity-laden voice mail message, only to have it quoted back to me on Monday morning. The same boss didn't have to yell or scream, nor did she fire me. Pure class.

In 2004 I left a good job because I was bored, angry, and stupid. After flailing for a few months, I found work as a junior lecturer at a computer college in downtown Johannesburg. A few days a week I would teach Java at a college comprised of non-white students, all of whom were on full scholarships. I discovered my love for teaching in the three months I spent there, and even through depressive episodes, the absolute joy on my students' faces when I walked into the class was my motivation.

At the start of the following year, following the teaching bug, I took a job as a high school teacher at a prestigious private school in the north of Johannesburg. There's nothing like earning the equivalent of $500 a month at a school where the annual school fees are $3,500 per student, in an area known for having some of the best horse breeding in Africa. I was teaching computer literacy to rich (mostly white) kids who had computers at home and wanted for nothing.

My life took another interesting turn here. Because I was at a rich school, and not qualified to be a teacher (I only started my Bachelor of Education degree the following year), my subject was not examinable. In other words, the kids were not being tested and they thought they were there to play on the Internet with adult supervision.

I realized really quickly, in the same way that I gamed my own high school experience, that I would lose the kids if I didn't engage with them in a respectful way.

I created the most expensive contest I could afford. I was earning practically nothing, and my teaching subject was pointless, so I developed a raffle where students could ask me general knowledge questions, and if I didn't know the answer I would enter them in a draw to win an iPod Shuffle. For all I knew, most of them might even have one at home already, but it worked because I have a pretty good general knowledge. All those years of reading as a child came in very useful. There were obviously a few kids who managed to stump me and that was fine, but the challenge of it was the thing. I earned their respect with my knowledge, and they learned something from their fellow students who tried to stump me.

I learned something in that job, too, ten years into post-Apartheid South Africa. There were around one or two non-white kids per class. Population representation was off by a factor of ten. One of the older girls was there on a scholarship, but most kids were there because their parents could afford it. Ten years in, only rich or lucky kids could get an education with the best resources money could buy. It wasn't the kids' fault, but they were still benefiting from a system that was supposed to have been dismantled already.

While I was teaching this fairly banal class, albeit with a great set of students, the headmaster asked me to take on a student who had recently moved from Taiwan and didn't speak much English. I was to mentor him in Computer Science so that he could improve his English while working in a subject he was good at. At the same time, I was also invited to participate in a Saturday School, where the school provided resources (classrooms and stationery) for underprivileged children from a local township. Aged 11 to 14, these kids would arrive by bus and they would have time with volunteer teachers to learn stuff they might not have been taught at their own school.

I had far more job satisfaction from Saturday School than my actual day job, and when I received an offer to work as a software developer at the end of the school year, I left computer literacy behind, but continued to do Saturday School for another three years.

Ignorance

This is a long way to go to get to the point of this chapter, in a book about diversity. This is not about me. I don't want accolades for working with underprivileged children. I don't want recognition for organizing a Pride event. I don't want a prize for having a positive experience working with women. These are experiences that are personal to me and helped me become more understanding of people in general.

This book is about you, Dear Reader. I'm hoping that relating my experiences can help you gain a new perspective as well. This last section is going to give you some homework, because I'm still a teacher at heart.

People look, speak, and act differently to you, and have different belief systems. Habits, strong opinions, and words in one culture that are forms of endearment, can be deeply offensive to people of other cultures. If the recipient is historically (or currently) oppressed, this becomes a method of control over that recipient.

As residents in an increasingly complex world, we are directly affected by the explosion of the Internet and its ability to allow people from many different cultures to communicate. Learn from them. Diversity and inclusion have been shown in study after study to improve working conditions, encourage innovation, and increase market share and profits. This extends to friends and family. Exposure to new ideas, to different perspectives, makes your own life experience richer. It all starts with how you speak.

Do you know what I hate? I'm turning 42 years old this year. I am an adult in the prime of my life, successful by any measure, extremely lucky (and let's face it, I look like I'm the right colour and the right gender), but I check myself whenever I want to show my affection to my spouse of almost eleven years in public. Nothing extravagant, mind you. Whispered "I love you"s and air kisses, hugs, holding hands. Any LGBTQ+ couples we see doing that in public is "brave". Why should it have to be brave, to be wary of ignorance? When I express my love for my husband, it's not your place to tut-tut and cross the road, mumbling under your breath. You already won.

The term "microaggression" was coined in 1970 by psychiatrist Chester M. Pierce, a Harvard professor, to describe the little putdowns that African Americans received regularly from non-black people. Over the years this term has come to refer to (usually subtle) insults and behaviour that denigrates any marginalized group.

This is a list of phrases I've heard through my life which hopefully you are now equipped to understand and respond to in a way that is meaningful. These phrases were directed at me personally, so they are specific to my gender expression and sexual orientation. It is a small step to relate them to sexism and racism, all of which stems from ignorance. The better educated you are, the less ignorant you become.

- You don't look gay.
- It's just a phase.
- Have you ever tried sleeping with a girl? Maybe that'll fix you.
- Why does your hair have a centre-parting? It's effeminate.
- Why do you like that singer? He's so gay.
- You should drink beer. Cocktails are girly drinks.
- You're one of the good gays. It's the flaming queers I can't handle.
- Be a man.
- That car is for girls.
- You throw like a girl.
- You run like a girl.
- You scream like a girl.
- Why can't straight people have a Pride Parade?

While the Wikipedia article I took the definition from also cautions against victimhood culture, the items in this list qualify as microaggressions which are insensitive and ignorant in the most generous of readings. And anyway, why is feminine behaviour bad? So what if I run like Caster Semenya, or hit a ball like Melissa Mayeux? Do you have rocks in your head if you think that's an insult?

The reason I don't look gay is because I've been trying to look and act like everyone else, to avoid micro and macro aggressions from ignorant people. I'M ONE OF THE LUCKY ONES.

I started this chapter with a lesson on race, gender, and sexuality, dipping into human history to give it some context. Gender and sexuality are inextricably linked to race, as Simon Nkoli said. Historically disadvantaged people have faced the same struggles to greater or lesser degrees, and I'm just a small voice in a big world, asking for some consideration of your own humanity.

I don't buy the argument that "we can't just say anything anymore because someone will be offended". We can't keep slaves anymore. We can't kill people who steal from us anymore. This is human progress. However, I do accept that there's a nuance that we are losing in common speech, and that's entirely the fault of social media, which loves to expose mistakes without any context. Where in the past we could have discussions about things, Twitter and Facebook relentlessly force us to summarize our thoughts in a few characters. Otherwise it's tl;dr (too long; didn't read).

We must find a balance between the right to say what we like, and how it affects other people. As children we learn that if we say something that hurts someone, we should apologise. In the same way, if we say something as adults that comes from a place of ignorance, we can no longer say it's "just a joke".

It's fine to make a mistake once or twice, but if a marginalized person or group explains why what we've said is wrong, or that it can be easily misconstrued as offensive, we should learn from that and modify our speech. It is no different to learning manners as a child. The right to speak freely does not include the right to be treated politely if we repeatedly say the wrong thing.

Finally, if you want to be an ally for LGBTQ people, you don't get to be racist. You don't get to take kids from their parents at the border. You don't get to conveniently forget that I'm a foreigner because I look like you. And please think before you speak.

CHAPTER 3

Finding Balance of Work, Life, and Soul

By: Sage Franch

I once stood in front of an audience of 200 young women and proclaimed confidently, "there is no such thing as work-life balance." At the time, I truly meant it. Like many young professionals, I was deep in the weeds of disorganization, juggling work and a full course load for my undergrad degree in Computer Science – the only difference was my job had me working remotely at one of the world's biggest tech companies.

The start to my career was unconventional to say the least. At 21 I was working as a Content Developer at Microsoft Learning Experiences, the team responsible for creating massive open online courses and first-party training content on Microsoft technologies. Our courses were being rolled out to tens of thousands of students and, as the youngest on my team by a generation, I constantly felt like I was underqualified for the role. Like most women nowadays, I am well versed in the ways of impostor syndrome; this was not the first time I experienced it, nor would it be the last. The courses I was creating dealt with concepts that I had learned through experience, but were still more advanced than the concepts I was learning in my classes. It was a strange and uncomfortable junction, a collision of my roles as both a teacher and a student, and I spent the entire last year of my degree living this double life.

For a long time, I felt divided to the core. Every aspect of my life had warring elements: school and work competing for my time, my degree in Halifax competing with my team in Redmond, a whole four-hour time zone apart, and somewhere in the middle, my home and family in Toronto. I'm an optimist, so I've always seen challenges as opportunities and nervousness as an indicator of excitement, and because of this I didn't realize how much this lifestyle was wearing me down until I graduated, changed roles, and saw how imbalanced my life had been.

I am honoured to be included in this book. My words, alongside those of some of my favourite women in tech, including Susan Ibach, my first sherpa through the tech world, and Lori Lalonde, whose tales of kickassery I am always begging to hear. I believe we as women in male-dominated industries need to tell our stories, good and bad, so the next generation of techmakers understands the past and can sort out the world so everyone feels welcome doing what they love. In 2013 I started Trendy Techie, my blog about navigating the tech industry as a young woman and, in the four years since, it has become an incredible community of people from all over the world, fifteen thousand strong. Through some of the darkest times in my life this community has been my breath, giving me purpose and positivity and often forcing me to paint my own life with a rosier tint. This has very much been a journey we've all been on together, experiencing the world as so many snapshots through the same kaleidoscope.

Trendy Techie began after a series of encounters with, as my friend Holly calls them, the "dude bros" of the tech world. In 2013 I had my first student internship working as an app developer (this was during the app dev craze, when a new app went viral every day and every young developer thought they were going to build the next Instagram). It was at this job that I learned the Windows development skills I'd be teaching two years later, but it was also where I encountered my first negative experiences as a woman in industry. I was the only student on the team and one of just two women, the other of which suggested I should learn about baseball to fit in with the guys. Most of our team worked remotely and would sometimes take the full day to respond to my questions on Lync, and the training videos for the technology we were using were available exclusively in Dutch. Already beaten down by my dismal work situation, I set out to the tech community to see if I could find peers closer to my age and experience. Within a week, I was told I didn't look like I could code, I was too pretty to code, and that I didn't need a high-powered computer because there's no way I could be doing intense workloads. Never having encountered such groundless discrimination before, I was wounded to say the least.

Like any millennial, I took to the internet, in search of someone telling the stories I so desperately needed to hear: not stories about fitting in with the guys, drinking beer at work, or learning the ins and outs of baseball. I needed stories about women in tech who were unashamed to be themselves, who were in this space because they loved it and were unafraid to stand up in a room full of men and contribute. I searched and searched, and was unable to find anyone telling these stories – so I decided to tell them myself.

Trendy Techie has led me to incredible opportunities over these past few years, and now I am grateful for the terrible experiences I had that summer, because they gave me a part of my identity I never could have found had I not been pushed to the breaking point. Because of Trendy Techie I got my internship at Microsoft, was invited to Parliament Hill to meet Prime Minister Justin Trudeau, and had the opportunity to speak on stage at the world-renowned Perimeter Institute for Theoretical Physics, where I gave that talk to those 200 young women.

It won't come as a surprise to you that I have since done a complete one-eighty on my philosophy towards balance. My mom always reminds me that life will keep trying to teach you a lesson until you learn it. The lesson will come to you again and again in different shapes and voices until you learn and grow from it. Though we may not necessarily subscribe to the same system of beliefs, I do believe you will keep making the same mistake over and over again until you learn from your failures. For many of us, and certainly for me, the lesson of balance is one we must learn from many angles before it sinks in.

I believe that the concept of work-life balance is necessary, but flawed. To say one has to split her hours between work and life puts far too heavy an emphasis on work and discredits the importance of, well, *everything else* we do.

This is the part of the yoga class where the instructor makes you stand on one leg. In this chapter, we will explore the underlying current that can make or break everything we do: balance. I am by no means going to pretend I am a master of balance, it is something I still struggle with every day. But in the time since I gave that talk, I have reflected a lot on what balance means in the context of living a happy life. In these pages we will explore key strategies that I use to find and maintain balance of work, life, and soul and, just like in yoga class, we will learn how to forgive ourselves and recover when we lose that balance and fall down.

My Journey

My journey of discovering balance is really rooted in that day when I stood on that stage and proclaimed the death of work-life balance. At the time I believed that work-life balance as a concept was an unnecessary and counterproductive notion. We've all heard that famous Confucius aphorism, "choose a job you love, and you will never have to work a day in your life" – while a poignant sentiment, it became the basis for my own flawed philosophy on balance. If you love what you do, I thought, work shouldn't feel like work, and therefore happy people shouldn't *need* to separate their work from the rest of their lives. Following this, I threw myself into my work and forgot that things outside of my jobs could make me happy, too.

The last year of my undergrad was the busiest year of my life. My career began earlier than most, and I began my first full-time role at Microsoft and my final year of undergrad on the same day. Over the weekend, I shipped myself and my belongings from my family home in Toronto to my bachelorette pad in Halifax, officially splitting my life between three cities. I would spend the next sixteen months calculating time zones and manipulating my schedule like plasticine to cram all my obligations into each day. I woke up an hour before my family in Toronto and four hours before my team in Redmond, so I scheduled my classes as early as possible so I could be online during the majority of the west coast workday. Of course, taking classes during the workday was impossible to avoid, so I scheduled meetings during the periods between classes and worked on my Microsoft courses during lectures. When I talk to friends and colleagues who knew me then, I am reminded again and again that no one knew quite how hard I was pushing myself back then. I'm sure if they did, an intervention would have been staged.

The thing was, on the outside, I didn't look overworked. I looked competent, driven, ambitious, and successful. The western view of success is flawed. We shine a spotlight on successful people and try to analyze their approach to attaining success, and replicate it for the masses. But success cannot be mass-produced. The media looks at people who are experienced and instills in us a sense of longing, of envy that we are not *yet* in that phase of our lives, not *yet* in possession of the elusive secret sauce to success. This implies two things: firstly, that we will, without exception, eventually reach that celebrity success stage; and secondly, that we *must* do so in order to be successful. We want so badly to reach that next stage of accomplishment, we can forget to spend time taking care of ourselves until it is too late.

For the first time in history, global-scale success seems attainable to everyone. Social media gives everyone a voice regardless of their proximity to industry hubs or family history with their craft of choice, and now the average person has the power to make a mark on the entire world, where before such reach was only achievable by politicians or celebrities. Young people see their peers blossom into paid Instagram stars, watch their classmates build apps that make the front page of Reddit, and favorite the tweets from the countless young entrepreneur accounts telling them to "stay humble, hustle hard." They do all this from their bedrooms, passively consuming the #inspiration, #motivationmonday, and #hustlelife with a double-tap, not realizing that the journey to success cannot be summed up in 140 characters. Success, clout, and influence come not just from how someone spent the tip of the iceberg hours that get distilled into their 500-word feature in *Fortune*, but from the days, weeks, and years spent under the water.

In the tech space, the archetype of a successful technologist still conjures images of a casually-dressed male with just the right balance of technical chops and personality. Bill and Steve were the first tech celebrities of this generation, heralding in a new age of computing and a new ideal for young people to strive towards. This has only been reinforced by the similar big-league success of Zuckerberg, Spiegel, Musk, et al. The map of successful technologists has sparked innovation around the globe - it gives young people the impression that impact is easy to make and disrupting an industry is as simple as building an app. We live at a truly exciting time in history, because information is more attainable than ever, and anyone with an internet connection can access countless courses to learn the skills needed to make their impact. Couple that with the communication power of social media, the cultural craving for virality, and the relatability of our tech-world rockstars, and reaching that level of success seems so easy that it is expected that we strive for it. This is both incredibly empowering and uncomfortably dangerous.

Characterized by an always-on mentality, a hunger for success, and an unhealthy appreciation for caffeine, hustle culture would have you believe that throwing yourself into your work and spinning endlessly on productivity is a surefire way to guarantee your success. Because of the accessibility of technology, there seems to be an expectation that, if you can code, you should be spending all your free time coding. The thing is, no amount of work guarantees that you will be next in line to the innovator throne. All it guarantees you is an unhealthy lifestyle and unpreparedness in the event that something goes wrong.

In 2014, just a month into my first co-op role at Microsoft, my mother was diagnosed with terminal cancer. It was a devastating shock to my family, and threw into question every plan I'd had for the progression of my life. I'd taken for granted the permanence of my parents, the expectation that they would live to see me kickstart my career, get married, create life, change the world. None of that was a given anymore, and I tumbled downwards through stages of grief, trauma, and depression trying to come to terms with this devastating unknown. Suddenly, the non-work components of my life, previously filled with maintaining my blog, maintaining my relationships with my life partner and our friends, and fulfilling my basic needs as a human, now also contained my role as a caregiver. Suddenly, work was far less important than the rest of my world.

As the months passed, the importance that work had previously held in my life shrunk, and for the first time I saw a distinction between work and life. I had been putting so much of myself into my work that it had ballooned out to consume other areas of my life. In amongst this emerged another distinction, one between the nitty gritty of life – which was now characterized by seemingly endless appointments and late-night trips to the hospital – and the few rare moments that brought true joy. Years passed like this, and time flexed and dilated around the few key moments that I remember. My memory of this time is faint, and I have to struggle sometimes to recall timelines. It was like living life half asleep. Looking back on that period now, the tapestry is a dark forest, with just a few joyful moments peeking through like fireflies. In five years I want to be able to look back on today and see a very different scene.

It is those fireflies, the moments of joy and fulfillment, that make life so worth living. When I refer to *soul* in this chapter, I am referring to the collection of fireflies we amass throughout life. It is a collection we must protect and nurture with all our might. The soul is the part of your life that brings you joy and makes you glow from the inside out. Sometimes we can light up our souls through work and life obligations, but true fulfillment comes when the soul is treated as an equal player and balance is maintained between all three. Treating the soul as equally important to your work and life allows you to take that control back and give yourself space to breathe and dream. This, I truly believe, is the secret sauce to happiness.

So, dear achiever, this chapter is about finding the sweet spot. Finding that elusive balance between the obligations of work, the responsibilities of life, and the duty you have to yourself. It is this nirvana that we should be striving for, for it is there that we can live a truly fulfilling life, and be, simply, happy.

> *"How we spend our days is, of course, how we spend our lives."*
> *– Annie Dillard*

We are always looking forward until our final hours, when we look back. Each of us only has one life to live, and at the end of my days, in my final hours, I hope to look back on years spent being inspired, living comfortably, and helping others do the same. I hope to look back on a tapestry of shared smiles, sun shining on skin, and moments enjoyed, not wished-for. Ask yourself, when it's your time to look back on your life, what do you want to see?

Balance is a lot like yoga. No matter how much you practice or how far you improve, there is no such thing as perfecting or mastering the art; the only boss to beat is your own current best. The same is true about balance; nobody can ever be an expert in balance because it is a different journey for everyone and each of us has a unique set of balls to juggle. All we can do is share our journeys with each other and learn from what we all have been through, and in doing so, pick up strategies that work for ourselves and our lives. Let's begin at a place most of us experience imbalance: the workplace.

Workplace unhappiness and job dissatisfaction are plaguing the working class. According to the Washington Post, only 13 percent of people in the world are happy with their jobs, and yet we are often told that simply finding a career we love will make us happy (as though finding job happiness is as easy as choosing to do so). But even if you do truly love your job, it's a misconception that loving your job equates to leading a balanced life. In fact, I would argue that loving your job puts you at risk for a different type of imbalance, in which you over index on your work at the sacrifice of your personal life. I know too many people who have made sacrifices in their personal lives in favor of work, sometimes irreparably damaging their family relationships.

One of my favourite tools for reflection is the work-life-soul Venn diagram. I love it because of its simplicity and easy replicability. You can plot your current state on this diagram by placing a mark on the place you think best represents the balance of your life. In the diagram below, I have marked the spot that represents the situation I described above, in which someone invests more time in their work than in other areas of their lives. Many students and people early in their careers fall into this trap because they think it leads to surefire, rapid success. And perhaps for some it does, but at the cost of personal relationships, free time, and pursuing their passions.

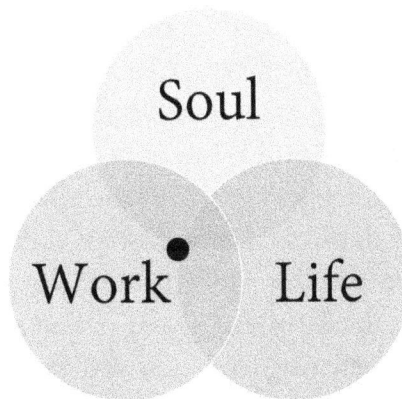

This is the state I was living in during my last year as a student. I loved my job as a Content Developer at Microsoft because I got to create courses that would be taken by thousands of people around the world - nothing makes me happier than equipping others with useful tools, and I suppose that's why you and I find ourselves bound together now through these words in this chapter. And I loved my job as a Computer Science student because I got to spend time learning and investing in skills that I could turn around and share with others. But loving your job is not sufficient to imply balance. Balance is more than enjoying what you do, it's taking your time and planning your life with intent, being sure to include space for things outside of work.

The onus is not just on the employees to balance their lives, however. Management has the power and the responsibility to positively influence the way their team members spend their time. Fair management is key to a happy workforce, and this is why it is so important to interview your interviewers when you are looking for a new role. Job happiness is more dependent on the quality of management than the day-to-day tasks, and high-quality management prioritizes employee balance in and out of the workplace.

My former skip-level (which, in corporate-speak, means my manager's manager) was an incredible senior-level leader. She had the ability to foster an environment that was equally inspiring and productive, and she stood at the helm of our organization like a Viking leader leading her team into battle - not superior to us, simply one of us whose direction we would follow. In the two cumulative years I spent working under her in both co-op and full-time roles, she always made very clear her commitment to us as people, not just employees. She and my direct manager pioneered a flexible work-life continuum, always made sure vacation time was taken and, most importantly, didn't shy away from recognizing the difficulty of the high-performance, high-volume expectations of our jobs.

I distinctly remember one particular team meeting when my former skip-level took the time to talk about balance. She spent a good ten minutes of our all-hands meeting talking about the importance of valuing our own time and taking time to step away from work. I was shocked! It was the first time I'd heard someone in management talk about the importance of stepping away to recharge so we can come back in strong. Seeing that our senior leadership had this mindset made a big difference in how I felt about my life. I no longer felt guilty taking time off and I no longer thought that people would look down on me for using my off-work hours for myself and my family. And though our team culture was set up to facilitate this quite clearly, not until I heard the words did I feel entitled to take care of myself and invest time in seeking balance.

Spending time on yourself invigorates you and builds a strong foundation of mental, emotional, and physical health so you can do better in all areas of your life, including your work. This is precisely why balance, and setting realistic expectations for our balance, is so important.

Being honest with others - and the consequences when we fail to do so - is something we learn early in life. Why, then, does it take us so much longer to understand the importance of being honest with ourselves? Professional workaholics lie to themselves all the time. *I have enough time, I'll get it done, I can make that work, I don't work too much, I didn't really want to go to that function anyways.* If we want to live balanced lives, we need to cut the bullshit and start being real with ourselves.

By the time I realized this, I was waist-deep in denial about my tendency to overwork myself. I constantly felt like I didn't have enough hours in the day, so one day I decided to sit down and calculate how much time I was spending in work mode and how much more time I had to play with. What I found truly shocked me: when I added up all the hours I expected myself to use - for work, school, and personal care - they far exceeded the week's total.

Work	40 hours
Classes	36 hours
Studying/Homework	16 hours
Transit	14 hours
Eating	14 hours
Hygiene	14 hours
Trendy Techie	10 hours weekdays + 8 hours weekend
Sleep	49
TOTAL	**201**

That's when I realized that feeling like you don't have enough time in a day is a product of not knowing how much time you have. I was living my life with the expectation that I could fill 201 hours in a 168-hour week, and that's without allotting any time to pursue art, fitness, or relaxation (I didn't include those at the time because they were last on my priority list). I effectively expected myself to fit 28.7 hours into each 24 hour day. No wonder I felt like there was never enough time! This is how the soul activities, the things we do for ourselves, get pushed to the ever-elusive "later."

I'm the kind of person who writes in the margins of paperbacks, so I have included some exercises in this chapter and I encourage you to grab a pen. In the chart below, write the hours you expect yourself to spend on each element in a week. I have included more fields than I had in my original chart because, well, I'm hoping you'll already have a better balance than I did when I first did this exercise. But know that there's no shame in putting a zero beside some of these items. The only goal here is to be honest with yourself.

Work	
Sleep	
Transit	
Eating	
Hygiene	
Fitness	
Family	
Hobbies	
TOTAL	

When you measure the week in available hours instead of in days, it quickly grows shorter. The exercise above is great for understanding your expectations of yourself (people can lie, but numbers can't), but not so great for helping you do anything about it. Let's now measure the week not in expected hours, but in available hours instead.

No matter how much you love what you do, a week only has 168 hours. Assuming you sleep a regular human amount of 7 hours per night, that leaves you 119 hours of waking hours to fill. How will you use them?

The chart below lays out the week in terms of work, life, and soul, with some ideas of what each category means. In the blank spaces, put in the immovable hours that you *must* spend each day. This is not meant to be an idealized look at what you want to spend on each, but a realistic analysis of the minimum you have already scheduled. In the "Total Allotted" line, add up the mandatory hours you included in the blanks. Subtract this amount from 24 and write that in the "Total Remaining" line.

	M	T	W	R	F	S	S
WORK Day job Side job Transit							
LIFE Sleep Hygiene Eating Other							
SOUL Fitness Therapy Hobbies Other							
TOTAL AL- LOTTED:	/24	/24	/24	/24	/24	/24	/24
TOTAL RE- MAINING:							

Now you have a realistic approximation of the hours you have to play with. How many hours do you have? Is it realistic? Is it sustainable? Most importantly, is it enough?

Looking at your hours laid out on the page, how would you describe your balance? Map it on the Venn diagram below:

Soul

Work   Life

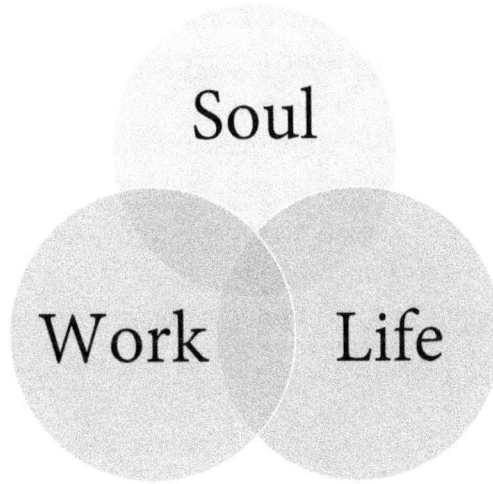

Understanding how you spend your time is a key step to being able to make change and rebalance your life. What you choose to do with this information is up to you - I like to check in with myself at least every quarter to see how I'm feeling about my balance and where I can improve. Our lives change so much week-to-week, it's good to check in and align your reality to your expectations. Your cadence doesn't have to be the same as mine, but checking in at least twice a year is a good baseline measurement. If you want to be even more prudent you can track your balance and graph it over time for a nice visual of your progress.

If your Venn looks like one of these:

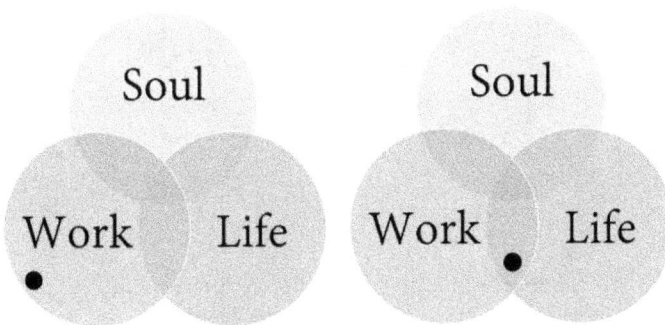

Soul   Soul

Work   Life   Work   Life

…you may be feeling a bit lost. I know I certainly was when I first did these exercises. My head was spinning because I had just realized how out of balance I was but had no idea how to fix it. It was then that I realized I didn't even have a good picture in my mind of what good balance would look like in my life, let alone a roadmap for how to attain it.

The center section of the Venn diagram, where work, life, and soul overlap, is the state in which all three components are balanced equally. To have true balance you must have:

- A source of income that brings in the money needed to fund the other aspects of your lifestyle;
- A home situation that allows you to feel comfortable that everything is under control when you step away from it;
- And frequent opportunity to explore your passions and do the things that reinvigorate you.

This seems simple enough but is quite difficult to maintain. Though I have made significant progress in recent years, I still would not say that I have perfect balance. I have a pretty good balance between work and life, but am still not doing enough to nurture myself. I find it difficult to step away from work and my family to do things for me, but I'm slowly learning how to do it more often. My Venn diagram currently looks like this:

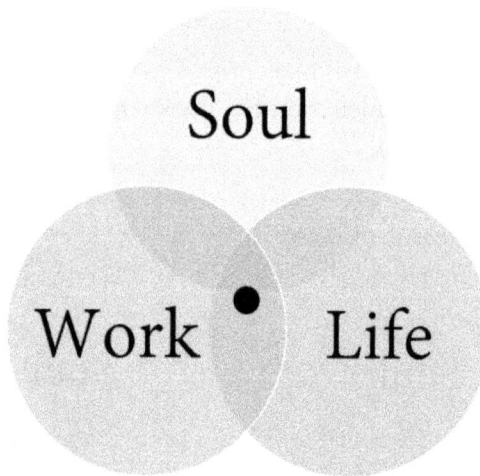

Soul

Work · Life

How I decided to place my balance is not based purely on equality of hours spent - in fact, it is highly unlikely that anyone with the right amount of balance can achieve an equal-thirds time split for the three areas. But it doesn't take an equal amount of soul hours to have balance, it's more about the frequency and quality of your personal investments than their duration. For this reason it is more fitting to look at your balance as a sum of the whole - numbers, feelings, and signs - rather than the individual parts.

Balance is a journey, not a destination; I can't emphasize that enough. So far I've been describing this journey as "finding balance," which is actually somewhat erroneous. Finding balance is not sufficient, for once it's found, we must maintain it, and this is the hardest part. Every now and then, do a sanity check and observe the signs of your balance level. Here are some indicators for reference:

Signs that you are out of balance:
- You keep working outside of work hours
- You feel guilty about spending time at home because it takes you away from work
- You feel guilty about spending time at work because it takes you away from home
- You can't remember the last time you engaged in your hobby
- You don't make meals a priority
- You go to bed at the end of the day with a laundry list of items you didn't get to that you will carry over to the next day
- You feel like you never have enough time

Signs that you are maintaining a healthy balance:
- You take off your work hat when you are not supposed to be working
- You take time to engage in your hobbies
- You eat regularly and maintain a healthy amount of fitness
- You go to bed feeling like you accomplished everything you had to in the day

These are just indicators and cannot be taken as infallible, only you can know if they are accurate indicators for your life. It all comes back to knowing yourself, and trusting her.

There is no get-rich-quick scheme for anything worth striving towards. Take your time with life, be intentional with how you spend your hours. You may feel you don't have time to do everything you want to, but you have as much time as anyone else does, and you should spend it in ways that fulfill you. Treat yourself with the same respect you would another person. Give yourself the same leeway you would give a colleague. Support yourself in the way you would support your sister, and love yourself in the way you would love your children.

> *"**The doing** is the **thing**. The talking and worrying*
> *and thinking is not the **thing**."*
> *— Amy Poehler, Yes Please*

I've never been able to keep an orchid. Around the time that I told those young women that balance didn't exist, my then-boyfriend would tease me every day because my orchids were in perpetual state of peril. Unlike me, my grandmother had an amazing green thumb. The woman could grow a full plant from a herb on a dinner plate. I remember traveling to Italy with her and watching her pick flowers in the mountains, only to see them pop up the next spring in her spectacular award-winning gardens back home in Toronto.

But nothing spectacular comes without commitment. My grandmother's award-winning gardens were spectacular because she spent hours upon hours from dawn till dusk tending them – checking the health of the soil, comparing the colour of the leaves, and picking the dead heads off the plants to allow the living ones to flourish - and every fall when the leaves started to turn she would pot up her perennials and store them in her basement till the spring thaw. She was practical, proactive, and dedicated to her craft, and she was able to create these stunning gardens not because she was lucky, but because she was committed to making it happen. Imagine the beauty we can experience if we cultivate our lives with the same love, determination, and patience that my grandmother gardened.

Like a garden, balance doesn't grow overnight. And balance, once grown, cannot be left untended. It must be constantly maintained in order to keep its beauty. This is, arguably, the toughest and most thankless part of the process. Keeping something the same is never celebrated on Twitter, maintaining your sanity rarely rewarded, because our society celebrates constant improvement – even failure, for that matter – over stasis. But maintenance is not a sign of a lack of progress, it is a sign of dedication and commitment.

We must hold ourselves accountable for our balance in the same way we hold ourselves accountable for meeting milestones at work.

A positive attitude towards scheduling is something I wish I could package up as a gift and give to every professional. What scheduling really does, beyond reminding you what you need to do, is takes the pressure of decision-making off of you in the moment and makes you accountable for your commitments. When scheduling meetings with others, this comes naturally to us - when a new email with "ACTION NEEDED" appears on your screen in the middle of a meeting, do you jump to it immediately? No, you continue through your scheduled meeting and get to it afterwards. But for some reason this is harder to do when we are dealing with our own time. We must learn to have the same respect for our own time that we have for other people's.

A day without a schedule can be modelled with a stack. In computer science terms, a stack is an abstract collection of multiple elements which are "pushed" onto the stack for temporary indexing and "popped" off the top to be dealt with. Stacks have a first-in, last-out priority order, so the first thing pushed onto the stack is the last thing popped off after all the later-pushed items have been dealt with. An unstructured day is like a stack, where throughout the day we continually push new, shorter-term responsibilities onto the top of our stacks, and pop them off one by one because they are easier to accomplish. This leaves the older items aging as we put them off in favor of our more immediate responsibilities, and this is where our soul time is disappearing to. We put ourselves on the bottom of our accountability stack and push all the other responsibilities on top to be dealt with first. Sometimes it is days, weeks, or months before we finally clear all the other responsibilities and get to that soul time lurking at the bottom.

The act of scheduling an entire day forces you to look at time in bigger blocks, and in doing so you can see your life from a bird's eye view. From this high perch you can get a better idea of how to add balance back into your life, by spacing out work commitments and blocking off time specifically for the fireflies. Think of this not as taking free time, but as scheduling time with yourself. Simply rephrasing the vernacular you use to describe your hours may help you prioritize yourself.

If it takes a calendar item to remind you to eat, block off three times on your calendar every day. Do the same for your hobbies and passions, and hold yourself accountable. In the beginning, you may still be tempted to blow off your commitment to yourself, but treat yourself like you would treat a colleague. If you're really resistant, enlist others to hold you accountable. Book lunches with people, find a personal trainer or a gym buddy who will expect you to be there, befriend people at the dog park and make plans to go together. Eventually you will be able to schedule time for personal items and commit to keeping those meetings with yourself.

Once you've committed to your schedule, you must also commit to staying on task within the time blocks that you've allotted. Even with a schedule, it can be difficult to stay on task. I believe this is linked to this era of short-and-sweet content, which conditions us to consume things in bite-sized pieces. Living in the information age, we have access to more information than humanity ever has. When we have access to so many different topics, it is impractical to consume longform articles about everything, so we publish news in snappy tweets and thirty-second videos that aim to condense a lot of information into a tidbit that takes minimal time and effort to consume. This scatters our minds and shortens our attention spans - if it's not consumable in a minute or less, we don't want it (those of us bound together in the writing and reading of this book are the obvious exception). This is why platforms like Medium have had such success with adding an estimated reading time to the subtitles of their articles. What results is an army of people who have been conditioned to consume things in bite-sized pieces – we know a little bit about a LOT of things.

With our attention spans shrinking, our ability to commit to things and see them through withers. While our ability to focus dwindles, the amount of work we must do remains the same. I've noticed it in myself as I've grown Trendy Techie; the longer I maintain my social media accounts, the less consecutive time I can spend in a single mode. Writing this chapter has shown that to be true, and has been great practice in stretching my attention span back out again.

With a shrunken attention span we can easily become derailed from the task at hand, even if we have allotted time for ourselves. There are tools to help structure time into shorter blocks to make them more manageable - many have turned to Francesco Cirillo's Pomodoro Technique, for example, in which time is broken into 25-minute working intervals with 5-minute breaks in between. Though I love the origin of the technique (which gets its name from the tomato-shaped kitchen timer Cirillo used to time himself as a student), it has never worked for me because my ability to be productive depends entirely on how I'm feeling in the moment, to an extreme level. If I'm in the mood to work, I'll skip the breaks; if I'm not in the mood to work, I'll take a break and keep extending it until five episodes of The Office have played by on my screen. Where I have found success, though, is in using productivity triggers to get myself back in the mood for work when I'm feeling unproductive.

Productivity triggers are repeatable micro routines that help you get in the zone for productivity. For many of us, one of those triggers is our morning coffee - it's not necessarily the caffeine that gets us ready to work, it's the Pavlovian association between the action and the subsequent productivity that reminds our bodies and brains that it's time to get in the zone. These actions are quick and unassuming, and can be performed at any point during the day when productivity starts to wane (a quick note of caution to my fellow coffee addicts, it is not wise to use this as an excuse to have eight cups of coffee in a day).

The effectiveness of these triggers ebbs and flows depending on how strong the association is, and certainly some will be more effective than others. To find your own productivity triggers, begin by observing your actions leading up to your work day and see which ones can be repeated throughout the day. Then, throughout the day, observe yourself for moments of productivity, and look back at your actions to see if there were any repeatable routines that could be injected throughout your week. Within a week you can effectively create a new trigger by adding or substituting a new micro routine to the period just before a scheduled time of heightened productivity like an important meeting or presentation. Before long, the association will stick.

Productivity triggers can also be used to hack yourself a healthier lifestyle. In an attempt to be more health conscious this year, my New Year's resolution was to do a quick vinyasa (a four-pose yoga sequence that stretches and lengthens the spine) every morning to prepare for the day. About ten days into doing this it became a routine part of my morning, and now when I find myself straying out of focus, I do a quick vinyasa or two to help myself re-center. Consider associating a healthy action like this with the start of productivity, like drinking a glass of water, taking a quick walk, or eating a piece of fruit. The concept of triggers can be extended outside of productivity as well, and you can condition yourself to get in the mood for virtually anything with enough repetition and positive association.

People tend to lean to one of two directions: you are either predisposed to fill free time with productivity or to fill it with procrastination. I'm the kind of person who defaults to productivity, and I used to be quite proud of how long I could force myself to work without breaking. Given an infinite amount of unstructured time, I will never run out of things to do, very few of which involve any kind of relaxation. As I have learned many times, however, this is not sustainable in the long term and is a direct recipe for burnout. When I burn out, I do a full 180 and turn into a procrastinator extraordinaire.

But it's not my fault and, fellow procrastinator, it's not your fault either. The fact is, we were born this way. It's how we evolved.

We procrastinate because it makes our brains feel good. Procrastination happens when the prefrontal cortex, a relatively newer part of the human brain, loses its battle against one of the oldest pieces of our brains, the limbic system. Also known as the reward center, the limbic system is old and dominant, and is the driving force behind survival responses like fear and anger, and the positive reinforcement responses we get when we do something that benefits our survival. These two parts of the brain must often compete because they are designed to want different things.

When we take on a task, we engage the prefrontal cortex, which is the practical planning part of our brains. But the prefrontal cortex is newer and doesn't initiate the same kind of automatic response that the limbic system does, so it takes more effort to activate it in order to continue to get things done. Since it takes effort to keep the prefrontal cortex in work-mode, the brain wants to let the limbic system take over and deflect energy. As soon as we lose that thread of motivation, our limbic system kicks in and tempts us with that sweet apple of procrastination, because turning off the prefrontal cortex's work mode activates the reward center, and makes us feel good.

Knowing this, you can identify when that animal instinct wants to close Visual Studio and switch into Netflix, and you can use that knowledge to keep yourself from giving in. I know, easier said than done, but you can also trick your brain into triggering that reward feeling while you're still being productive.

During my hectic final year as a student I learned how to trick my brain into feeling the reward of procrastination without losing the productivity: when I felt like I needed a break from one project, I'd switch to the other, and back and forth until they were done. Doing this seemed to satisfy the instinctual search for reward by switching off the first task, while allowing me to enter the next task feeling good.

This method of productivity by procrastination is not a long-term solution to laziness, and it is certainly not a solution that leaves you with an intentionally balanced life. It should really only be used as a last resort when you need to aggressively meet a deadline. When I first started doing this, I would just go, go, go for weeks at a time, morning till late night productivity. I became addicted to work – in retrospect, being productive satisfied my need for control at a time in my life when I felt I had lost all control. Getting things done combatted the stress and depression I was feeling from coping with my mom's diagnosis. When I was working, I was accomplishing, and when I was accomplishing, I could finally be in control. But this always-on hustle mentality led to some of the worst burnouts I had ever experienced, and in those days the depression would take over like quicksand.

I opened this section with that excellent quote by Amy Poehler because she's right; thinking and worrying and stressing about "the thing" is just an unproductive attempt to buy more time before we do it. We put so much energy into imagining all the possible outcomes and focusing on the worst-case scenarios, but if we instead put that energy directly into planning our lives and accomplishing the task, we could erase from possibility a significant amount of the outcomes we worry about. Further, if we instead channeled that energy into ourselves, into doing things to destress and re-center, we replace worry with joy and enter our productive times refreshed. You are, in a way, a team all on your own, a team of instincts and intuition and needs that must work together to make the whole cohesive human that is you. Be a good manager to your team, and hold yourself accountable for every team member's success.

You are Not Perfect. But You Don't Have to Be.

We get so caught up in what we're supposed to do, we forget to pay attention to what we're doing, sometimes until it's too late. This is how the devil of regret finds its way onto our shoulders. We look to the future for what we don't have yet, we dwell on the past where we made mistakes, and we forget to look at the wrinkles growing deeper in our family's faces. I'm not quite sure where it came from, but somehow my family instilled in me the ability to live in the moment and, twenty-three years into this journey of life, I find myself with comparatively fewer regrets than my peers. I don't think that any healthy person has absolutely zero regrets, but minimizing regret frees us from the invisible cages that keep us from achieving our goals.

There's no recipe for a regret-free life, but there are ways to proactively and reactively handle regret. Assuming you believe in free will, our lives can be reduced down to a series of decisions, a very long path down a huge decision tree. We are pressured by immediacy to weigh our decisions based on what benefits us most in the short term, like choosing to work late instead of making it home for family dinner. Eventually, these decisions add up and you suddenly realize you messed up the big mosaic when you were focused on the individual pieces of glass. Instead, we can proactively evade regret by weighing each option based on its *potential for regret*, and at each decision point choosing the path of least regret. This may lead us to make mistakes, let others down in the short term, but have greater happiness and fewer regrets in the grand scheme of our lives. An apology today is better than a regret tomorrow.

Even with this, we are sometimes blindsided by regret. We burn out, we don't see the big picture, we don't spend time with a loved one until they are terminally ill. These regrets can't be erased, but they don't have to ruin you. There is an antidote for regret; that antidote is forgiveness.

Combining prioritization and forgiveness, you can live with minimal regrets. It is much easier to forgive yourself for your past decisions when you know that, whatever you did or said, you made the choice because you thought it would have the least negative impact based on your knowledge at the time. We can't time travel and give ourselves knowledge retroactively, but we can trust ourselves today to make the best decisions for tomorrow.

"You can do anything, but not everything."
– David Allen

Technology is evolving so fast, it is impossible to keep on top of every development. Blockchain, artificial intelligence, virtual reality, it's all so exciting and complex, and impossible to learn it all in depth. I do believe the day will come when it is standard to augment our brains with machine intelligence (and that there will be a subclass of regressed humans who have not augmented their brains or bodies, whether because of financial inability or unwillingness to meld man and machine, but I'll save that for another book). But until that day comes, we simply can't learn it all.

As a young professional working in this fast-paced space, I feel the pressures of industry bearing down on me. Being the youngest person on my team means I'm constantly surrounded by people who have vastly more experience under their belts than I do, and it can lead to feelings of inferiority and impostor syndrome.

It was at the Grace Hopper Celebration in 2014 that I first heard of the concept of a "T-shaped person." This is the notion of having a bit of proficiency in each of many areas (the top of the T), and deep proficiency in one area (the stem, under one specific category). Altogether, this T is your portfolio of skills including your specialization. Here is my T for development skills:

Web & App	Blockchain	Artificial Intelligence	Mixed Reality	Security
		Machine Learning		
		Deep Learning		
		Data Science		
		Conversational Agents		

My current manager, Tommy, who is very supportive, often reminds me, "You can be a bold T but you cannot be a bold square." You can be an expert in some things, but you can't be an expert in everything. Using this T model is not only helpful in guiding your learning, but also in guiding the projects and tasks you decide to take on.

In my job as a Technical Evangelist, there is no average day-to-day. Every week looks completely different because my job involves both short- and long-term projects across a variety of technologies and audiences. Our small team gets looped into projects from all around the company, working with different customers and partners to implement Microsoft's latest technologies. It's a thrilling experience, so in the beginning I said "yes" to as many opportunities as I could, and promptly burned out. I wanted to learn and contribute right out of the gate, but I spread myself too thin too fast and broke like bubble gum.

The T model helps me be more strategic about which projects I say yes to and which ones I turn down. Because I specialize in AI, I am confident that I can contribute well to AI projects. When projects in my other skill areas come up, I can assess whether or not I have a deep enough understanding to contribute meaningfully, and elect not to participate if I don't. When you're striving for success, especially early in your career when your success feels like it's in the hands of people with more seniority, you won't want to turn down an opportunity to prove yourself. I've always approached new projects with this mindset: say yes to opportunities outside your comfort zone, and prove yourself by learning and executing to the best of your ability. This is a great way to upskill quickly in new areas, but it's also a great way to put yourself in a pressure cooker. It took a long time and a lot of encouragement from Tommy for me to be okay with saying, "that's just not my thing," but it's an important sentence to know and use. Say it out loud, "that's just not my thing, *and that's okay.*"

Understanding your skills and accepting your T as it is helps keep you in positions that best complement your interests. Proficiency comes with experience and time, so forgive yourself for what you don't know right now and understand that you can target your learning so you eventually reach expert understanding in your chosen areas of depth. In short, forgive yourself for what you don't (yet) know, and you can better avoid the beast of burnout.

The first time I experienced burnout in my career, I couldn't get out of bed for three days. I had just returned to Halifax from a three-day trip filming courses in Seattle, and every last bit of my energy had been spent. My approach to work travel was very unhealthy; I hated wasting hours in transit so I would book early morning flights in order to be in Seattle by 11am, and would work for the entire duration of the two or three flights it would take to get there. This meant leaving my apartment at 3:30 AM to make it on the first flight to Toronto, from where I would, on a lucky day, catch a direct to Seattle or, more often, head to Seattle by way of Vancouver. I would take my laptop out and work on content for our Windows 10 app development courses, or if it was near exam time I would study hard for the courses I was taking at school, and I would get a good six to eight hours of solid work time on the plane rides before touching down in Seattle.

From the airport I would head to the studios on campus, stopping at my hotel only to drop off my carry-on and get camera-ready, and commence a full day of filming course content. If you were one of the tens of thousands of students to take a course with my videos in it, you now know that it was a travel-induced state of delirium that led up to the corny jokes and intro gags between me and my co-host, Chris.

When I first joined Microsoft as a co-op in 2014, my mentor-turned-close-friend Vincent told me that work travel would eventually get old. I didn't believe him at the time, but here I am just a couple years later, dreading the next time I have to cramp my 5'10 frame onto a plane for the four-and-a-half-hour flight to the west coast. It's as hard on the body as it is on the balance; traveling for work is a very good way to throw balance out the window. When you travel for work you are spending a significant amount of time on work and not much else, and back then I worked overtime and exhausted myself trying to prove myself to my team.

This particular trip, I had a fever coming on by the time I got on the plane back to Halifax, and when I got back to my apartment I left my bags in the hall and passed out on my bed for fourteen hours. Waking up to dark windows, I wished the night would stretch out for another week so I could recover before it was time for my next class. The only saving grace was that the trip had been short enough for the food in my fridge to not yet have expired, and that it was sometime between Saturday and Sunday, meaning I could decompress without guilt for a day.

Very few people have ever seen that side of my life, and if you look at my Instagram feed from around the time of my work trips, you would never be able to tell just how hard I burned out when I did. Social media is a threat to the mental health of our youth. I'm not as concerned for those of us in our mid-twenties and above (twenty-three counts as mid-twenties, right?), but considering that, as of writing this, approximately one third of my audience on Instagram self-identified as 13-24, I am seriously concerned about how my social feed affects my followers.

Social media influencers have a direct line into malleable minds; that's why brands like Samsung, Ford, H&M, and many more will pay big bucks to have influencers advertise. Even Tim Horton's has an aggressive influencer program! The culture around social media influencing is becoming less of a culture of positive rallying around like-minded individuals, and more an opportunity to obsess over and covet other people's lives. Brands know that people will fork out their hard-earned cash to buy something that makes them feel more like their favourite celebrity, even more so when that celebrity is "just like them."

Influencers are different than traditional celebrities because their lifestyles are inherently more attainable than those of actors and pop stars. Because of this, the things we do and say online can more directly influence the way people behave in their own lives. I wish I had realized sooner how unrealistically I was portraying my lifestyle – until late 2016, I only ever shared the moments I deemed exciting, positive, and inspiring, and I intentionally refrained from posting about the times I was struggling or burning out. As my following grew, I began getting messages from other young women asking for advice on how to get a life more like mine. One day I sat there reading the messages that had piled up in the message requests inbox, baffled. I had done such a great job of obscuring the difficulties of my life, that people wanted my hectic lifestyle. Some days even I didn't want my life, and yet I had young women reaching out from all around the world to know my secret.

My secret was that I was practically drowning myself in work so that I would forget about the realities of my personal life. Of course, I couldn't tell them that, but since then I have been much more conscious of how I portray my life on social media. It is so important to talk about the times when things go wrong and not just show the perfect, covetable moments.

The first time I posted publicly about being burnt out, I was shocked by how many people contacted me to ask if I was okay. Colleagues pulled me over in the hall, people sent me encouraging messages, and even my manager offered his support to pull me out of burnout and prevent me from getting back to that state. I was shocked; all this time, I could have had this support if I'd just opened my mouth and been honest about the burnout! I had been in this situation so many times before, it had become normalized to me and I'd devised my own strategies to quietly and quickly climb out of the hole, but here were my friends, my teammates, and even complete strangers offering to help me build a ladder.

Burnout is nothing to be ashamed of. It's like falling off a bicycle; not a sign of weakness, just a sign of imbalance. Even Olympic cyclists fall down sometimes.

Dwelling on things you cannot change is counterproductive. Once burnout happens, you can't simply erase it, you need to work through it. Here is my four-step plan to recovering from burnout.

Step 1: Identify the Cause

The first step is to identify the cause of your burnout. Do you have too much on your plate? Is something happening in your life that is causing more stress than usual? Sometimes it's not being out of balance that causes you to fall. Sometimes it's the weight of all the responsibilities you are balancing that causes you to crumble and drop it all. Whatever it is, forgive yourself for letting it happen. Forgive yourself with the same kindness you would offer a friend, and accept that what happened, happened.

Step 2: Recharge

Once you've identified the cause of the burnout, give yourself permission to recharge. Disconnect from whatever it was that caused you to burn out, and allow yourself to do so without guilt. I've seen many young professionals burn out and hide it – we feel guilty or ashamed that we were unable to power through everything on our plate, and we don't want it to reflect poorly on our overall performance. Especially in early career, where the pressure to prove oneself is always bearing down, it can be difficult to accept that we can't do it all. But sometimes we simply can't, and we need to know that that's okay.

Step 3: Seek Help

This is the one most of us forget to do. Until my community rallied around me, I never expected that people could be so compassionate and supportive. Don't be afraid to ask for support from people in different areas of your life. Family and friends, of course, can offer a particular kind of support, but your coworkers and leadership at work may be able to provide support as well. Can your manager or team step in to help share the load while you recover? Even if nothing can be moved or pushed, a conversation with your manager can help them understand what's going on in your life at that moment and give you an opportunity to discuss realistic expectations for everyone involved. Hiding your burnout from your team is a missed opportunity to identify a problem in balance that may be affecting overall team productivity. Your manager should know when burnout happens so they can work proactively to correct the situation for the future. And if you're a people manager yourself, encouraging your people to share their honest feedback with you can help you build trust and foster a happier, more productive team.

Step 4: Reboot and Realign

This whole burnout recovery process is like hard rebooting your computer, making sure you start up properly once you're ready to start running processes again. The last step in making a full recovery is realigning yourself to your goals and priorities. This is a great time to revisit your T, your work/life/soul Venn, your time expectation chart, and your goals. Do these snapshots of your lives complement or conflict? Reevaluate with honesty and forgiveness, and then take a look at the weeks ahead and plan your return, building yourself a gradual ramp up instead of jumping right in to a deep pool of mixed responsibility.

A tree stands tall because its roots are stronger than the wind. —Unknown

To this day I still fear that I was responsible for some young women adopting a flawed approach to work-life balance. Dear reader, if you were there that day I stood on stage in front of 200 young women, I would love to hear from you, whether it's to tell me you took it on board or saw it for what it was, a reflection of how imbalanced my life was at the time. I don't regret saying what I did that day - that moment was the root of so much reflection that started this journey of discovering real balance - but if I could stand on that stage again, I would sing a very different tune.

Balance isn't just important, it is THE MOST important. Balance is the best gift you can give, to yourself and to others. When you live a balanced life, you gift not only yourself, but everyone around you. Your family benefits from your undivided attention when you commit to being present in the time you share together. Your teammates feed off your energy when you feel happy to be at work and aren't bogged down thinking about all the things you still have to do. Your quality of work goes up, serving as validation to both yourself and your colleagues because you are a valuable member of the team.

When you live a balanced life, you begin each day with a fresh, well-organized slate, and end each day with an empty stack, having dealt with all the responsibilities - at work, at home, and to yourself - that were on your plate for the day. When you live a balanced life, your everyday happiness improves, and with that your life adopts a more positive shine, your glasses tint rose. When you live a balanced life, you can survive anything the universe throws your way, because you have strong roots and feel fulfilled in your work, life, *and* soul.

CHAPTER 4

Confidence: Fuel for Success

By: Melody Zacharias

Life is not easy for any of us. But what of that? We must have perseverance and above all, confidence in ourselves. We must believe that we are gifted for something and that this thing must be attained.
– Marie Curie

Just Say Yes

For as long as I can remember, even as a child of uneducated alcoholic parents with very little money, I have always felt that if I wanted to accomplish something, I could. I just had to determine how. It did not matter what it was. I remember being 10 and wanting a particular pair of jeans for the new school year coming up. They were more than my parents could afford, so they said they would not buy them for me. I accepted their answer but did not feel that was the final answer. I found a job. I babysat for a family that had a small boy and before school started I had earned and saved enough to buy the jeans I wanted.

That summer I also entered a radio contest for a Sony Walkman, another thing that was too expensive for my parents to buy me and also out of my financial league. I had never won anything in my life and I'm not sure what prompted me to make the effort required to enter the contest. While making the effort, I was not under any delusion that I was likely to win. So, after entering the contest I did not give it much thought.

On the first day of school wearing my new jeans, a boy much older than me said "Hey! I heard on the radio you won a Walkman. Can I have it?" It was a joke, but a not a funny one. I was intimidated by the older boy and as a shy younger girl did not want the attention. I immediately said no, but I had no idea what he was talking about. Later that week I had a new Sony Walkman!

It was then that I first realized I could control the outcome of my life through my own actions. For some things there was a direct correlation – I worked, and I purchased my jeans. For other things, like much of life, there is a strong luck component. However, by putting in effort, I increase the odds of something good happening in my life. It was the first time I had any sense of control over a life that was, until that point, wholly dependent on my parents.

During this part of my life, we lived in a research town where most of the adults were university educated professionals. In fact, most families had at least one person with a Masters or PhD in Physics. My parents were poorly educated and worked very hard to earn a meager living. I was often looked down on by other kids and pitied by their parents. Having something no one in town had, a Walkman, gave me a glimpse into the world of status, class, and money. I was not, and never will be, interested in any of those things, but I knew I did not like how people looked down on me and I saw that education was the way to change it.

I didn't know why or how, but I absolutely knew I had to rise above my current situation. Not rise above in status or class but in the sense of taking the high road. I did not want status, nor to be a part of a particular class or to flaunt wads of money or expensive baubles. However, deep in my core, I knew I did not like how people treated me when they viewed me only as a poor kid with alcoholic parents. It was not a conscious decision to take the high road; it was more of a coping mechanism. I often felt powerless as a child when I was thrust into situations out of my control where I had no help or place to turn.

For example, one of my babysitting jobs was for a family that had recently had a baby. I was 11 and had no business taking care of a 6-week-old! Those were the days before there was any training for babysitting, no book, guide or course you could take. No Google to search for tips, tricks, or checklists. If you seemed mature, adults assumed you could take care of their child. I remember being terrified! I was the youngest in my family and had zero experience with babies, especially any that young. Taking on challenges like this was something I just did. Somehow the child and I both survived that night and many more after. Challenges like this come up in everyone's life. The key to these challenges is to say "yes" and work hard to ensure you succeed. Yes! has become something of a motto for me. If a client asks if I can do something, I say yes. Then I make sure I figure out how to do it. If I want something, I say yes. Then I figure out how to get it.

When I was thirteen, I was doing all I could to earn some extra money. Back then, delivering newspapers door to door was a common way for kids to do this. Unfortunately, I had one customer that would insist on greeting me at the door at 5:30 AM to get his paper. Normally this would not be an issue, however, he was a very large man over six foot seven, a professional football player, and would open the door wearing nothing below the waist.

At this age, not only was I buying some of my own clothing, but I was also buying sandwich meat and fruit to make my lunch each day (did I mention we were poor?). This man became my worst nightmare! I was terrified to approach his house. Each day was a challenge for me to try to figure out how to sneak up to his house so he could not see me coming. That way, I could deliver his paper before he knew I was there. This went on for a few months so he changed his tactic. Now, in the evenings when I would go to collect payment for the newspapers he would again open the door with no pants on. So I stopped collecting payments. Eventually my boss called me to ask why I was not collecting from him. I told him why, and they stopped selling him a paper.

In hindsight, I should have called my boss when it first happened, but I was young, naive, and worried that because he was a football player they would not believe me and I would lose my job. I needed that job. I wanted to eat lunch. In the end, I believe that although traumatic, the experience was confidence building. I pushed through the adversity and in the end the paper believed me. I proved to myself I could once again triumph over adversity.

The 7 to 1 Rule

> *I fall asleep feeling beautiful. Then, in the morning, before I leave the house, I say five things I love about myself, like 'You have really pretty eyes.' That way I can go out into the world with that little bit of extra confidence. It's a feel-good protein shake in my back pocket in case someone messes with me that day.*
> *– Jennifer Love Hewitt*

With each new obstacle I survived, I not only got more money but I became more confident. I now see this same confidence growing in my daughters. Earlier this year, my youngest daughter was concerned about completing a course for school over the summer. I asked her if she was worried that she could not do it without the typical supports of the school system. Her answer was perfect, she said; "No mom. I know I can do it. I am just struggling to figure out how." To me, THIS, is confidence. In life, we will not always have the answer to how we will accomplish something but knowing we will is the most important piece. Have confidence in yourself and you can accomplish anything.

This has led me to one of my favorite quotes: "Life has no remote. Get up and change it yourself."

This is not much different from the Nike motto, "Just Do it". However, the quote has the added quality of letting you know you are accountable for your situation. That is not to say that a poor beggar in Calcutta is responsible for being destitute. The lottery of the womb, and a lot more of life's randomness plays an enormous role. At the same time, if you are reading this book, there is a good chance that you have more control over your life situation than 90% of the people on this planet.

You likely have not had experiences like mine that have helped build my confidence. But if you look back at the experiences I described, you will see that they weren't particularly positive – I just turned them into something positive.

Perhaps your experience has led you to have a lack of confidence. Studies show that for every negative experience we have, we need **seven** positive experiences to counteract that negativity. I am thankful that I had enough positive experiences to build that confidence. Most of those positive experiences were of my own making, or a result of how I viewed the situation.

Girls and women are subjected to daily experiences that strip their ability to grow confident, much more so than the average male. Often, people do not realize that what they are doing has a negative impact; it is simply normal in our society. The barrage of western media insisting how we should look and what we should wear is a flood of negativity directed at women. You may think marketers are selling a new lipstick by telling women their lips are not full enough or the correct colour. Marketers know better. They know they are attacking a woman's self-esteem in order to create the imperative for the viewer to go out and buy that lipstick. Buy our lipstick and you too can have the confidence and appeal that our model is portraying. (For commercials directed at men, they skip over the attack on self-esteem and instead tell you that so long as you drink our beer or wear our body spray, gorgeous fun-loving women will simply throw themselves at you no matter how you dress or look.)

This is just one example of the many negative messages that bombard women every day. There are movements and organizations that work against this type of message (Dove soap for example has been running a self-esteem program for years), but going back to my quote, we need to change it ourselves. Paraphrasing Gandhi, we cannot change the actions of others, but we can certainly change our own. For example, I limit the number of commercials my kids and I watch by not subscribing to cable TV where there is a lot of negative messaging.

Your mind works just like your body: You are what you eat. You limit the amount of junk food you eat because it is going to rot your body. Take the same care with your brain. Ensure your brain gets a healthy diet of positive messaging, and don't rely on others to feed it to you.

Limiting the number of negative messages is one side of the coin. We know some negative messaging is going to get through all your filters, so we must also address the other side of the coin and ensure we are getting enough positive messages. One way we can do this is to support the women and girls in our lives by adding to the positive messages they receive. A couple of years ago, whenever a girlfriend would phone, I would answer the phone with an enthusiastic "Hello Gorgeous!". I am always sincere; each and every one of my girlfriends are amazing, gorgeous women. The reactions I got from this positive message was not at all what I expected. Some were startled and ignored it, some just laughed, and one tried to argue with me about how she was not "gorgeous". Clearly, some of my girlfriends need more positive messages from more people. Also, it is clear that no matter how many positive messages you get from others, your attitude is capable of filtering them so you never get to enjoy the benefits.

We all thrive on positive feedback and when we have amazing women in our lives there is absolutely no reason not to celebrate it by telling them how great they are or giving them a sincere compliment. My teenage girls are often asking how a particular outfit looks on them. It is not because they think it looks awful, but because it makes them feel safe, and secure in their choice and gives them a little more confidence to venture out into the world. This does not mean you always tell them it looks great. They are not stupid. Nine times out of ten, they know what you should respond with, and want to hear it to confirm their thoughts. This confirmation builds their confidence in their own thought process. So always be honest! Be careful though. You can be honest and not kind, please choose to be kind as well.

Each and every experience we have in life can be seen as a success or failure. If we see the positive in each experience we can learn, grow and build our confidence. If we dwell on the failure, like my inability to get the money for the papers, it diminishes that confidence. Our reality comes from the stories we tell ourselves. Nothing in life has any real meaning except the meaning you give it. A funeral, for example, can be viewed as a celebration of someone's life, or a time to mourn a death. You get to choose the meaning of an event. By understanding that things and events can be interpreted any way you want, you can learn to improve the quality of your thoughts and therefore the quality of the messages you are receiving.

I don't think of myself as an optimist, but as a realist. There are lessons to be learned in everything. I truly believe those lessons are best used to grow and move forward, not to dwell and wallow. Which is why another quote I am fond of is, "What doesn't kill us makes us stronger".

I have succeeded in life for many reasons. For example, I was the first in my family to go to university. As soon as I knew what university was, it did not occur to me that I would not go. In hindsight, this is odd since nobody in my family or in my life at that time was in or had gone to university; however, it never occurred to me not to go. Discussions with friends, colleagues, family and my own research has lead me to adopt this key trait for success: confidence. The more successful people I learn about, the more I have come to realize that confidence drives most other traits people use to define success. Books, research, and papers all talk about the keys to success as being:

1. Determination
2. Drive
3. Tenacity
4. Ambition

These are all things that are derived from confidence. Since confidence is so important, it is surprising it is not taught in school. So once again, it is up to us to figure out how we get more, make more, build more. To answer these questions, we have to first understand what confidence is and look at where it comes from.

What is Confidence?

Confidence is going after Moby Dick in a rowboat and
taking tartar sauce with you.
– Zig Ziglar

Confidence is the feeling you have about your ability to do something. Many people do not feel confident about being able to present an idea at a seminar or convention (public speaking). But they may feel very confident that they can build a great website. So, "confidence" can be specific to a situation.

On the other hand, there is the confidence that gives you the feeling that even if you cannot currently do something, you are sure in your ability to learn how to do it. Again, I will use the idea of public speaking.

I have gone through the better part of my life eschewing any and all public speaking. I didn't like it, and, to be honest, it terrified me. Then I came to a crossroads in my life where, in order to achieve what I wanted, I was going to have to start doing some public speaking.

I had a choice:

1. Give up on what I wanted to achieve.
2. Get over myself and learn to speak in public forums.

I now speak at SQL Saturdays, PASS Summit, and other venues many times each year. It has gotten to the point where I often lament that I only have one hour to get my point across. I went from not being confident about public speaking to being very confident. The thing that got me there is the same thing that allows men to apply for a job when they have very limited qualifications for the position. That thing is confidence in my willingness to learn. I say "willingness" instead of "ability" because we are all able (some a little more quickly than others), but many of us are not **willing** to do what it takes.

I looked at the situation and understood that people who stand up and speak in front of a crowd do not have some magical ability. I've seen some great speakers, but I've also seen some poor speakers. They both managed to survive the ordeal. I was confident that even if I am not a gifted public speaker like my daughter, I can still, at the very least, be a competent one. I found a couple of coaches, and I practiced, and practiced, and practiced. I had to practice a lot because I was nervous as hell and needed to know that if I blanked, my speech could go on in auto-pilot mode.

I survived my first speech, then my second, then more. Eventually, through coaching and practice, I was no longer "surviving", I was thriving! I was willing to work hard and suffer through the initial fear because I knew that I was able do it. If others can, there was no reason why I couldn't.

The confidence I am talking about in this chapter is not the confidence to build a website; that is too specific. It is the confidence in your ability to do almost anything that someone else can do, and your willingness to do what it takes to do it. This does not mean that I believe I can be the next Picasso. It does mean that if I put my mind to it and practice, I could be a competent painter. By the way, I currently suck at drawing / painting.

There is an important but subtle difference between "confidence" and "self esteem". Confidence addresses your abilities. Self esteem addresses your respect or admiration for yourself. You can have low self esteem, yet still feel confident in your ability to do something. You can feel confident that you can solve a specific math problem and still have low self esteem. The confidence that I want you to have is a lot easier to come by if you have high self-esteem. They are two different ideas, but they can be dependent on each other.

Confidence can be derived from self-esteem, but it can also work the other way around.

Where Does Confidence Come From?

I was always looking outside myself for strength and confidence,
but it comes from within. It is there all the time.
— Anna Freud

There are psychology studies that claim that confidence is between 25% and 50% genetic. This of course brings up the whole "nature vs. nurture" debate. Rather than simply dismissing or wallowing in these studies, let's assume they are correct and look at them at the most pessimistic end of that statistic. Let's assume that confidence is 50% genetic. Like the glass is half full or half empty question, this is a question of optimism. You can view it two ways:

- Oh no! I know I got short changed in the genetic confidence basket because I am not currently confident. I will never be as confident as Joe. Or,
- Wow! At least 50% of my confidence comes from what I do and how I think. These things are 100% within my control, so I get to be the master of my own confidence. Genetics only dictates where I start on my confidence journey, not where I end.

So, now that I know that even if confidence is 50% genetic, my confidence level is 100% under my control. Where do I start?

I think you know where I sit on these two outlooks.

So, to answer the question of where confidence comes from, it comes from you and the stories you tell yourself. Having others tell you that you are great can be helpful, but the last thing you want to do is rely on others for your level of confidence. It is too important to leave to chance! Take control and don't let other people decide who you are. Don't allow negative thoughts to dominate. Replace them with positive thoughts and start working on your confidence. At the same time, pay it forward. Confident women don't hate other women. Be confident enough to instill confidence in others.

Why is Confidence So Important?

Experience tells you what to do; confidence allows you to do it.
— Stan Smith

In the 7 to 1 Rule section, I said that the generally agreed upon factors for success are derived from confidence. So, no matter how you define "success", it is confidence that is the best route to achieving it.

Your portrayal of confidence allows others to feel confidence in you. If you are sitting in the board room and are unsure as to whether you can complete a project, your manager or client is going to have a very difficult time giving you the budget and other resources to succeed. On the other hand, if you portray confidence in your ability to complete a project, your manager or client will also feel confident in the project, allowing them to easily sign the authorization to get started.

Personal confidence promotes the feeling of confidence in others. Studies have shown that confidence even trumps IQ in terms of how competent people come across. This can be particularly important in business where many decisions are made on feelings of trust and competency. Often these feelings go hand in hand. If you aren't sure you believe me when I say that confidence trumps IQ, I'll bet you can instantly picture a confident manager in your past, who is also completely incompetent. Checkmate! Mark Twain is quoted as saying, "All you need is ignorance and confidence, and then success is sure."

If I am confident, I appear more competent and that gives people the feeling of trust, and therefore more confidence in the decision they must make. A Carnegie Melon study shows that confidence is even more important than reputation. Have you ever wondered how that co-worker with a reputation for getting nothing done, managed to get promoted? Wonder no more. Confidence trumps reputation and gives managers the confidence to promote them.

Finally, confidence is the fuel for action. How often have you thought about wanting to do something and thought you may not be successful at it, so it then became too much work to try? The American Pastor Robert Schuller famously asked a very powerful question: "What would you do if you knew you could not fail?" Sit back for a couple minutes and think about that question. If you spent fifteen minutes pondering this question I bet, you would have a list of at least three amazing things that you would do. I say only three because you will probably get lost in the details and thoughts of accomplishment for each thing you think about.

That is what confidence does. It allows us to dream big and gives us the fuel to escape from a world of apathy. It gets us out of bed ready for action; ready to do something that will move us towards achieving whatever goal we set for ourselves. Without the confidence to at least try, we are sure to fail. If we try, but only halfheartedly because we lack confidence, we will likely fail.

So, if it is just a matter of confidence, why isn't everyone painting on a smirk and walking with a swagger? It's because it isn't easy. If it were easy, everyone would be doing it. It requires sustained effort, and despite all the benefits, not everyone is <u>willing</u> to make the effort.

Now a word of caution. There is a fine line between confidence and arrogance. Confidence is knowing you can do the job. Arrogance is knowing you can do the job better than anyone else, because you are better than everyone else. It is the prejudice or feeling of superiority that some people have that turns confidence into arrogance. It is the difference between knowing you can learn what you need to in order to complete the job versus knowing it all.

The Look of Confidence

Confidence is the sexiest thing a woman can wear.
— Aimee Mullins

Picture what a confidence looks like to you. Science says you are likely to see a 30 - 50 year old male who stands at least six feet tall, is Caucasian, and wears a dark suit. Google agrees with this. If you google "confidence male" and check out the images, you have to scroll exceptionally far to find images outside this stereotype.

Now picture what a confident woman looks like to you. Science says that there are almost as many answers to that question as there are people you can ask. Most often you think of someone specific in your life and generalizing a specific image is not as easy. Google will agree with you again. If you google "confidence woman" and check out the images, you will immediately see far more variety. There are different races, ages and clothing types. The sad part is that this search turns up lots of images of women in very little clothing. Welcome to modern Western cultural stereotyping.

The good news is that stereotypes are not true confidence. If they were, then how is it that your friend who is 5' 2" and likes tan coloured suits is so confident? And ladies, I don't know about you, but going to work in a bra and thong would not be a confident look for me.

What is true, however, is that body language, not your height or race, does make a difference in looking and being confident. If you go back and look at the images for both women and men, you can see that none of them are slouching or making themselves look small. Their body language is such that they are taking up lots of space, especially females, and they are all smiling. A smile goes a long way towards portraying confidence. That is because when you are confident, you are in control. When you are in control, you almost have to be happy, since control implies that everything is going according to your plan.

The Voice of Confidence

When you think of confidence, what voice do you hear? Is it a deep base male voice or a high pitch female voice? We want to guess it is the deep male voice, but that doesn't ring true in describing confidence. People are generally more comfortable answering with, "I can't describe it, but I know it when I hear it". That is because confidence comes in all voices. The genetics that gave you the voice you have plays zero part in whether you are perceived as confident.

What is important is the body language you see and the cadence of the voice that tells you whether the person speaking is confident. In this section, I am focusing on the cadence.

Consider this situation. You have two friends over for dinner, you individually ask them the question, "What would you like for dinner tonight?" You get the following two answers:

1. Let's have chicken for dinner.
2. Let's have chicken for dinner?

The words are identical, but the meaning and perception of the listener are far from identical. It is easy to guess which one sounds more confident.

Research shows that it is more likely that the first answer came from a man. This is because, when men hear a question they tend to answer the question with a statement. Conversely, women tend to provide you with the answer but at the same time, want to know what you think as well. So, women are more likely to answer in a questioning tone. Although you may think that you are being polite by inviting participation and indicating your willingness to be flexible, what you are really doing is coming across as wishy-washy and throwing the cognitive load back on the person asking the question. When someone asks you a question, they are looking for an answer, not a question in return. If you answer a question with a question, not only does it imply that you do not have the answer, but it also paints you with an aura of diffidence.

When polled, both women and men agree that answer #1 shows more confidence. Again, the words are the same, and the voices could be those of identical twins, but the cadence makes the two sentences completely different.

Confidence is not a stereotype but still has a definite look and sound to it. So, lets take what science has learned about the connections between confidence and body language and voice, and start filling our confidence glass. Start paying attention to your body language and practice the things that are going to help build confidence.

What Do We Do to Build Confidence?

I've already pointed out that your level of confidence is 100% under your control. So the question becomes, what specific things can I do to start building a more confident me? There is both good news and bad news in answering this question. I like to end on good news, so, first the bad news. Many of the things you need to do aren't easy. If you are looking for a magic pill that will instantly give you confidence (while allowing you to lose a few pounds), you will have to look in the fiction section of your pharmacy. The good news is that there are lots of things you can do, and some of them are easy.

Fake it Till You Make It

You gain strength, courage, and confidence by every experience in which
you really stop to look fear in the face. You are able to say to yourself,
'I lived through this horror. I can take the next thing that comes along.'
– Eleanor Roosevelt.

In a previous section I talked about overcoming my fear of public speaking. I was not a confident speaker, but I am now. The path I had to walk that lead to becoming a confident speaker is one where I had to face that fear head on. Paint on a smile, and fake it till you make it.

In the comfort of your living room, you know that people do not die from bungee jumping. Driving to the facility is infinitely more dangerous than jumping off the bridge. We know this to be true, but at the same time, most of us know that driving there is easy and we wouldn't think twice about it. Taking that single step off the edge is close to impossible for us to do, and we would be thinking more than twice as we stood there looking into the abyss. Yet if we face that fear and take the step, we know that doing it again will be just a little easier. Do it enough and you will be looking for new ways to make it thrilling again by going backwards or doing flips.

That first time isn't easy, and it isn't bravery that allows you to take the step. You cannot say, as you are shaking and your mind is screaming at you to go crawl under a rock, that you are being brave. It is your ability to convince yourself to trust the bungee that allows you to muster up enough fake bravery to step off the bridge. The same applies to public speaking. You know you will survive, but you must paint on a smile, practice, and pretend like you don't want to run away and hide. Eventually it gets easier, but the first several times is almost always an exercise in "fake it till you make it." Are you willing to face your fears?

If you have ever been to a personal growth or leadership seminar, you likely had to do something crazy. Some of the things you do in these seminars include a "trust fall", "eat fire", walk on fire, or even bungee jump. The reason they have you do these things is they want to prove to you that you can do things you thought were impossible for you to do. The idea is that from that point forward, every obstacle you face is small compared to walking on fire. You should be able to tell yourself that if you can jump off a bridge, you can do anything. As you go through life facing your fears, new fears start to look insignificant.

Adopt a Better Attitude.

Optimism is the faith that leads to achievement.
Nothing can be done without hope and confidence.
– Helen Keller

Girls and boys get completely different messages as they grow up. The other day I saw a boy, around twelve years old, wearing a T-shirt that said, "If you aren't the fastest, you are losing." This boy was considerably overweight and didn't look like he would win many races. Yet he had the confidence to wear this in-your-face T-shirt. And you know it was his parents who bought it for him. Now think about how an overweight twelve-year-old girl would feel and the societal messages she would be receiving. Would parents buy a shirt like that for their overweight daughter?

In part, this is one of the reasons men are more confident than women. Society often gives boys a pass in areas where girls are judged harshly. This leads to boys seeing events in an optimistic or more confident way. Studies show that when a job posting comes out, and a man looks at the list of ten qualifications on the posting and sees that he meets three of the ten he will apply for that job and feel relatively confident that he will get the job. A woman on the other hand, will look at the same posting and if she meets less than seven out of the ten, she will not apply at all. Women are often not confident enough to even apply! This pattern is a big reason why women are not advancing to the corner office like men. In this instance, the only thing holding us back is our own bad attitude.

How often has a woman mentioned to you that they received a promotion, award, or accolade, and they say they were surprised. Likely, you thought it was well deserved and easily justified, but the recipient doesn't see their own talents. They are too focused on their shortcomings. I have friends who do this all the time. The people around us see our abilities, we just don't recognize them in ourselves, or we brush them off and don't use them to cultivate the confidence we need.

Our glass of confidence needs to be filled by first acknowledging our successes and second, underline accepting them. A great friend wisely pointed out to me that by not accepting a compliment graciously, you are insulting the person or organization that gave you the compliment or award. When you think about it that way… stop being rude and say thank you! There is nothing that says we need to justify, or worse, reject another person's feelings by projecting our fears and feelings on to them.

If this is difficult for you, start by simply acknowledging the compliment and saying thank you. It is that simple when you think about it. But don't stop there. Recognize the angst you feel, and tell yourself a better story about how hard you worked and the things you did to help bring you the accolade. Work on that inner voice and bring it to heel.

We, as women, need to stop diminishing our actions or down playing them. Some women think that by downplaying a compliment, they are remaining humble and avoiding being seen as arrogant. This is simply wrong thinking! There is nothing arrogant about accepting a compliment. Just do it graciously.

When you find yourself downplaying your accomplishments, or surprised by an accolade, those should be red flags for you to realize that you have a bad attitude. Put those dismissive thoughts aside and adopt a better attitude. You deserve all the things you earn.

The Power Pose

I have a confidence about my life that comes from
standing tall on my own two feet.
– Jane Fonda

We already talked about the look of confidence. Your body language affects how people perceive you, and in particular, their perception of how confident you are. Now here is a little secret for you: Your body language also affects how confident you feel.

Imagine you want to portray a look of determination. What is the first thing you do? Likely, you clench your fists. You thought something, and your body reflected what you thought. Researchers conducted an experiment to see if it works the other way. They provided students with a tough problem to solve. Half the students were told to clench their fists for thirty seconds just prior to starting the problem, the other half just started in on the problem. On average, the students who had clenched their fists worked significantly longer on the problem before giving up. In other words, their body language affected their own brain and made them more determined.

While your body language is communicating to others, it is also communicating to you. Your non-verbal body language can actually govern how you think and feel about yourself! You become what your body language is communicating. It affects your thoughts, feelings, and even your physiology.

Throughout the animal world, power and dominance is displayed through body language by opening up or spreading out. A snake rears up as high as it can, a cat's fur stands on end and humans stand tall and spread their arms. This form of body language is so dominant that even blind people who have never seen anyone doing it, will raise their arms wide in triumph when they win at a physical competition.

Now, as I said earlier, our body language affects those around us, but it also affects ourselves. In order to change your thoughts and feelings about how powerful you are, you really need a change the hormones coursing through your brain. In particular, you need to increase testosterone and decrease cortisol (small wonder that men are generally more confident than women).

Studies have shown that after a two-minute high-power pose, testosterone levels in your brain increase by 20% and cortisol levels decrease by 25%. With a low-power pose, the hormones go in the opposite direction. So, a two-minute pose can either leave you feeling assertive, confident and comfortable … or shut down and stress reactive.

What do you do when you go to an interview and are waiting to be called in? You sit in a chair, hunch forward, and check your phone or read. What you really want to be doing is stand up with your arms up and legs apart.

In a study done at Harvard, they ran this experiment. They put participants through a very stressful interview. For two-minutes, half the participants sat in a low-power pose and half assumed a high-power pose. The participants were judged by a panel of people who later watched tapes of the interviews. The judges were completely blind to the purpose of the study.

Overwhelmingly, the panel chose to hire the people who had struck the high-power pose prior to the interview.

What was driving this preference was not the content of the interview. It was their presence! They were comfortable, captivating, **confident**, passionate, and enthusiastic. In other words, these people were able to bring their true selves to the interview. They were able to be present, without the enveloping stress that can *paint* over everything you say or do.

Our bodies change our minds. Our minds change our behavior. Our behavior changes our outcomes.

Eye Contact

I like getting to the meat of things. You can't get it in a five-minute
interview. I like to hone a person. I like to make eye contact.
– Larry King

Eye contact is not just something our mothers told us to do to ensure we were paying attention. It is a human connection that promotes oxytocin, a hormone that creates trust. Eye contact can build trust in the relationship and with trust comes confidence in that relationship. Whether with a significant other or a client, trust is critical in building the relationship and will help promote your confidence.

Even five-day old babies prefer faces that make direct eye contact over faces with an averted gaze. This preference is genetically coded into us. You want to hold eye contact for about three seconds. Any more than that, and people start to feel uncomfortable, unless you are particularly trustworthy in their mind; then a little longer is fine.

One trick used by social gurus is, when you are first introduced to someone, look into their eyes and try to make a mental note of their eye colour. The deep gaze and added time helps build instant trust.

Once you have some now what?

Once we believe in ourselves, we can risk curiosity, wonder, spontaneous delight, or any experience that reveals the human spirit.
– E. E. Cummings

Once you have a little you will want more. Once you begin to see how confidence can work for you and with you, you will want more. The wonderful thing about building confidence is that it builds on itself. The more confidence you have the more you accomplish. The more you accomplish, the more confidence you get. It becomes a virtuous circle. So how do we get from a trickle to a fire hose full of the stuff? We do it by taking control of our thoughts, who we interact with, and by trying really hard to face our fears.

Once we have done all that and are starting to feel the virtuous circle taking hold, we quickly run into a society that views confident assertive women as a bitch. Both men and women have bought into this fiction. Overcoming this hurdle is going to take patience and more than just a little finesse. Don't be discouraged when you do everything right and some people still label you a "bitch!". Some people feel the need to attack when their masculinity or competency is challenged by a woman who has the temerity to speak.

In all cases, you must take the high road (the Gandhi approach). If you:

- keep your assertions to areas in which you have at least some knowledge,
- keep an open mind as to whether you may be mistaken,

- avoid hysterics, hyperbole, yelling, and other histrionics, and
- use logic, not emotion, to make your points,

you will hopefully be seen by those around you as being the reasonable one in the room. For now, that is all we can hope for.

Summary

People spend a good part of their lives chasing something. When we were young, it was boys. After that it might be education, followed by a job, then career, and for most or all that time, money.

Like so many things in life, what we want cannot be attained directly. Researchers point out that one excellent way to find happiness, for example, is to make others happy. If you want a car, you don't go chasing cars; you chase after money, which means you need to find work, a promotion, or perhaps education.

Success means something different to everyone. However, whatever it means to you, there are likely a variety of things you need that will help you attain that success. I believe that confidence is one of those indirect things that everyone should be spending time cultivating because it leads to attaining virtually every other goal you hope to achieve.

I hope that I have convinced you that you can and should work on improving your confidence and that I have given you the tools and motivation to start working on it right now.

CHAPTER 5

Mentorship for the New Age, or How to do Career Development on the Sly

By: Elizabeth Hosang

This is the story of how a meeting invitation, a car accident, and a stack of old training materials changed my attitude about my role in industry, and led to me running the Professional Women's Network at my company.

I went to Engineering school in the late 80s. At the time, women made up only ten percent of the student body. We had worked hard to get there, along the way ignoring joking, and sometimes out-and-out serious, advice from teachers and guidance counsellors who told us that women didn't go into Engineering. Once we arrived we continued to work hard, and adapted ourselves to the new environment. We laughed along with some of the racy jokes, rolled our eyes at those that were a little more risqué, and turned a blind eye to the truly obnoxious in order to fit in. We shouted down any attempt by the professors to say we should be treated differently. It was going to be hard enough to get hired and taken seriously without the professors telling potential employers that "women need to put their feet up once a month." Yes, an actual male Engineering professor said that, at a meeting they called with female students to discuss how to promote women in Engineering. My mother, a head nurse at the time, also disagreed. That was certainly not the way she or anyone else made up work schedules for the almost exclusively female nursing staff. While she supported me going into Engineering, we still disagreed over whether it was appropriate for women to wear pants in the workplace. Skirts and high heels were still the office norm.

Eventually my classmates and I graduated, getting jobs where again we worked to prove ourselves. Over the years I have often been the only woman in the room, both with clients and with co-workers. For a few years I was the only woman in the building, which housed only the personnel on my project. I worked my way to a senior position, running projects and supervising junior employees. Along the way I tried to share the benefits of my experience, but no formal opportunities came along.

Then one day, I got an email inviting me to a meeting held by the Professional Women's Network, or PWN. It was the company's initiative to retain female employees. Apparently, in the years since I had graduated, someone had decided to do something more than just talk about recruiting more women. More impressive still, someone also found research money to study trends in industry. One of the things they proved was that there are long-term benefits to companies with diverse workforces. Diversity encourages innovation and resilience in a workforce. This research had raised the issue in such a way that large corporations were responding with workplace initiatives.

Unfortunately, another thing they found was that women who managed to achieve careers in high tech didn't always choose to stay in high tech. At my company, a decision was made by upper management to create an initiative to support their female employees. This initiative was the Professional Women's Network. The idea was to provide career development opportunities, as well as building support networks. A handful of women were approached to organize the network, with the support of management for resources, such as email lists and a web site for announcements and resources.

I was not among the first group of women approached to organize the meetings, and when I got the email, I hesitated. As I mentioned before, my generation of Engineers learned not to draw attention to the fact that we were female. And yet, I went.

At first, the presentation went about like I expected, a lot of shiny promises about all the activities that would take place. Over the course of my career, I had seen a variety of extra-curricular initiatives start strong and then fade over time. If anything, I was mostly curious as to how long this one would last. Then they asked for volunteers to run some of those activities, including someone to run the Mentorship program.

I don't know if it is the big sister in me, or the mom in me, but when I saw the word Mentorship up on the screen, I stared, transfixed. Over the years I'd tried informally to coach junior team members, but it mostly took the form of conversations during drives to client sites. I had been very excited at one company when they started a formal mentoring program. Those of us designated as mentors were assigned three or four people to meet with on a regular basis. We were to receive a budget and a time code so we could go for coffee once a quarter and discuss career plans. Unfortunately, someone started doing the math and decided the program was going to cost a little too much, and everything ground to a halt.

This new PWN program was a voluntary affair, as in come to a meeting over your lunch hour, no billing codes, no budget. The good news was that this meant less chance it could find itself in the cross-hairs of a cost cutting effort. In the end, I emailed the woman running the PWN, saying I was willing to fill the position of Mentorship prime. Committed, I set forth to work out the logistics of matching up mentors and mentees.

My first step was reading up on mentorship. It was like learning how to set up a dating service – matching mentor and mentee based on their backgrounds, experience, and interests. The problem with this approach is the same problem facing women in STEM: lack of numbers. It was hard enough to get anyone to attend the lunchtime presentations. There was no way we were going to get enough senior women to volunteer to be mentors. Complicating my situation was the fact that the PWN was open to everyone: engineering staff and administrative staff. Different backgrounds meant different career paths requiring different advice. The logistics of this approach quickly became far too complicated.

Plan B was group mentoring. Technically, group mentoring means gathering in a group, with a senior person leading a discussion on a given topic. My situation was complicated by the fact that the PWN was for the Canada Region, so we had people in Nova Scotia, Ontario, and Saskatchewan, meaning three different time zones. It's hard to build a group dynamic via conference call – it seems like talking on the phone is almost as bad as public speaking for some people. The lack of being able to read body language just makes it worse. This meant that a meeting focused on group discussion was probably not going to work.

In the end I went with Plan C, a series of six presentations called Building a Life Plan, based on things I wish I had known early in my career. I put together power point presentations, recruited the PWN representatives at the various sites to book meeting rooms, and sent out my own meeting invitations. Now all I had to do was cross my fingers and hope that I could attract an audience. At least I was confident that the presentations were good, because I had a lot of material to draw on. One benefit of starting in my career in the late eighties / early nineties was that it was the era of Big Tech.

For those of you who don't remember the days when cartoons were limited to Saturday morning, let me explain. Once upon a time, life in the high tech industry was good. Companies were flush with cash, and the perks flowed. Christmas parties were subsidized. Major releases were celebrated with catered off-site parties, and everyone on the project was given swag like desk clocks or key chains with the company logo and the product name. During this golden age, regular training was an expectation. Every year as part of setting your performance objectives, the boss handed you a catalog and told you to pick a certain number of classes. Sometimes you got to attend courses outside of work, at a hotel or the training company's office. If you worked for a really big company, they might have their own training department, offering classes customized in-house courses. Not just technical courses, either. Soft skills were taught, too, things like presentation skills and conflict resolution and time management.

Sadly, around the turn of the century, the bubble burst. Stock prices plunged, and bottom lines were highlighted in red. Luxuries like training and free coffee went away. If it didn't boost the bottom line, it didn't happen. Employees were on their own when it came to developing new skills, meaning you spent your own time and your own money. If you were lucky, and you could make a business case for how the class would benefit the project you were working on, you might be reimbursed after the fact, and after passing the class, of course.

Fortunately, I had started my career at one such large company. By the time the PWN meeting invite came along, I had amassed a small stockpile of training materials, and had augmented the pile through my own reading and the occasional Continuing Education course. Thanks to becoming a single parent when my daughter was very young, I had added books on child rearing and personal finance to the pile, and had compiled a list of references on parenting that I thought everyone should have to read.

On top of all that, one snowy day six months before the PWN invitation arrived, I was in a car accident around the corner from my office. At an L-shaped corner, another car slid across the centerline and plowed into my driver's side front panel. Two feet and half a second made the difference between me walking away, and me being pried out of a badly mangled passenger compartment. My steps were a little shaky, but thankfully I walked away from the written-off wreck of my car.

After the shock wore off, one question kept rolling around in my head. If things had gone differently, would someone else be able to run my life for three or six months while I recovered? What if someone had to take over completely? Who would pay the bills? Where was my will? My Power of Attorney? I knew I had updated these things after the divorce, but would anyone know where to find them? As a result, I spent the next two weeks searching for all my important papers and putting them in one place. To my disgust, it took me a full week to find my will. It was on the floor of a closet I didn't use very often. As the responsible adult in the house, I should have done better. If I couldn't find it, how could my grief-stricken friends and family?

When I look back on that time, I am a little disappointed that my close call didn't lead to one of those free-spirited, shopping spree / wild adventure montages you see on television sitcoms. Instead, I bought a life organizer. I put all my important papers into it, wrote down important names and phone numbers, and filed it someplace more sensible than the floor of the closet. I even updated my will, since I was no longer the parent of a toddler. The one sit-com cliché that I did suffer was the burning need to share my newfound wisdom. The evangelical spirit filled me: Update your will! Collect your warrantees in one place! Change your furnace filters on a regular basis!

All of this went into the first of the six presentations, called "Developing a Plan for Your Life". It focused on the importance of having a plan that covered all aspects of your life, and not just your career. Family, friends, community, finances – all these things need to be taken into account if you want to make it from first job to retirement with your sanity intact and a sense of achievement. Knowing my longer-term goals has helped me survive the chaos in my own life, so much so that I wanted to help others figure out theirs.

The presentation was a good hour long, had way more material than can reasonably be absorbed in one sitting, and included a reference section at the end with a long list of recommended reading. I blame the information density on my fear that it would be the only presentation I would ever give. I've seen a lot of employee-led initiatives across many companies fail due to lack of momentum. I was also worried that we would draw the attention of someone who wasn't part of the group that originally sponsored the PWN. The fact that we were doing career development on company time (during business hours, anyway) might make them see it as an official corporate activity. That same someone might decide that the program needed official corporate oversight, but wouldn't be sure who should provide it, or how things should run, and the entire program would end up on indefinite hiatus while they thought about it. I was afraid that my first presentation would be my last.

In the end, no one ordered a halt to my little lunch-time session. Feeling brave, I put together the next five presentations, each touching on a single theme. I scheduled the meetings, one a month, to create a sense of continuity. Determined to see this happen, I joked with a manager friend about being committed to sticking with the schedule, come hell or high water. As it turned out, Fate tried to call my bluff. I made one presentation while sick (no fever, but I went home to rest right after), and I once drove to the office through a snowstorm to do the presentation. The storm wasn't affecting Saskatchewan and I didn't want to disappoint anyone. (High water in the form of two feet of snow on the roads is still high water.)

In the end the presentations were well received. I don't know if anyone has updated their wills yet, but at least a few of them started thinking about it. (If you've got kids, but don't have a will, consider this scenario: your most obnoxious relatives end up with custody of your kids. Trust me, when you finish reading this, call a lawyer.) We even found a spot on the internal corporate website to archive the presentations, so people could look them up later.

I finished the last presentation in time to take a break from the PWN over the summer. The next fall I was asked to take over as the Chair of the PWN. The woman who had been the Chair had to step down due to other responsibilities, and the Mentoring presentations had been the main PWN activities the previous year. Between company activities and project deadlines, it did not make sense to have more than one PWN session a month, so we decided to stick with the Mentoring presentations. We put together a survey and sent it out via email to find out what topics people wanted to see. Management skills were the most popular topics, so we went with those.

After two years of informal presentations, we did finally meet with the upper level management, and were happy to discover that there was still corporate will to support the PWN. We had started holding book club sessions, discussing non-fiction books on management topics. Since most people didn't have time to read the books, one person does the reading and gives a presentation. Yes, we are doing book reports, but they are voluntary. Our Vice President offered to buy copies of the books so that people could read them. We now get several copies for each site. That same Vice President has promoted the PWN during all-hands meetings, acknowledging our efforts and encouraging people to attend. With his support, we have sent emails to the resource managers, asking them to suggest giving a PWN presentation as a way for employees to develop presentation skills. In addition, we've sent occasional newsletters giving goal setting advice. We'll be holding another survey soon, using the corporate survey account to ask what topics people want to see next.

I realize that this is not mentorship in the traditional sense. We do not have one-on-one sessions where a senior person offers advice specific to the mentee's situation. What we do have is guidance for skills development. I am hopeful that at some point we will have built enough of a network that we can start matching mentor/mentee pairs. In the meantime, we continue our monthly presentations, and encourage our members to invest in themselves.

The evangelical fire I felt after the car accident has faded, although I still like to remind people to make a will. I strongly believe in the importance of having a bigger plan, of looking at your life as a whole and working on all parts of it. Maybe that is because in the aftermath of the car accident, I found I did not have to make any major changes. I already had a good sense of what I wanted from life, and was working towards some of these goals. Being a mentor was always something I wanted to do, so when I got that first invitation email it was a case of right place, right time. With that opportunity came personal growth. Nowadays I am willing to stand up and be counted as a woman in high tech, especially if doing so can encourage others to enter the field and remain here.

The high tech industry is one of continuous change. The current industry is a lot different from the one I entered as a new-hire straight out of university. The internet has created an environment where small companies can start up almost overnight, with one good idea, crowd-sourced funding, and online advertising and distribution platforms. High-tech workers no longer expect that they will spend their entire career at one firm. Everyone needs to own their careers. Whether you want to develop new technical skills or go into management, you need to be prepared to drive your own career. We are creating new traditions, and new models for career paths. Those of us who have been doing this for a decade or two should consider what guidance we can offer to those who are coming behind us. And until someone sets up Mentors.com, or eMentorship.com, we are going to have to find non-traditional ways to offer this guidance.

CHAPTER 6

The Parenthood Penalty

By: Lori Lalonde, Author / Community Leader / Conference Speaker / Mentor / Code Whisperer

How many ways can discrimination rear its ugly head in the workplace? Women are discriminated against for being <insert random excuse here>. From age to physical appearance to education level, it seems there is no shortage of what the world criticizes women for and demands from them. There isn't a woman on Earth that meets the exacting requirements that are laid out in the corporate world for the type of career progression that many of us seek. And then of course, there's the parenthood penalty.

You know what I'm talking about. How many times have you seen your coworkers roll their eyes, or let out an exasperated sigh, when a coworker announces her pregnancy? Soon after, the whispers start, and speculation begins about whether or not Sarah will return from maternity leave, how much of her workload should be reduced during her pregnancy, or how absent-minded she seems to be now that she has "baby brain".

When Sarah does return from maternity leave, the speculation now moves towards her fitness as a team player. With a set schedule from 8am – 4:30pm, Sarah isn't able to attend spontaneous after work socials at the pub anymore, or work overtime from the office on a moment's notice. Sometimes she needs to work from home, and the rest of the team makes jokes about whether or not she's "really" working. Sarah actually uses her sick days now, when she rarely used them before, and this seems to upset her peers.

From the moment Sarah announced her pregnancy, the probability that she would be put on stretch assignments or considered for a promotion is drastically reduced. Does this sound familiar? This is what is known as the parenthood penalty.

But how does this situation play out for a male coworker? His suitability, loyalty, or fitness for his current role are never called into question. He can take time off from work to drive his wife to doctor's appointments during her pregnancy, he is able to take paternity leave, duck out early to pick up his kids from school, or work from home when one of his children is sick without any discrimination. In fact, more often than not, his peers will revere him saying, "What a good, loyal, and doting father and husband he is!"

He isn't removed from consideration for promotion or stretch assignments. In fact, there is a greater likelihood that as a working father he's considered more responsible. Opportunities expand for him, while the opportunities for the mother dwindle.

It's really frustrating to have spent the last 20 years watching this scenario play out over and over again.

In my case, I didn't have to wait until I entered the workforce to experience this type of discrimination. I experienced it firsthand, directly from my family, when they learned I was pregnant.

Why Can't You Just…

"Stay at home. You can't go back to school now. Forget about having a career! You have a responsibility."

That was my father's response when I broke the news to my parents. I was 19 years old at the time. Enrolled as a political science undergrad at the university. I was hoping it would be a program that would prepare me for law school. However, I had no interest in being a lawyer, and I was bored of the program by the time the first semester wrapped up. Law school was the dream my parents had envisioned for me.

During the second semester, I stopped going to class, I partied too much, and I was in a toxic relationship that ultimately ended with my pregnancy. This situation woke me up in ways I could never have imagined. The party was over – literally.

"Are you crazy? THIS is exactly the reason I need to go back to school. The only way that I can ever hope to be a good mother is by having a career, earning my own money, and not relying on anyone else to support us", I shot back.

"Well, you have to get married now", my mother said matter-of-factly.

"Married? No way! I'm not ready to get married", I proclaimed.

"What do you mean? If you're not ready to get married, how can you be ready to have a baby and take care of that baby while you're in school? How can you manage a career?", she said angrily.

I couldn't believe I was having this argument considering the importance my parents placed on education throughout my childhood. At this moment, they seemed to think that my potential was diminished because of this baby growing inside of me.

Not only did they underestimate me, but they also decided that they knew what was best for me. According to them, I was no longer capable of making my own decisions. It was time to focus on the baby and give up on my own dreams. My life was over and the only way to make it right was to raise this child in the hopes that he, or she, turned out better than I did. I was a complete failure in their eyes.

"There's no way you will land a husband now", I recall my mom saying, shaking her head in disappointment.

I was in utter disbelief. She was more concerned that I had lost my chances at finding Prince Charming than she was about my education. Finding a husband wasn't at the top of my list of priorities. I checked the calendar. Yep, it's 1994. I hadn't travelled back in time with Marty McFly in his DeLorean.

I tried to understand where my parents were coming from, but I just couldn't grasp it. They came to Canada from Lebanon in the late 1950s, dropped out of high school, and toiled away in the factory for decades. They grew up during a time when unwed mothers were considered damaged goods.

I'll agree the situation I found myself in wasn't what I planned for my future, but I wasn't ready to throw in the towel and just give up on carving out the type of life I wanted. This was a mere speed bump, not a road block. This battle was just the first of many during an extremely long nine-month period.

During my pregnancy, I lost count of the number of times family members, friends, and even complete strangers would give me their unsolicited advice about what I should and should not do. Working part time at a diner, one of the waitresses I worked with had no shame in telling me that I should consider an abortion. I didn't ask for her advice, yet she was so keen on sharing it. I just wanted to scream at the top of my lungs and tell everyone to just shut the front door already.

At the same time, my family was still trying to convince me that being a stay-at-home mom was the right option. "If you want to be a good mother, you will quit school and focus on raising your child instead of having a complete stranger do it for you."

<queue exasperated sigh and excessive eye rolling>

No matter how many times I tried to reason with my parents that being a good mother does not equate to the number of hours you clock in at the home office, they did not want to hear it. I was sick and tired of the old-school mentality and how everyone else seemed justified in telling me what to do. Being a stay-at-home mother is a great option if you are 100% committed to it. I wasn't. I knew that if I sacrificed my dreams to be a stay-at-home mom, I would not feel fulfilled. Resentment and regret would cloud my ability to be a good parent.

The more they pushed, the more determined I was to push right back. I was adamant that I was going to pursue my studies after the baby was born. I just had to figure out exactly WHAT it was that I wanted to study. It was time for me to step up and figure out what truly made me happy. I had a baby growing inside of me that would soon make his, or her, grand appearance in the world, and I wanted to have my shit sorted out before then, or at some reasonable time soon after.

Nine months and 36 pounds of pregnancy weight gain later, my firstborn son arrived on Christmas Eve. I decided to take some time to adjust to this new life of mine with a baby boy in tow, and to contemplate what my next steps would be. What kind of a career did I want to pursue? What kind of role model did I want to be for my child? Where did I find true fulfillment?

It wasn't long before I realized where my true passion resided.

····

When I was 11 years old, my parents had purchased a Commodore 64 just for me. I had been pestering them for months about it, and when I landed on the Honor Roll list yet again at the end of Grade 6, they came through. I loved my new computer and found the most joy teaching myself BASIC using the computer manual that came with it. I would spend countless hours experimenting with the different types of programs I could create. My mother would often scold me for spending too much time indoors on the computer instead of going outside to play with the neighborhood kids.

During high school I juggled a part time job, a social life, and my homework assignments. Somewhere along the way I just stopped programming.

····

It was in this moment of introspection that I realized what I needed to do next. I applied to the Computer Science program at the local college. They had just revamped their program to bring in updated technologies. This was what I wanted to do for the rest of my life.

The years I spent in college were the happiest I had been in a long time. My daily commute was 2 hours by bus each way, mainly because my travel time consisted of a detour in the mornings to drop off my son at the baby sitter. I would then take that same detour on the way back home to pick him up.

To make ends meet I applied for a student loan and worked part time waiting tables at a local night club. This was where I would meet my first husband.

<sigh> Yes, you heard me. <eyeroll>First</eyeroll> husband. </sigh>

By the time I graduated from college, I had a second child – a baby girl – and a soon-to-be ex-husband. He was as equally unsupportive of my ambitions as my own parents were. He had carved out his own ideal of what our life would look like together. He wanted me to drop out of college and work as a waitress, like his mother did.

He began to plead his case, "My parents were happy at their blue-collar jobs. My job is stable at the casino. Why can't you just…."

Before I continue with what was said, let me tell you how much I hate the phrase "Why can't you just….". Throughout my entire life, that phrase was used as a bullying tactic to get me to succumb to whatever demand the person who uttered that shitty phrase was making. I think every strong-willed woman has heard that phrase at least a million times over the course of her lifetime. Whenever I heard that phrase, I knew I was following the right course and it only served to strengthen my resolve.

"Why can't you just be happy with being a waitress? We make enough together to pay the bills. What more do you need than that?", he questioned.

"Yes, we make enough to pay the bills with both of our paychecks combined. What happens if you lost your job, or got sick and couldn't work anymore? I would never be able to support us alone working minimum wage. I'm doing this for all of us.", I explained.

"You're just being greedy and selfish. You don't care about the kids or me. You only care about yourself!", he yelled before he stormed off to the bedroom and slammed the door.

I'd like to say that was the beginning of the end, but truth be told, the warning signs of our doomed relationship were visible a lot sooner than that. I deliberately chose to ignore them, thinking that things would sort themselves out. My bad.

Eventually, he became so frustrated with my ambitions, that he spent more time away from the family. Whether he was working on his side gig in a bar band, wrapped up in the latest video game at home, hanging out at his friend's place, or pursuing other women, he just lost interest in the marriage and in the family unit as a whole. One day, he finally packed up his belongings and walked out the door.

I was devastated and felt betrayed. It took quite a bit of time to heal after that, but I knew that no matter what, my children and I would be just fine.

Little did I know there were more challenges ahead which I would face in the work place. I was a woman in tech AND a single mother.

The odds were stacked against me.

The Sick Day

Early on in my career I worked at small companies, or startups as we now refer to them. In those companies, everybody knows your business and you know theirs. My coworkers knew I was going through a divorce and living paycheck to paycheck with two babies to support.

The company I worked for was a small software consulting business that operated as a factory-style environment. I was hired on as a junior software developer at a rate of $15/hour. The software platform that I worked on was targeted towards the construction industry, which we customized for each client. We were required to "punch-in" at 8am and "punch-out" at 5pm. Lunch was from 12pm – 1pm and we were required to sit in the designated lunch room during that time. We weren't allowed to leave the office unless we were going onsite to meet a client, and we needed to be accompanied by the development manager if we did. Those were the rules that the owner set. For the sake of this story, we'll call him Joe.

We worked on laptops because we were expected to take them home and complete tasks that were assigned at the end of the day. We weren't paid for this time even though we were considered hourly employees. The owner only paid for work that was performed in the office. So, even though I often worked 12-hour days between the office and home, I was only getting paid for 8 of those hours.

The men in the office generally had a forgiveness-factor for being 10 minutes late, leaving a few minutes early, taking extended lunches, or stepping out for appointments. The women in the office, which consisted of myself, one other female developer, and the female receptionist, didn't have those privileges.

Joe would often make conversation with the women about how terrible his wife was, except he didn't use the word "terrible" to describe her. He was far more explicit and derogatory. Other times, he would lash out and throw a tantrum in the office if a sales call didn't pan out as he expected. For the most part, we just ignored him and carried on about our business.

It was a toxic work environment but I was able to make ends meet and I had the ability to interact directly with customers that were using the software we built. Although client interaction was something that the other developers cringed at, I enjoyed it thoroughly. There is no better way to learn how a product is being used than by sitting with the people who use it. Understanding their pain points, and gaining insight from them on how we could make the product more usable, was extremely valuable.

I felt that the antiquated office rules were somewhat bearable at this company. Ignoring Joe was a skill that I acquired over time, which made it slightly more tolerable. That is, until the sick day.

It was a morning that started off like any other. I was deep into my current development task when my office phone rang.

"Hello, may I speak to Ms. Lalonde please?", said a voice on the other end.

"Yes, this is her. Who is calling?", I replied.

"This is Anna from ABC Day Care. Your daughter has a fever and it's not going down. It's at 104 right now. You will need to come in and pick her up as soon as possible."

"I'm on my way", I said.

I walked over to Joe's office to let him know that I had a family emergency. I assured him I would take my daughter to the doctor and then place her in the care of a family member afterwards so I could return to the office within a couple of hours. I knew asking for the rest of the day off would be out of the question, so this was my compromise.

"Well I'd be a real prick if I said you couldn't leave, wouldn't I?", he proclaimed.

Without batting an eye, I responded with, "Yes you would. And I would go anyway."

I didn't wait to see what his response was to this. I quickly spun around, walked out of his office, grabbed my belongings and left the building.

Considering I had only been in the workforce for a year at this point and had no other job prospects or connections to land another job if this one went sour, it was a pretty bold move on my part. But then again, you just don't mess with a mother when it comes to her child.

Two hours had passed between the time I left the office and the time I returned. When I was settled in at my desk, Joe marched over and demanded that I mark the day as a sick day in the time tracking system.

"Are you kidding me? I was gone for 2 hours, one of which was over the lunch break. I work 12-hour days for you, and I only get paid for 8 of them. Tonight will be the same as it is every night. I'll be working another 4 hours to get my tasks done by the morning", I said in disbelief.

"You can't bank your hours here. That's not how it works", he bellowed.

"I'm not losing a full day of pay over this by logging it as a sick day. I'm here and I'm working. If you want to track my hours worked, then pay me for all of the overtime hours I put in since I started here", I said with finality.

He stormed off muttering "We'll see about this." I was relieved that he finally left me alone to get back to my work.

. . . . .

When payday rolled around, everyone had a paycheck on their desks except for me. Yes, you heard me... paper paychecks. Remember those?

I stormed over to Joe's office and found him sitting there in gleeful anticipation of my inquiry about the missing check.

With a smug smile, he stated, "Well, I told my accountant to withhold your pay until you corrected the error in the time tracking system. You didn't work a full 40 hours in the building during the standard office hours. Go back and change that day to a sick day, and you'll receive a paycheck for the hours you actually worked." Seemingly satisfied with himself, he reclined back in his office chair, stretched his arms, and folded his hands behind his head.

"I have children to support. I rely on that money to feed them and keep a roof over our heads. This isn't a game" I said, while trying to maintain my composure.

"You're right. You have a choice and you have to do what's in the best interest of your children. So, go make that change in the system, and I'll cut you a check right now", Joe refused to back down. Unfortunately for Joe, he underestimated my resolve.

Looking him straight in the eye, I spoke clearly and slowly to be sure he understood what I was saying, "My parents were factory workers and the one lesson they taught me was never to work for someone who refuses to pay up. I'm going home and I'm not returning to work until you pay me what I rightfully earned. If there's no check in my hand come Monday morning, I'll be looking for a new job. I don't have time to play your games. I have a family to support."

For the second time that week, I grabbed my belongings before the end of the work day and walked out.

While driving home, I contemplated my next move. It was time to update my resume and start looking for another job since I was newly unemployed. Joe didn't care about the type of employee he was losing. After all, with the way he spoke about his wife, and the way he treated his female employees, it was painfully obvious he had no respect for women.

As I entered my apartment, I could hear the phone ringing. Glancing at the call display, I recognized the number. It was the office calling, most likely Joe himself. I was exhausted at this point. There was no way I was going to continue the argument while at home. Especially, not in front of my children.

I picked up the phone and slammed it back down. I wanted to send a clear message. What happened at the office wasn't up for discussion. The phone rang again. Joe calling. I picked it up and slammed it back down. This happened two more times before he finally gave up.

I spent the rest of the day enjoying my time with my kids. It was rare to have this kind of quality time with them during the week. I relished in these extra hours that I reclaimed.

By the time dinner time rolled around, the apartment buzzer went off. It was the development manager, Theo. He was friends with Joe, so I wasn't sure what he was up to. I reluctantly buzzed him in. Puzzled, and slightly suspicious, I opened the door and asked if he had come by to bring my personal belongings. In my haste I forgot to pack up my photos from my desk.

He looked a bit nervous as he replied, "No, I'm here to deliver your paycheck. I talked to Joe and I told him he was being unreasonable, so he decided to make an exception this one time. I just don't think he wanted to show any weakness in front of anyone at the office. Anyway, here it is and it's for the full amount. Maybe if a family emergency comes up in the future, could you have someone else on standby to handle it?"

"Absolutely not. The next time my kid gets sick, I'll just leave for the entire day and leave my laptop behind. Jobs come and go, but family is forever. I already hate myself for leaving my daughter that day when she needed me the most", I was livid. How could he make such a stupid request?

"Ok. Fair enough. Will you be at the office on Monday?", he asked, looking uncertain.

"Yes, I will. And I am going to start looking for a new job in the meantime. I can't work for someone who doesn't respect his employees", I stated and then I closed the door.

When I look back on that, I am surprised that Joe conceded in that instance. He must have either realized the impact I had to his current project, or that he was going to be losing out on twenty hours of free software development each week.

True to my word, I returned to the office on Monday morning. I continued my job search, and not long after that unfortunate incident, I landed a role at yet another startup. I was more than happy to leave that company, and Joe, behind.

Unfortunately, I found out that leaving a bad situation in one company resulted in dealing with a different, and equally bad, situation at another company. A recurring theme throughout my career was being put in a position to choose between my children or my job.

The Town Hall

"There comes a time in your life when you have to make a choice between work and family."

Here I was sitting directly across from the CEO of the company, as he uttered that very statement. Being a working mother of two, this was a battle I pushed back against relentlessly throughout my career and I was not about to back down now.

What brought me to this room, in the middle of this face-to-face confrontation with the CEO – let's call him Donny – all stemmed from the company town hall that was held earlier that day. Apparently, Donny really wanted us to hear about some sweeping changes which were going to propel the company forward and drive continued success.

. . . . .

It was a bright, sunny Wednesday afternoon when the employees gathered in the main hall. The room was buzzing with excitement, as 200+ employees congregated. Side conversations were taking place all around me as everyone speculated what the announcement would entail. When Donny stepped up to the podium, the room fell silent.

The town hall started off as any other. Donny rambled on about the company's financials and talked at length about a new acquisition of a company in Europe. All of this was just corporate speak to me, and I wasn't interested. Instead, I was anxious to return to my desk to work on a licensing issue that had come up just before the town hall. I worked on the internal business development team and I had inherited a shoddy licensing system that was built using a combination of ASMX web services, VBA scripts, Great Plains Dynamics, Onyx CRM, and a SQL Server database. During my time with the company I had managed to rewrite parts of the system to stabilize it, but there were still the oddball bugs that cropped up from time to time.

As Donny was about to wrap up the town hall, he decided to make one final announcement. He was rescinding the company's policy on flex time for all employees, except for 10 guys on his R&D team, which he referred to as his "A-Team". All employees, except the A-Team, were required to be at the office at 9am and stay at least until 5:30pm. No more flex hours, no more working from home. This policy was to go into effect on Monday.

The room fell silent and there was an uncomfortable tension in the air, which Donny seemed oblivious to.

"Any questions?", he asked, smiling from ear to ear.

Not a single person raised their hand. In a company that was filled with working parents, I was surprised at the lack of reaction to this announcement. As the full weight of his words bore down on me, my heart started racing, my thoughts were moving a mile a minute. This was not something I could work around. My commute to and from the office was 45 minutes in each direction. My children's after-school program closed at 5:30pm. I lived in a city with no immediate family that I could lean on for support, and finding other options would take me longer than simply a few days. Being able to arrive at the office at 8am and leave by 4:30pm was the only way I was able to make this work. In fact, the flex-time policy was one of the major factors in my decision to accept a job at this company. Without it, I would have to quit my job.

"Yes, I have a question.", I proclaimed as I thrust my hand up to get his attention.

I heard a few gasps from the crowd, while someone was whispering at me, urging me to put my hand down. "Don't do it, Lori. Don't ask a question".

Donny, looking a bit confused but more irritated, said, "Yes, you in the back. What is it?"

I ignored the muffled requests to stay quiet. "Many of us are working parents, and removing this flexibility will make it difficult for us to keep to this strict schedule. Daycares and after school programs close at 5:30pm with no exceptions. Is there a reason you are instituting this change?"

"Great question!" Donny said, as his face began to take on a bright pink shade. It was obvious to everyone in the room that he did not think this was a great question at all.

"Well, we need to buckle down and really start producing more on the sales end. With the increase in sales, we'll need all hands on deck during our core hours. And to be honest, I have noticed that there are people in the company who have been taking advantage of the flex time policy. They just come and go as they please, spend all afternoon in our company gym, and they are not putting in the full 40 hours a week that it takes for us to really drive this ship forward."

He was beaming, looking satisfied that he had fully answered the question. Nevertheless, I persisted.

"Well if you have a few people who you feel aren't putting in their full work week, shouldn't their managers talk to them directly and work with them on a case by case basis? It's not fair to punish the entire company, since the majority of us come in early and work overtime on evenings & weekends when needed. More often than not, we are putting in well above the standard 40 hours. This policy is going to make it difficult for working parents to maintain any semblance of work/life balance since child care centers and after school programs close at 5:30pm. And if the policy is affecting all of us because a few people are taking advantage of flex time, then why is the R&D team exempt from this change? That's not really fair."

Donny's face was turning a darker shade of red, as he mustered up his final answer of the day, "Because they are the backbone of this company. I'm going to take this line of questioning offline for now. We can discuss it at a later time."

Over the course of answering a few unexpected questions, Donny managed to convey the message to the company that:

- he didn't trust the 200 employees that worked for him,
- he didn't value what his employees did for the company,
- the only team he truly valued was the R&D team, and as a reward, they were exempt from this sweeping change,
- this policy was in effect to make it easier to micro-manage employee arrival and departure from the office, and
- he had no care or concern for how parents were going to find alternate childcare arrangements on such short notice.

As I headed back to my desk, a handful of my coworkers applauded my courage, and shared their relief that I was able to verbalize what many of them were thinking but were too afraid to say out loud.

An hour after the town hall wrapped up, Donny's executive assistant summoned me to the boardroom. Donny wanted to meet with me privately.

As I entered the boardroom, we exchanged pleasantries, then Donny quickly got down to business. "Lori, I've spoken with your manager and he told me that you have a great reputation here and you've done some great work with stabilizing our internal business systems over the past year. But today, I think you lacked good judgement which really surprised me. Do you think it was appropriate to ask me those questions at the company town hall?"

"Well, you did open up the floor to questions after announcing a major policy change which affects almost every employee in the company. That's what the questions were related to, so I'm not sure I see what the problem is here."

At this point, I was feeling a bit confused. I did not understand how my actions lacked good judgement, as Donny had so bluntly put it.

"You embarrassed me in front of the entire company and I think you owe me an apology." With his hands neatly folded together on the table, knuckles turning white from the tight grasp he was maintaining, I could tell Donny was holding back.

"Yes, I am a good employee. I have gone above and beyond in my role here, as have many of the other employees. I think putting a policy in place to punish everyone for the bad behavior of a few is not the right approach, especially when you exempt an entire team.

"If I can speak honestly here, the guys that are in the gym all afternoon are from your A-Team. The working parents that make up the vast majority of this company don't have time to waste during their work day. We have a family to go home to in the evening that needs our attention. So, when we are here, we are focused on getting as much done as we can. When overtime is needed we log on from home to work, sacrificing time that rightfully belongs to our families. You are putting a policy in place that will make it impossible for working parents to continue to work here." I stared back at him blankly. I was no longer just speaking for myself, but for the collective.

It was at that moment that Donny verbalized the sentiment that we know many old-fashioned, high-powered executives think, but rarely ever admit out loud, "There comes a time in your life when you have to make a choice between work and family."

Without hesitation, I shot back, "Family wins every time".

The smile from his dry, cracked lips faded quickly. He cocked his head to one side, sizing me up. I could see in his expression that he was choosing his next words carefully. "Well, then we're at an impasse."

"And that's what is called constructive dismissal", I said with finality. I knew that I was losing my job. I wanted to let him know I wasn't naïve, and I was fully aware of the direction this conversation was heading.

"Go back to your desk, we'll discuss this another time."

· · · · ·

Needless to say, we didn't discuss it another time. In fact, I lost my job the very next day. I walked out of the office with a severance package in hand. One that was just good enough to ensure that I would not sue the company for wrongful dismissal. They just wanted me to go away.

I walked out of that building with my head held high and a smile on my face. On the drive home I cranked the radio up and sang along at the top of my lungs. I felt elated and liberated. No one at the company enjoyed working under Donny's rule and I no longer had to deal with that.

I pulled in the driveway right around noon. The kids were on their lunch break at school, and my second husband was still at work. I walked through the front door of the house. It was a rare occasion to find myself at home alone and I was immediately uncomfortable in the silence that surrounded me. The big, satisfied smile I had plastered on my face earlier in the day disappeared as the thoughts of my recent undoing washed over me.

I was just fired! FIRED! For what? Asking a question at the company town hall? Refusing to make my job a priority over my family? This company touted that they believed in work/life balance, and here I was cast out like garbage because I questioned a policy that would remove any semblance of work/life balance? Was this really happening? What kind of a person throws out an ultimatum like that?

I tossed the big manila envelope containing the details of my severance package on the coffee table. I threw myself onto the sofa and I broke down.

Feeling completely and utterly helpless, I sobbed uncontrollably for what felt like an eternity. I sobbed over the countless hours I had given to yet another company, how hard I had worked towards... towards what? I worked evenings and weekends, sacrificing time with my family. Like a fool, I proclaimed to Donny that I would never choose work over family. I had demonstrated exactly the opposite during my time at that crappy place.

I had been blind to my own shortcomings. Of course, I had made work the priority. It just didn't feel that way, because it was on my terms and at my convenience. My children noticed that I worked "all the time". Rather than being rewarded for my efforts, I was squeezed. The more successful I was in completing the work assigned, the more work I was handed. I was nothing but a work horse – a cog in a very big wheel.

Here I was, well into my career, with nothing to show for it. Instead, I was pink-slipped because I could not work within the rigid schedule the new company policy imposed. It wasn't personal. It was just business.

"This never would have happened if the person running the show was a woman or if Donny actually had any kids of his own," I thought to myself.

Boy, was I wrong.

The Double Agent

I found myself at yet another small company interviewing for another software development role. I was particularly excited about this prospect because the Development Manager was a woman. This would be a great opportunity to learn from her and hopefully look to her as a mentor, I thought.

During the interview process, I made sure to question whether or not the company enabled its employees the option of working from home. When I posed this question, the CTO, Boris, proclaimed, "Absolutely! We do allow our employees to work from home from time to time. It's at the manager's discretion, but we've never had a problem with it."

The Development Manager, Kathy, who was also participating in the interview followed up with, "Yes, it's not a problem. I actually work a reduced schedule, 4 days a week. We're very flexible. As long as you get your work done there shouldn't be a problem."

This set my mind at ease and I happily accepted the new job offer. I even negotiated a higher salary than what I was earning in my previous job. Everything was coming up roses. In my first few months at the company I excelled in my role while being able to work with leading edge technology. Not only was I implementing new features in the company's product suite, but I was able to have a voice in some of the design and architecture decisions. I finally found a place where I would thrive. Or so I thought. It wasn't long before the warts began to show themselves in this new place.

During this time, my second marriage had unraveled. Like an idiot, I confided in my new manager, Kathy, that I was in the process of going through a separation and looking to sell my house.

"I'm sorry to hear that. But I have some good news for you!", she proclaimed. "I know the perfect real estate agent that could help you to sell your house!"

"Oh, that's great. If you have a recommendation, that would help a lot. Who is it?", I said and then immediately regretted it.

"It's ME! I work as a real estate agent part time. I usually ONLY sell houses for family and friends, but I'll make an exception just for you. I'll even give you a discount on my rate! I'll charge 2% instead of the usual 3%."

I sat there for a moment, stunned that she was pitching her services to me. We sat in an uncomfortable, awkward silence for what felt like an eternity, as she was smiling at me like a fool before I was able to reply, "I'm sorry, I'm just not comfortable with that. This feels like a conflict of interest to me. I think it would be best to have someone else handle the sale. I hope you understand."

But Kathy didn't understand. She pestered me a few more times over the course of the next week before I finally agreed to broach the idea with my soon-to-be second ex-husband.

"This is a bad idea," he said.

"I know, but she just won't leave me alone about it. I don't know what else to do. If I can get her off my back, and she can sell the house, then we both win. I just started at this place a few months ago. I have a feeling if I don't let her try, then she's going to hound me even more", I said reluctantly.

"Well, I'm not happy about it. But we can try it with her. If she can't sell the house in three months, then we find another agent. Ok?", he asked.

"Yes, of course", I agreed.

It wasn't a good plan, but it was a plan nonetheless. I thought that if I at least gave her the first opportunity to list the house, that should make her happy.

Throughout this ordeal, my daughter was getting sick regularly. Not just sick, as in having a cold sick. But sick, as in visits to the ER kind of sick. She was lethargic, unable to stomach much to eat or drink, and making frequent visits to the bathroom. I was beside myself with worry.

It wasn't long before she was hospitalized and put into quarantine. After a series of blood tests checking for C. Difficile and H.Pylori, the doctor confirmed that she didn't have either of those infections, and she wasn't contagious. However, she needed to be under the care of specialists to determine the source of her illness. She was transferred to another hospital that specialized in gastroenterology. She went through another round of tests before the doctors concluded that she had Inflammatory Bowel Disease – more specifically, ulcerative colitis.

She was given a course of steroids, and then put on proper medication afterwards to help keep her in remission. This was a condition she would now have to live with and manage for the rest of her life. By the time a diagnosis was made, and she was stabilized, I had expended all of my sick days. I hoped that now that my daughter was on the right medication, she would be ok.

Several months later, she experienced a relapse. I was at work when I got a phone call from my daughter, letting me know that she was exhibiting the same signs during her initial flare up. I knew I would have to leave work for yet another hospital visit. A visit that could result in an extended stay for the second time that year.

Reluctantly, I walked over to Kathy's office to discuss this with her.

"Hi Kathy. I just got a call from my daughter and it sounds like she is experiencing a relapse. I'm going to head out now to take her to the hospital. I'm not sure if she will be hospitalized again, but if she is, would it be ok if I worked remotely during that time? I've used up my sick days for the year, and I would prefer to keep up on my work while still being able to be with my daughter. The hospital has WiFi so I can log on and be productive."

I could tell from the expression on Kathy's face that she was growing impatient with me.

"Well, Lori, your daughter has to realize that you have a job and you can't always take time away from your job to sit with her in a hospital room. You can leave now to take her to the emergency room, but if she does have to stay there for an extended time, then she'll be in good hands with the nurses and doctors taking care of her. She doesn't NEED you there during the day. You can just visit her after work. I'm sure she'll understand."

"I don't understand why I can't work remotely. I'll have an Internet connection and I'll be just as productive whether I'm there or here. I don't think that's an unreasonable ask.", I pleaded, "You just sent out an email this morning that Mike is working from home to take care of his sick child. What's so different about my situation?"

"You have been here less than a year. Mike has worked here for 5 years. He's earned the privilege to work from home", she said flatly. "And besides, this company pays you a lot more than what some of these other guys are getting, myself included. So, you really shouldn't be asking for anything else."

"We discussed working from home privileges when I interviewed here. That was a major deciding factor in whether I accepted the job offer. Now you seem to be walking back from that. I'm asking for this because I'm backed into a corner between choosing between my job and my daughter. What would you do if you were in my situation?", I tried to reason with her as one mother to another.

"I have both my mother and mother-in-law to help me. Don't you have extended family that can be there? What about the father? Why can't he be there?", she chided.

My heart sank. I knew this wasn't going to end on a good note. Did I bother to tell her that my mother had passed away the year before? Would it have made a difference? I could sense that nothing I said would change her mind. Kathy was determined to stand her ground.

My daughter's father lived 3 hours away and he didn't drive. He also had no intention of sacrificing any of his sick days or vacation time for my daughter. I was certain of this because I had asked him if he would be willing to do that the first time that she ended up in the hospital. He was not.

My daughter's stepfather, my second ex-husband, had also expended his sick days to be there for my daughter when he could. He worked in a factory so working remotely wasn't an option he could exercise.

"There's nobody else" I said, feeling utterly disappointed that my manager, who herself was a mother to three young children, was unable to empathize with my situation.

"Ok, well it's decided then. Go take her to the hospital today. I'll see you back in the office tomorrow morning", she said with finality.

It played out exactly as Kathy had requested. I took my daughter to the ER and spent the remainder of that day with her. She was admitted to the hospital, as predicted, and was expected to spend the next 5 days there until she could be stabilized.

Even though she was 15 years old at the time my daughter pleaded with me to stay with her. It broke my heart to leave her there and head to the office each day. I would head out of the office at 4pm every day to trek over to the hospital and sit with her during the evening visiting hours. It wasn't enough that I was visiting for a few hours a day. She was angry and felt that I deserted her when she needed me the most. I hated myself for it just as much.

Each night I sat in her room at her bedside trying to force a conversation. She would just give me the silent treatment. She would log onto Skype to chat with her friends and ignore my presence. She wanted to make it clear that she was angry with me for abandoning her.

Our relationship wasn't the same after that for the remainder of her high school years. She felt unsupported, and no longer trusted me.

I eventually quit that job, but the long-lasting damage to the bond I had with my daughter persisted in the years that followed.

This whole work/life balance fallacy was something I had chased for a long time in my career and failed miserably at time and time again. No matter how hard I tried to juggle the pressures of work with the needs of my children, I seemed to end up with egg on my face. I had no clue what the right thing to do was.

Was I a failure as a mother, a working professional, or both? Any parent will attest that it's impossible to know how any given day will play out when children are involved. In many instances, my male colleagues weren't put on the spot when asking for some flexibility in dealing with family issues. As I pointed out to Kathy, Mike was able to work from home to take care of his sick child, no questions asked.

She didn't extend the same courtesy to me. Instead, she penalized me and reminded me that I was paid well to tow the line at work. It didn't matter that I had never had a problem delivering my work on time. There was no justifiable excuse for denying me the ability to work remotely while allowing another colleague that privilege. This was a power play. Nothing more. Nothing less.

I experienced the same discrimination in a few of the other companies I had worked at before ending up in this company, with Kathy at the helm. Working from home privileges seemed to be stripped from mothers, but the fathers could work remotely without pushback. Each time I pointed out the difference in the way I was treated in comparison to my male counterparts, the manager would respond with a random lame excuse that really didn't excuse the injustice.

The Parenting Plan

I naively thought by the time my children became teenagers, it would be easier to focus more on work. For the most part, they were now self-sufficient. They were able to get ready for school in the morning, catch the bus, and head home on their own. My days at the office were becoming more predictable, which reduced my stress levels. I was no longer in a battle with my managers over whether my parental responsibilities were negatively impacting the team.

Rarely did the school call for emergencies, and when the kids were sick, they were able to remain home on their own and take care of themselves until I returned in the evening. I had hit a real stride at my current company. I had just surpassed my 2-year anniversary without incident, and I finally felt settled into my role and with my team.

It was a typical weekday morning in August, as I was getting ready for work. My son, Michael, was supposed to be getting ready for summer school, but he had not yet emerged from his room.

I called out to Michael across the hall, reminding him that he needed to get up and get ready for school. The next thing I heard was a dull thud, and Michael screamed out. I ran over to check on him and could see that he was not able to stand up on his own. During his attempt to stand up, he immediately fell down in excruciating pain.

My first thought was to get him to the car, and drive to the hospital. There was no way I could help him to the car on my own.

"Taylor, I need your help. Michael is hurt.", I yelled out frantically. The next thing I knew, Taylor was on his right side, and I was on his left. We helped him to stand up and tried our best to support his weight as we walked down the stairs, out of the house, and into my car.

"Taylor, you can stay home. I'll call you from the hospital", I told her.

To be honest, I can't even recall the drive to the hospital. When we arrived at the emergency room, I helped Michael into a wheelchair, and rolled him to triage. Once the intake was complete, Michael was placed in a bed immediately, hooked up to an IV drip, given some medication for the pain, and then wheeled away for x-rays and ultrasounds.

Somewhere in between, I pulled out my phone to email my manager and let him know I wouldn't be at work for the day and why.

Four hours later, as Michael was resting, the doctor arrived at his bedside. "Hello, are you Michael?", he inquired. Michael smiled and nodded yes. "Well, Michael, let me tell you that you are full of shit!"

"What?", I asked. What the hell was this doctor trying to say?

"Michael, you are literally packed full of shit – from end to end. How long has it been since you've gone to the bathroom?", he continued.

"A few days, I think", my son laughed awkwardly.

I let out a chuckle at the doctor's play on words, and a sigh of relief. His appendix hadn't burst. He wouldn't need surgery. He was just constipated.

What we had learned was that even though it sounded trivial, this situation could be serious if it persisted. It was the summer, and he wasn't very active. He wasn't eating a healthy diet, and his system was stalled.

To spare you the details, the doctor recommended we address it at home and I monitor him closely to be sure he was able to empty out his system sometime over the next few days. Otherwise, he would need to go back to the hospital so they could empty it out for him.

This meant no more solid foods until he was regulated. His diet would consist of yogurt, lots of water, and more importantly, Metamucil. Unfortunately, Michael was a typical teenage boy. There was no way he was going to stick to that diet. Which meant that I needed to be home to ensure he followed the doctor's orders.

No problem, I thought. I'll email my manager and let him know the situation. I will just work from home for the rest of the week.

When I returned to work on Monday morning, I had a meeting request that the Director of Human Resources, Sally, had setup between myself and the CEO of the company (we'll call him Harry):

Subject: Discussion for plan going forward
When: Wednesday, August 19, 2009 8:30am – 9:30am
Location: Harry's office
Message: To include discussion on Lori's plan going forward to deal with family issues, possible absences from work, working from home, etc.

What the actual fudge? Except I didn't say fudge.

I read that meeting request over a few times to fully understand what was happening. Is this a joke? Does Harry think it's appropriate to talk to me about a parenting plan? I worked at this company for 2 years with no drama, until now. This was absolutely ridiculous.

To add insult to injury, there was another email in my inbox that morning, from my male co-worker, Ernie, to the entire team with the subject line, "Working from home".

I wonder if Ernie is going to get put on a parenting plan, I thought to myself. You can rest assured, the answer to that would be a firm "No".

By the time Wednesday morning rolled around, I had planned my approach to this meeting. Under no circumstances, would I lose my cool. I wanted to remain calm and have a rational conversation around this irrational topic. As I walked into Harry's office, I could see Sally was already seated across from his desk. There was one open chair on her right for me to take a seat. As I sat down, Harry got down to business.

"Lori, I know that you've had some issues with your troubled teen lately, but I'm going to have to pull back your work from home privileges"

My inside voice was replying, "Of course you are. This isn't my first rodeo."

My outside voice calmly asked, "Why is that?"

This gave Harry the soapbox that he needed to explain that the company was hitting a rough patch. Not only did they need to reduce everyone's salaries by 10%, but they expected overtime on a regular basis now. Harry went on to explain how it's really hard focus on work when you're working from home to babysit a "troubled teen" as he had so blatantly put it. In that case, it's impossible to give the project the full and undivided attention that it needs right now.

After he was done rambling on about the dire straits the company was in, I stated my case, "I have been here for 2 years. During that time, I have worked overtime whenever we needed to meet deadlines. I've been here nights and weekends with the team no questions asked. And I have performed my job above and beyond every time. In fact, the last project I just wrapped up, I spent 3 months straight working 60 hours a week to ensure we met our deadlines. That work was done in the office and from home. It didn't make me less productive. I don't understand why there's an issue with it now. If you want to formalize my work schedule so that I am only able to work from the office, then I will only work my regular work week. From what I recall, the company policy's standard work week is defined as 37.5 hours. So I guess I'll just do that from now on.", I said.

He leaned forward, and his voice become a bit louder, a bit more menacing, "You listen to me. The company policy on work hours is the MINIMUM number of hours you work for me. You will work as many hours as I tell you to work in order to deliver your project on time."

Maintaining my cool, I shrugged my shoulders and said, "Well I'll have to check the Canadian labour laws on that. But I'm pretty certain that you can't force your employees to work an unlimited amount of overtime as you see fit."

His face was turning red at this point, either in frustration or anger, or a little bit of both. "You are nothing but a low rate junior developer. You will work however long I tell you to work, otherwise I will have you replaced with a single phone call", he threatened as he picked up his office phone for effect.

"Ok. Go ahead then", I urged, "Make the call."

I motioned towards the handset he was holding. I was disappointed that he had sunk to a level of name calling and idle threats. I was a senior developer at this point, and he was trying to antagonize me by attacking my experience and my abilities. I wasn't having any part of it.

He stared at me in disbelief and slowly put the handset back on the receiver. "Go back to your desk," he said.

"Sure, no problem," I said.

I guess we weren't going to work on that parenting plan after all.

I didn't get replaced with a single phone call, as Harry had so dramatically put it. But I did start looking for a new job. I had a feeling my days with this company were numbered. It was better to proactively search for a new opportunity, rather than just wait for the inevitable pink slip to make its way to my desk.

Within a few short weeks, I was packing up my desk, saying my goodbyes to colleagues, and preparing for my new role. When I arrived home, after my last day at the office, I received an email from Harry to my personal email account.

From: Harry
Subject: Bye for now
Hi Lori. Thanks so much for the time you invested at my company. You have great talent and managed the recent work/life challenges maturely and with style.
Thanks and perhaps our paths will cross again :o)
All the best! Harry

I can happily proclaim that it's been over a decade, and our paths have not crossed again.

Family Court

When my son was 16 years old, he decided he didn't want to live with us anymore. He was moody, rebellious and resentful. He did not have a real relationship with his father and somehow I was to blame.

When he visited his paternal grandmother over the Christmas break, both she and his estranged father had convinced him that he should live with her, instead of returning home. When school reconvened after the holiday break, the principal called to inform me that Michael had requested his school records to be transferred to a school in his grandmother's town, a two and a half hour drive from where I lived. I was heartbroken, but he was legally at the age where he could make that choice. There was nothing I could do about it. After a few failed attempts to contact him by phone, blocked by his grandmother, I accepted his decision.

Not long after, I discovered that his grandmother was suing me for child support. This, during a time, when his father owed me $36K in back child support. He had refused to pay child support for most of Michael's childhood, and had done everything possible to avoid it. If he tried to claim support, there was a good chance the judge would apply the back child support to offset the claim, reducing the amount of money that he would be able to collect from me.

All of this was unfolding just as I had passed my 3-month probationary period in a new role as a Technical Lead. The company's headquarters were based in the Greater Toronto Area, but they wanted to expand in Waterloo to absorb the tech talent here. The role enabled me the opportunity to both staff and lead this new office. It felt like the kind of opportunity that would change the trajectory of my career and set me up for a management opportunity in the near future.

When I landed the role, I had successfully negotiated a higher salary and an additional $5K increase to my salary upon passing my probationary period. I had just received a stellar performance review from my manager. It was a bittersweet moment. My career was progressing in a positive direction, but my relationship with my son had fallen apart.

On top of that, I had to figure out how I was going to ask for time off work to head to Windsor to attend family court. Knots formed in my stomach as I remembered how this played out in past roles, and I wasn't confident it would end well with this one.

After receiving the subpoena to attend family court, I emailed my manager, Sandy, to request the planned court date off from work with a brief explanation. I followed up on the email by submitting a formal request to the company's internal employee management system.

As anticipated, Sandy's reply was not supportive and she rejected my request for time off. She said that with the new project deadlines in place, nobody would be allowed time off between January until April. I let her know that I would not ignore a request to appear in court, and that she could not deny me the time off to do so. I was willing to book an unpaid day off if it was that much of an inconvenience for the company.

Eventually, she relented and approved my request for time off.

A couple of days later, I saw a flood of email messages in my inbox containing resumes, related to a job posting for the Waterloo office. The posting was for a Technical Lead.

Oh FFS! Seriously? Was this really happening?

I emailed the office coordinator to ask why there was a live posting for my role in Waterloo. She assured me that there was nothing to worry about and that the posting went up in error.

The next day, the office coordinator arrived in Waterloo to meet with me one on one. She handed me a letter that explained I was being dismissed without cause, and without severance pay. I was angry, speechless, and yet not completely surprised that this was the end result. I was disappointed that Sandy did not have the decency to fire me directly.

That wasn't the last I'd hear about Sandy though.

Years later, she provided a negative reference about my work ethic when I was going through the interview process at another company. Luckily for me, they were willing to hear my side of the story and it did not cost me that job opportunity.

I can go on and on about how I've dealt with bad bosses, particularly when it comes to trying to find a balance between excelling in my career and raising my children. Truth be told, I have made my fair share of mistakes as a parent as well.

The Drill Sergeant

When both of my children were in school full-time I was thrilled for two reasons. I no longer had to manage the cost of full-time daycare which was extremely expensive. It also meant that I only had to make one stop in the morning to drop off my kids, and one stop after school to pick them up, making my life just a little bit easier each day.

I enrolled them both in the before and after school child care program that was available at the school. Every day, like clockwork, I would drop them off at 7am and head off to work. The after-school program was open until 5:30pm, but I was usually able to make it there by 5pm to pick them up.

However, it wasn't long before my kids started getting into the habit of dragging their feet in the morning, and it was disrupting the daily schedule I had in place. The later I got on the road to get to work, the more likely it was that I would be stuck in rush hour. Arriving at the office later, meant that I stayed at the office later, increasing the likelihood of getting stuck in rush hour traffic on the way home. I ran the risk of not being able to make it to the after-school program before it closed. The consequences of showing up late to the after-school program were expulsion. This situation was too good to screw up.

When the kids were dragging their feet in the morning my anxiety went through the roof and I grew impatient with them. I didn't want to get into the habit of yelling at them in the mornings, but I was starting to yell more often than I was comfortable with. I had to make a change.

What were my options? I thought them through quite a bit:

1. Get to the office later, work a shorter day, leave early enough to pick up the kids and avoid rush hour, then log on from home later in the evening to make up the daily short fall.
2. Get to the office later, work a full day, risk arriving at the after-school program after they close resulting in the kids being removed from that program.
3. Find alternative home daycare options that would be more flexible in pick up times.

4. Enforce a strict schedule in the morning, ensuring that we left the house on time to get the kids to the before school program by 7am – no ifs, ands, or buts about it.

Let's start with option #1. I had a few days here and there where I exercised that option. These days were the worst because my co-workers would chide me as I headed out the door at the usual time at the end of the day, "Oh, so you're working banker's hours now, eh? Must be nice!", they would say sarcastically, and loud enough for my manager to hear.

They didn't see the additional work that I was putting in from home in the evening, and they didn't care. Out of sight, out of mind. Right? Even though the company offered flex hours and work-from-home privileges, I knew it would only be a matter of time before my manager eventually decided to talk to me about this. Been there, done that, got the pink slips to prove it. I didn't want it to get to that point.

Option #2 wasn't really an option. I recall when I was in school, how much I would hate being the last kid picked up after school.

. . . .

My parents were factory workers, and their schedules could be unpredictable at times. We lived about a 20-minute walk from the school – right on the boundary of where the buses would pick up the other school kids. But we lived on the wrong side of the street, literally. So, we were "walkers".

In decent weather, we would make the walk. During winter, it was a bit much, so my dad would pick us up from school. I hated those days when he was late in picking us up, after all the other kids had already gone. I vowed when I was a parent, I would not do that to my kids. I never wanted them to feel like I forgot about them or abandoned them.

. . . .

I had considered home daycare options when thinking about option #3, but in my neighborhood, they were all at capacity. So that was not really a viable option.

I convinced myself that option #4 was the only way to go. With that, I put in place a strict morning routine that the kids had to adhere to. I became the drill sergeant.

Every day, I would wake up at 5am, have a shower and get myself ready before waking the kids up at 6am. Once the kids were awake and seated at the dining table, they had 20 minutes to finish their breakfast. I set the kitchen timer so they could see the countdown. This resulted in less chatter and bickering amongst them. It worked! I was so proud of myself.

While they were eating breakfast, I would lay out their clothes on their beds so they didn't waste time trying to decide what they wanted to wear that day.

When the timer went off, whether or not they had finished their breakfast, they would have to move on. I would reset the timer for 20 minutes. During this time, they would need to wash their faces, brush their teeth and get dressed.

Once that timer went off, if they weren't dressed, they knew that they would be grounded later when we got home. That meant they couldn't watch their favourite TV shows at all that night.

The last timer was set for 5 minutes. This final timer was set to ensure they got their coats, shoes, and school backpacks on. Then it was time to head out the door and get in the car.

The school was only a 5-minute drive from our house, right in the same neighborhood, so if we made it out the door on time it was smooth sailing from there. With this new timer-driven schedule, I was able to keep the kids focused on what they were supposed to be doing in the morning. There were the odd occasions when they were distracted or dragged their feet. I was so pleased thinking that I had this parenting thing all figured out.

Looking back on it now, I feel like a bit of a hypocrite. While seeking to protect flexibility in my schedule at work, I had become inflexible with my children. I had instilled a timer-based routine that moved them from station to station with no room for conversation or connection with each other, or myself, at the start of each day. I worried more about impressing my managers and co-workers, and less about how this type of routine made my children feel. It didn't occur to me at the time that mornings were the greatest opportunity to connect with them and relish in the time we had together before starting the day. I always justified it by thinking to myself that I would make it up later, but later panned out less frequently than I had planned.

How did it get to this point?

For the first half of my career, I felt like I was being pulled in opposite directions. Trying to balance the needs of my family with the demands of my job was extremely difficult, but I managed the best I could. I became the drill sergeant out of necessity. I walked away from jobs that forced me to make work a priority during times when my family needed me the most. I demonstrated that, against all odds, I had performed my job above and beyond the normal call of duty. At least that's how I rationalized it at the time to make myself feel better.

After fifteen years of struggling to fit into traditional full-time roles that demanded more of my time and provided less flexibility, I moved into the consulting world to reclaim some control over my own schedule.

I'll be the first to admit I didn't always handle every situation with elegance and grace. I stumbled along the way, not always making the best decisions, but doing the best with what I had. I had performed a juggling act that spanned over the course of the first fifteen years of my career, and it was exhausting. It was messy, it was ugly, but it was my version of success. Most importantly, I debunked the working mother myths that were so often parroted to me by family, friends, co-workers, and managers.

The Working Mother Myths

Myth #1: "You Can't Do Both"

As I mentioned in the beginning of this chapter, my parents truly believed that I had to make a choice. In their minds, I was going against the grain trying to pursue my career while raising my children. They argued that there was no way I could excel at both, and my duty was to my children.

They were right in that I had a duty to raise my children. But they were wrong to think there was only one way to be a mother. This was especially galling coming from my own mother who had worked in a local factory throughout our childhood. She was also the CFO of our house. She managed the finances and made sure all the bills were paid. If anyone taught me to be a strong, independent woman, it was her. She didn't want me to struggle like she did. She didn't enjoy having to do it all. She was right in that I would struggle, but then again, I never expected anything worthwhile to come easy.

Myth #2: Working Mothers Are Less Dedicated, Productive, Efficient

This was a sentiment that was expressed by some of the managers I worked for. Generally, the smaller the company, and the younger the team, the more they held this notion up as truth. It was extremely difficult working under people that held this belief.

Every single day I felt like I was in a fight for my life. Every day, I had to prove that I was completely capable of doing my job. Being a mother didn't make me any less skilled in software development. In fact, being a mother made me more efficient and productive while I was in the office.

Working mothers have more disciplined schedules. They don't have the luxury of dealing with silly distractions. They have to focus on work while at the office, knowing that they don't have the option of staying at the office later to make up for unproductive time.

In my case, I would arrive at work by 8am, while my fellow developers would stroll in anytime between 9am and 11am. By the time the late-comers logged on for the day, I had already worked a solid 3 hours of uninterrupted time.

I was hyper-focused on the work that needed to be completed while at the office. At the same time, my fellow male colleagues would take multiple breaks throughout the day to play foosball in the lunch room. Whenever I did take a break from my monitor to engage my team mates in small talk, someone would inevitably walk by and jokingly proclaim that I should stop distracting the boys with my chatter and let THEM get back to work. <insert extremely hard eye roll here />

How many times did that joker walk into the lunch room to tell the boys to stop playing foosball? Zero. Exactly zero times.

At 4:30 PM, as I'd pack up to leave the office, someone would inevitably comment, "must be nice working banker's hours". I got tired of explaining that I had actually started my work day early and had worked a full day by that point. My pleas for sanity usually fell on deaf ears.

Their perception was greatly skewed from the reality, and this stunted my career progression. I've seen similar scenarios play out with the other working mothers in those same companies. We were just as productive, if not more so, than our male counterparts. But they didn't see it that way, and that was all that mattered.

Myth #3: Work/Life Balance

During the beginning of my career, I believed it would be easy to balance my career and motherhood as long as I had work-from-home privileges. Most job postings today use work/life balance as a way to attract new talent. However, depending on how the company policy is worded, you could find yourself in a bind when it's too late.

In my case, I had seen firsthand work-from-home privileges being abruptly revoked, either for the entire company, or select individuals. Generally, this was a move that was meant to assert control over the employees, because management distrusted him/her/them. This was short-sighted on the company's part.

The reality I experienced when being given the opportunity to work from home was that I ended up working far more hours for the company – above and beyond the standard 40-hour work week. Evenings and weekends were not off limits. I had set the tone that I was available 24/7. I worked during times when I should have been helping my kids with their homework, or paying attention during their dance lessons, soccer games, and karate tournaments.

I brought my laptop everywhere, because I could. I felt justified in doing so because I was physically present with my family during those times. What was the harm in having the laptop open for a few hours? The reality was that I was both mentally and emotionally checked out from the experience. I didn't see this until it was far too late to make it right; but my children noticed.

In the back of my mind I knew that if I didn't put in those extra hours for work, the freedom I experienced in my daily schedule would be revoked. And I was right. In many cases, if I didn't complete the impossible tasks that were constantly mounted on me, my work-from-home privileges were rescinded at the discretion of my jilted managers.

Myth #4: The Tech Industry is a Meritocracy

This chapter touches on only a few of countless negative experiences I have encountered in the tech industry, and only focuses on the setbacks I have faced as a working mother. However, this issue isn't limited to women. People are discriminated against based on their gender, gender identity, skin color, religion, sexual orientation, disability, and even age.

We all want to believe there has been forward progress and that the tech industry serves as a meritocracy, rewarding everyone for their hard-earned achievements. We only need to look as far as the latest news reports coming out of Silicon Valley that proves that bright, talented people are subjected to toxic work environments, harassment, and unfair treatment. Unfortunately, this isn't just a Silicon Valley problem. This is a worldwide epidemic for which there is still no cure.

It's 2018 and yet many people go to work every day to pursue their passion and earn a living, only to be:

- bullied,
- harassed,
- ignored,
- interrupted,
- silenced,
- overworked,
- contradicted, only to have their ideas stolen and parroted by someone else later,
- paid less than their male colleagues who hold similar roles & responsibilities,
- passed over for promotions,
- passed over for career development, mentorship and training opportunities, and
- passed over for roles they are qualified, or even over-qualified for.

The tech industry is not a meritocracy yet. There is still a long way to go before we achieve equality in the work place.

In Retrospect

Over the course of my career, I have seen and felt the toll the parenthood penalty takes on working mothers. I encountered discrimination in many forms in the work place so I worked harder in my role in order to be respected and seen as equally capable as my male counterparts.

No matter how many times I went above and beyond to demonstrate my capability, it all seemed to be reset at the stroke of midnight, only having to jump through the same hoops the very next day. From hero to zero – every single day. This wasn't just my problem and my experience.

I witnessed firsthand as other female co-workers were discriminated against and disrespected in the workplace when they became mothers. Some of those women eventually left the field because they were tired of having to prove themselves over and over again. They were tired of being passed over for promotions, raises, and stretch assignments while our male colleagues experienced accelerated career advancement in the field.

My struggles as a working mother were only one set of challenges among many that I faced in the industry. I, like those other women, experienced discrimination in all its ugly forms. But I refused to be pushed out. I dug my heels in, determined to remain in this industry to pursue my passion, even when so many others told me I did not belong here.

It feels like a punch in the stomach whenever anyone reduces my efforts to a simple explanation of, "Well you stuck it out for this long, so it must not have been that bad."

I didn't simply stick it out.

I fought for my rightful place in this industry.

I pushed back against anyone that underestimated my skills based on my gender while overlooking my education and work experiences.

I persevered in the face of adversity.

I persisted.

I am winning, in spite of it all.

CHAPTER 7

Embracing Your Role as Role Model

By: Susan Ibach – Microsoft program manager

I would like to share the tale of how initially, I really didn't see any need to contribute to the women in tech community. I thought the work was already done. But as I went through my career, I discovered the need for female role models and realized that I was a role model and that I should get out there and be more visible.

Priest or Rocket Scientist?

Like many high school students, when guidance counsellors and friendly parents asked me "So what will you do after high school?" I had no clue. In grade 11, I took a computerized aptitude test. I answered a series of questions and the program suggested possible careers. The list suggested rocket scientist and priest! Okay, I was the youngest daughter, and I know that historically there was a time when families sent their youngest child to serve the church, but I didn't think that was my calling. I went to a small high school in Eastern Canada which did not offer calculus, so I was missing a pre-requisite for all the big tech universities. As a result, getting into rocket science seemed a little ambitious. So, despite the helpful advice from the aptitude test I remained unsure what to do next.

Our local university had a good engineering program. I really had no idea at all what engineering entailed, but I knew it involved a lot of math; my strongest subject. I also knew that most of the graduates got jobs, so I figured that was as good a choice as any. I still had to decide what type of engineering to pursue. Chemical, Mechanical,

Electrical, Civil, Forest, Geology, Survey or Computer. Apparently picking a degree program was going to be more complicated than I realized.

I didn't know it at the time, but my final choice was influenced by my first female role model in tech: my older sister. My sister graduated with a degree in Electrical Engineering and accepted a job offer at Bell Northern Research in Ottawa. She was good at math. I was good at math. She seemed happy with her job. So, that September I started studying electrical engineering along with about 80 other students including about 8 women.

The Perception of Female Engineers

Among the women in my engineering program, I found some friends for life. Occasionally the topic of being girls in engineering came up. Honestly, we didn't think being girls in engineering was a big deal. We truly believed the generation before us had paved the way for women in STEM (Science, Technology, Engineering, and Math) and the fight was over. We could choose any profession we wanted. We were just engineering students who happened to be female. Our classmates and professors didn't seem to treat us any differently and that was how we liked it! Rather than being offended, we were amused in our 3rd year mechanical engineering lab when the teaching assistant insisted on doing all the work for us because he was worried the group of girls might hurt themselves with the machinery. We didn't think being a girl in engineering was anything to get excited about.

On December 6, 1989 I was in the third year of my degree program. I was home in the basement watching tv and waiting for a phone interview for an internship when I heard the news. A man had just entered a mechanical engineering class at Polytechnique University in Montreal. He separated the male and female students and shot the women! He claimed he was fighting feminism and called the women a bunch of feminists, and feminists had ruined his life. He killed 14 women and injured 10 women and 4 men.

This was one of the first school shootings. It was in Canada. The gunman was targeting female engineering students. My friends and I were deeply affected. You might think it made us want to stand up and shout out we are women in engineering and we stand strong! Oddly enough, it left me with a strong aversion to the word feminist and to being singled out as a female. I just wanted to finish my degree and get a job.

I didn't see myself as any sort of role model for women in engineering, but I did take pride in being an engineer, and I did enjoy sharing my passion for engineering with others. I volunteered to go back to my high school to talk about engineering as a course of study. I presented with a female professor, the chair of Women in Engineering at my university. About 20 students came to our talk, three of them girls. I talked about my courses and the workload in engineering. During our talk, the professor singled out the three girls, telling them how important it was for them to pursue engineering because of the shortage of women in the field. I could tell the girls were uncomfortable. I don't think the average high school student wants to be made the center of attention and told the future of women in STEM depends on their degree choice. Looking back, I understand what the professor was trying to do. She had been hired as the chair of women in engineering and clearly there was an expectation that she would increase female enrollment in the program. These girls had attended the presentation so there was a chance they would enroll. Surprisingly, it hadn't even crossed my mind that I was likely invited to speak to my high school because I was a female engineer myself. Without even knowing it I had already been held up as a role model.

Where Are the Role Models?

When I graduated, I took a job at Andersen Consulting, a worldwide consulting firm. The pay for a new hire wasn't particularly good, but the model was simple: work hard and move up! As you move up, the pay gets better. Your goal is to become a partner and bring in the big bucks. There were no girls in my start group from Ottawa but there were other girls at our worldwide orientation in Chicago. I didn't notice any discrimination towards women at the company. But, when I joined, Canada had no female partners or associate partners. For the first couple of years it didn't bother me, I was just trying to work my way up to manager. All my managers had been men, but I did cross paths with a couple of female managers. I even asked one of them to be my mentor, but unfortunately our personalities and styles clashed. I was trying to find a female role model to help me picture the path for my career, but she was not the right role model for me, so I continued to rely on male role models, many of whom were very helpful.

After a few years, I started to think about the path to partner. The rumour was that partners at Andersen had a 90% divorce rate. (I have no idea if that was true or just a company myth like the story that Arthur Andersen, the founder of the company, was killed by being hit in the head with a golf ball.) What I did know to be true was if you wanted to move up in the company you had to pursue the right opportunities. The right opportunity frequently involved long hours and working out of town. Some Associate Partners and Partners managed two projects in two different cities at the same time. I was already living on the road. I lived in Ottawa, but I was working in Montreal, Fredericton, Calgary, or Halifax. My regular taxi driver would pick me up every Monday morning and drive me to the airport. Friday nights I would fly home and meet my boyfriend for dinner. I was having trouble imagining the future I hoped for as a partner at Andersen. Would I ever get married and have kids with the heavy hours and constant travel?

During my third year at Andersen, a woman associate partner transferred from the US to Canada. She was assigned to my project. She had two young boys, and her husband had moved to Canada with her to support the opportunity to become an associate partner. I liked her, she was smart and successful. She was an associate partner at a consulting company and raising two kids. I had found a role model on how to balance career and family at Andersen.

About a year later, my boyfriend and I got engaged. We sat down and had a serious conversation about our future. My role model at Andersen had a husband who followed her from city to city so they could still be together as a family. A partner at Andersen makes good money. If I chose to pursue that path, my husband would not have to work, but we would constantly move from city to city. It was that last aspect in particular that led me to leave Andersen. We decided I would quit Andersen to cut down on my travel. My husband would be the primary income, and that would give me the option of staying home with any kids. I had no idea if I wanted to be a stay at home mom, but it was nice to have the option.

I found a job teaching databases and programming. Ironically, I was still travelling, but there was no more overtime. I enjoyed the new job. I love learning new technology and sharing that knowledge with others, and all modesty aside, I am pretty good at it.

There were a number of female employees at the training company, but they were in sales, marketing, and administration. Female technical trainers are few and far between. I am happy to say that I did not have any issues in the classroom with the students disrespecting me because I was female. I think it helped that I was a confident presenter and I knew my material. I was in demand as a presenter. I got married, I had two kids. I had a job with 9-5 hours that worked well with motherhood. I even managed to negotiate a part-time work arrangement so I could spend more time with my kids!

Unfortunately, one drawback to life as a technical trainer is there isn't much of a career path. I was getting bored teaching the same courses over and over. So, I started volunteering to help or speak at conferences. At the conferences, I met other women doing technical training. Most of them would reschedule their shifts to attend the women's networking luncheon at the conference. I had no interest in attending. My career was going well. If anything, I felt being female had worked to my advantage. I was a very good technical trainer and when a company was selecting staff or speakers for events, I knew they were happy to have strong female candidates. I envisioned the women's networking session as a luncheon where a bunch of feminists would sit around complaining about being underpaid or mistreated. That wasn't my experience, I didn't need to be a part of it.

The 'AHA!' Moment

Fast forward ten years or so, my career as a technical trainer led me to a job at Microsoft as a technical evangelist. I was the only female technical evangelist on the team, and when we had new openings on the team I started to hear more about diversity. I began to understand diversity is about more than just hiring a mix of men and women; it's about having people with different backgrounds and perspectives who can contribute to discussions so you can make better decisions.

I had an "aha!" diversity moment when a good friend of mine was interviewing two candidates for a job on his team. One of the candidates was easy to talk to; they had a lot in common. They got along well in the interview and it was pretty clear they would work well together. The other candidate was very capable and intelligent but had a very different personality from him, and they clashed a bit during the interview. He knew if he hired him, it would result in some occasional heated discussions. As he described to me the two candidates I thought it was clear who he should hire! But he looked at me and explained his dilemma: the guy who thinks and works like me is great, but I already have me on the team, do I need another me? Isn't it better to bring someone to the team who is going to contribute new ideas, challenge my ideas, and ask questions I haven't thought of? That is the true spirit of diversity! Women and men do have different life experiences, perspectives, and communication styles. When you have a team with a diverse set of perspectives and ideas, you are more likely to reach a better solution. It's good to have male teachers and male nurses; it's good to have female engineers and programmers.

I continued to work as a technical evangelist (great job title, isn't it!) and was assigned to work with university students. My job was to encourage students in computer science and engineering to try out Microsoft developer technologies. It was a lot of fun! I got to visit universities and colleges across the country. I delivered guest lectures. I presented tech talks at hackathons and I noticed the number of girls in engineering and CS really hadn't changed since I went to university. I was shocked! 20 years later and girls still only made up around 10% of the students in CS and engineering. Sure, some universities and some programs had increased female enrollment, but overall there had been no improvement since I was in university. Girls had the power to choose technology as a career, but they simply were not choosing that option. Why?

This was the turning point for me. There were lots of bright girls out there capable of doing computer science and engineering, but they were choosing law, medicine, chemistry, and biology. Hey, if that's your passion, awesome, go for it, but it was becoming clear to me that many girls were not choosing engineering or computer science because they didn't seriously consider it as an option. They met female nurses, female teachers, female doctors, wildlife biologists, but day to day most of them never met a female working in high tech. There was a shortage of role models.

Something else started to happen when I visited universities and talked to professors. Because I was a female in a technical role at Microsoft, I started getting requests to speak from woman-focused groups. I ended up on the agenda as a presenter at the Ontario Celebration of Women in Computing. As the day of the conference approached, I was not looking forward to it. But hey, it was my job, so I would go and I would present. No doubt the conference would be full of women complaining about the advantages men have over women in the workplace and how we all have to fight for our rights. That simply wasn't my experience. My male managers and co-workers had been supportive, and my managers actively sought out ways to help me in my career. I went into the keynote, fully expecting to tune out and start checking email on my phone within minutes.

Finding My Place

Surprise! I had it all wrong. The first session was a keynote where Maria Klawe, President of Harvey Mudd College, talked about how simply changing the way they taught computer programming to first year students helped them go from 10% to 40% female enrollment. They split up the introduction to programming course based on existing coding skills. Don't put the people who have been coding on their own for 5 years in the class with the student who has never written a line of code just because they are both in their first year! They shifted the course focus to coding as a tool to solve problems.

The next presenter talked about imposter syndrome. A syndrome that affects men and women but tends to affect more women. When you start a job or enter a meeting room and think "I don't belong here. I am not as smart as these people. I am not as good as they think I am. At some point they are going to realize I am not that good and then I will be in trouble". I was successful in my career, but when I started presenting at conferences I frequently found myself looking at the other presenters around the speaker room talking about their books and their various speaking gigs and thinking they know so much more than I do; at some point someone is going to figure out I don't know this stuff as well as they think I do, and I won't be invited back to present.

I honestly thought the other presenters (who of course were 90-95% male) might be smarter and better than me. Maybe I had just been invited because they wanted some women on stage. Doubts still plagued me despite the fact I had battled a couple of friends for top speaker score at a recent conference. Until then, I thought I just lacked confidence and skills. I didn't know my self doubt was so common it had its own name.

Later at the Women in Computing conference, I presented my session to a standing room only crowd made up entirely of women studying Computer Science. This was a whole new experience for me. In 20 years I had frequently presented to rooms with a large technical audience that was 90-100% male. I had never presented to a large technical audience that was 100% female! I'll be honest. It threw me off a bit, and I found myself commenting out loud that I had never before had the opportunity to present to a room entirely filled with women in CS before, and they burst into spontaneous applause. They all appreciated that this was not a common occurrence for the audience or the presenter, and it was something to celebrate.

In the final session of the conference there were some humorous debates delivered by some wonderful women. Female CS professors and professionals debated whether it was better to wear a skirt or pants in the workplace, making jokes about not having to shave your legs! I had to wear business suits long ago at Andersen Consulting, and I don't miss dealing with nylons. I laughed out loud when the 'pro-pants' debater argued you can't wear skirts because it can be very awkward if you need to crawl under a table to reconnect cables. (That's exactly why I stopped wearing skirts as a technical trainer!) These women were awesome. They were successful. They were smart, they were fun, and they all shared a passion for increasing the number of girls in tech. I had found new role models, and this time the role models were showing me how I could be a role model!

What Can You Do?

I started thinking about what I could do to encourage more girls to consider careers in technology and to help those who had chosen STEM as a career to be more successful. I had learned a few tricks along the way: how to network, how to negotiate work-life balance and how to teach technology to others. I had knowledge to share and I am fortunate to have a job that gives me the opportunity to go to universities and meet students. I started volunteering for not-for-profit organizations to teach kids or women to code. I started creating content to teach coding to beginners to inspire more people to explore the world of coding.

When I joined the women's networking groups at Microsoft and in my community, I discovered they included a lot of people like me. When we meet up we might compare notes on how we helped our kids deal with mom travelling for work, or what the heck you do when a random stranger proposes to you on social media because they saw your video on how to code. Or maybe it's a friendly debate over whether kickboxing or yoga is better for relieving stress after a long day at work. In their own way, all the other women in the group are role models for me in how to deal with different challenges in my career, big and small.

I remember hearing an interview with a black actress who said she cried when she saw Whoopi Goldberg acting on TV, because up until that point she did not know a black woman could be an actor on television. I don't remember her name, but she was being interviewed because she was starring in a TV show. Simply seeing another black woman on TV opened her eyes to a new career.

You could be the first female in tech a young girl meets. You could help someone discover the world of coding. You might be the person who opens up a young woman's eyes to the possibility of a career in tech. Oh, and here's another secret: It's fun and it's rewarding! Watching a 12-year-old girl laughing as she adds sound effects whenever the unicorn in her game jumps. Helping a high school student train a data model to predict who would live or die on the Titanic and watching her grin as she tests her trained model by entering the name of her English or Physics teacher to see whether they would survive. Having a female business student thank you on Twitter because your video helped her finally get started programming. Getting an email from a student telling you your advice helped them land their dream job!

So get out there! Find the women's networking group that works for you. Teach kids to code. You have the power to inspire the next generation of girl coders.

You are a role model!

CHAPTER 8

The 800 lb. Gorilla

By: Kellyn Pot'Vin-Gorman, DBA Kevlar

I've somehow managed to make it a pastime of pointing out how often incredibly skilled women are passed up for recognition while average men are promoted around them. When removing gender and getting down to skills, experience and accomplishments, it becomes quite clear just how heavily we scrutinize and limit women while most men pass them by.

We belong to a society that loves to shoot the messenger any although I'm constantly pointing out we shed light on this topic, it's a good thing I've been nicknamed Kevlar, because I'm going to need all the bullet proof material I can get. A previous mentor once said of me, "Kellyn won't just tell you there's an 800 lb. gorilla in the room, she'll name him George and demand you find him a zoo". We don't like discussing these uncomfortable topics and it's just easier to point out the person who's identified it.

I'll be tasking the reader to absorb a few facts backed by considerable data- such as citing an extensive study published in the Proceedings of the National Academy of Sciences, who discovered when senior faculty across the US, were presented with identical resumes from candidates for an open position, demonstrated bias against the female candidate vs. the male. Both male and female faculty were more likely to offer a higher salary and opportunities for mentorship to male candidates. As stated, although there was bias shown towards the female candidates, it was demonstrated by both genders. This chapter will touch on numerous areas surrounding why we all show bias towards women at some level and how its limiting women in their career progression.

As much as the upcoming paragraphs are focused on women, these same challenges are also faced by all minorities, no matter if we talk with people of color, differing sexual orientation, or from other various backgrounds that fall outside the expected traditional ones. Research also demonstrated that when women and minorities engaged in promotion of diversity, they were rated less positively than when their white, male peers were to promote it. Culture and bias, although at the core of these challenges, are less straight forward to identify. When faced with racism or discrimination, it's commonly easier to identify, often having laws and policies to address it, letting others know it's unacceptable. As the center of the debate, communication is a complex combination of words, facial expressions, vocal inflections/tone and even posture, involving two or more individuals, that when combined, can change an interaction to be viewed from benign to hostile. These complexities leave it difficult to navigate and to set policies around bias and culture that provide clear guidelines and recommendations everyone can agree upon. What was acceptable in years past, may not be acceptable today and as culture is one of the most difficult things to change, slow to evolve. As we inspect what, by today's standards are clearly unacceptable, generations can collide and to move forward as humans means that someone is left behind.

Growing Up Girl

I was the first girl of my generation already populated by tall, sandy haired boys, nourished on Upper Michigan venison and Wisconsin cheese. As a child of the 70's, I took after the small stature and small-boned French of my family. I stood in contrast of these tall, blond cousins, but as I lacked the self-awareness to know my role as a girl in society, I felt no different than the boys around me. I quickly began to compete with them, demanding I keep up on their adventures. I recall my cousins standing in the ice, cold creek by our house, challenging each other to see who could stay the longest in the freezing water. I'd quickly join them, but only I'd be scolded by relatives to come out of the water and dry off. I would stubbornly refuse and ask why they were allowed to continue while I was asked to leave. The adults would attempt numerous explanations until exasperated with my persistent questions and unyielding will, they'd exclaim, "Because you're a little girl!" By the time I was five, I wanted nothing more than to be a boy because the only data my young mind could reason was boys were allowed to have more fun than girls.

As a grown woman, these were cast away memories until I began to hear similar stories and was surprised by how often other women had similar stories to my own. I was now a performance specialist in a technical field and I was known for identifying patterns that most others missed. Along with discovering incredible performance gains and increased revenue for companies, it leads me to offer insight to my managers when I'd identify patterns in behavior and how to improve team relations. This naturally included noting cultural and bias issues, which I was so rarely wrong about that one manager started referring to me as the "psychic DBA". Having a sixth sense for recognizing these types of challenges often left me anxious, as anyone who's dealt with it knows, it's not pleasant to know what's really going on when people would prefer you to be oblivious. It felt as though the 800lb gorilla was everywhere, even if I thought he was, at first, a figment of my imagination.

This lead to requests for frank discussions with management to ask them to resolve problems and becoming the person identified to have the discussions with those experiencing these difficulties. I would repeatedly lose respect for managers that relied on me to resolve bias problems, as it seemed so straight forward to me on how to do it successfully:

1. Give everyone the benefit of the doubt to their intentions.
2. Don't allow others to hide behind the façade of bravo or insensitivity. Have real conversations and demand that people show each other respect.
3. Stress that respecting each other is as important as the technical skills they bring to the position.

While some of my managers hid and asked me to take on these difficult discussions, I naturally adjusted my speech to keep the other person(s) open to the conversation. I rarely stepped back from difficult topics unless I discovered the manager supporting bias or disrespectful behavior. At that time, I would quickly discern this was the manager's problem and not mine from that point on. With the increased experience working with diverse people of different backgrounds, cultures and beliefs, the more my skills at addressing bias continued to improve. By ten years into my DBA career, I was almost always the only woman on my team, so the conversation I was brought into most often was challenges with women in technology from other groups. The groups included how to get more girls interested in technology to how to achieve more in a technical career and how to retain more women in the industry once they entered the field. The source of the problem often came back to upbringing and the bias everyone has. It wasn't just how girls were brought up, but how we were taught to interact with women, that we still prepare young women for a more traditional role in life, and how to raise boys to be men.

I've heard every excuse of why there aren't as many women in tech as men. I won't entertain the physical differences in gray matter, white matter or how the left and right hemisphere are connected in the brain between the genders as proof to why. Recent research shows that on average, men and women have the same IQ, so it is pitiful to try to prove one gender is better than another when in truth, they are both essential to the field. My focus is on upbringing and how we raise boys to take more risks, rely less on other's opinions and be more assertive. As was my own experience, these types of traits, when demonstrated in a girl, are more likely to be received with a negative response and correction from the adults around her. The same negative response is often experienced by boys when they demonstrate sensitivity and/or timidity. They are often corrected, and a more aggressive response is promoted. If girls are more inclined to engage in risk behavior, they're more often to be held responsible for any negative outcome, where we'll be told, "boys will be boys" when boys take risks.

Along with numerous, small differences, these hinder women from taking risks as easy as men later in the business world, too, which is an important part of career growth. It sets an expectation that women will take a safer, less risky or assertive role at work, leaving many women expected to take a more administrative role, even when they are part of a team of peers with similar skills.

It's All About Culture

There is a cultural tendency and a comfort level in letting the women of a group, a team or department utilize their soft skills, (administration, project management, communication) more than the technical skills they may possess. The percentage of women that have experienced an incident where there were expected to take notes for a meeting, the organizer for a group event or the one to "entertain" a guest at the office are incredibly high. Women are asked to take notes in meetings, build out spreadsheets and project plans, while their male peers are busy writing code, performing system administration and installations.

More often found in male-dominated fields, women find they become the "mother" and caretakers of their group, (a topic discussed in depth in a later chapter.) Men may still hold the official titles of leadership, but women are the ones managing the day-to-day administrative tasks. In turn, when interesting, technical opportunities arise, there opportunities are offered to their male peers and if too many of these experiences pass them by, women's technical knowledge can be impacted.

Engaging in higher profile technical knowledge sharing, such as blogging, authoring or presenting, may present women with ambition the opportunity to surpass the glass ceiling, but new challenges wait. There is an assumption that once women accept a promotion to a lead or management position, that she'll no longer have interest in engaging in technical challenges. Sometimes it's a simple misunderstanding of what deems technical. For some companies, formatting a spreadsheet is viewed as technical work, but we quickly need to squash this foolishness and reassign it to administrative work that is assigned across all the team members.

If the woman has always found true technical work fulfilling, the removal of these kinds of challenges can create a barrier to future career fulfillment. As I've gone through this multiple times, I began to despise title promotions that would remove me from the day-to-day technical challenges. I would joke that my career goal was to "...walk right by the corner offices to get to the server room." It wasn't that I minded administrative work- there's always going to be specific tasks that aren't preferred that are part of a role, but I entered a technical career because of my passion for technology. To only assign technical tasks to my male peers will quickly impact the moral and as I spoke to other women, I discovered it was a substantial reason behind them leaving the industry after appearing to achieve success.

In November 2014, I was recognized in my home state of Colorado, awarded the Women in Technology APEX Award from the Colorado Technology Association. I was heavily involved in their events to foster involvement from women in the industry. I met some of the women that I continually network and collaborate with years later, but the interactions with many of the women left me realizing the significant amount of bias impacting our conversations, task assignment and career development in the technical industry.

The women I spoke to over the years were starved for networking opportunities, but the ones offered to them were always lesser than ones occurring in their company networks. We were still celebrating them with "Women in Technology" lunches, but some assumed the only way to get them involved was to create opportunities for coffee, book clubs and yes, even knitting circles. Most of the women who were deep tech, welcomed the female companionship, but recognized that these events rarely, if ever would grant the networking opportunities to solve the problems we were up against. These events, unlike most of the men's networking opportunities, didn't discuss further information about positions, mentoring, technical skill enhancements or business connections. All of this, combined with the limited time these women had available, outside of personal and professional responsibilities left many incredibly frustrated.

Although Women in Technology initiatives are a big deal, your time is valuable and my professional recommendation is to spend time on them only if they provide the following:

- Locating mentors or even more importantly, sponsors.
- Discuss high impacting topics of how to be successful in the industry.
- Networking opportunities regarding salary, potential job or networking opportunities.
- Further technical skills or certification.

- If a company WIT event or group, there must be a plan an analysis to show greater inclusion of promotions, leadership positions and opportunities for diversity at the company.

Women in technology initiatives must walk the walk, not just talk the talk. Just as we want career advancing tasks, we also don't want to waste our time at events that consume our personal time that isn't going to provide professional value.

Alas, we continued to attend meetings where we were handed notepads to take notes, we're unsure if we'll be heard when contributing or had contributions credited to those around us. We stayed onsite while our male peers attended events that promoted their careers. I had refused to do anything other than what my male peers were doing, emulating them and expecting to be treated like them, but there were a number of disagreements that occurred when I did stand by this expectation. The few women who'd started out with me two decades ago started to slowly leave the industry after about five years into my career. In future conversations over coffee or drinks, I asked them to return to the reasons behind their departure from their technical careers. When they began their stories, most sounded unique, but as we dug into their personal reasons behind the experiences, I found eerie similarities. Having the luck of parents who possessed a supportive and incredibly equal partnership to serve as an example, I realized that only small differences in mentor opportunities and sheer persistence may have all that created a story of success and not one of career abandon.

Being born the oldest child of three girls, I was driven, directed and understood what I needed to do to take care of my career and family. My ex-husband was the best friend anyone could have, but he shied away from most family responsibilities and when I went from girl "friend" to wife, I quickly cascaded down his list of priorities. As a natural follower and supporter, people liked him right off and he continued to live his life after our children were born just as he had when he was single. The follower he was, he rarely if ever disagreed with people and to use the analogy of a dog breed, reminded many of America's favorite, a golden retriever. He was just happy-go-lucky to be allowed to be in your presence and was happiest in large groups of people. Although in many ways we complemented each other, culture impacted us heavily. Society expected me to be the baker of cookies, the attendee to every school event, community involvement and yes, note taker in meetings. With the demands of my career and clear understanding of what our family of five required, my analytical mind clearly understood and made logical decisions about what was necessary and what was secondary, often with a clear strategy to get ahead and make my way up the technical ladder. I was the more natural bread winner of the two of us.

Recognizing this and attempting to take on a more traditionally maternal role, he received negative feedback from his family and friends. They viewed it as less manly and that he wasn't living up to his responsibilities. They didn't understand why he wasn't approaching his career as I was. He was offered very little to no support from his family, friends and peers. This is just one more way that culture and society impacts the ability for women to be full contributors to the workforce- even if women do embrace their ambition, especially if it correlates with the natural skills of the couple, we continue to expect a more traditional role for each.

This lead to challenges in the workplace, too. My managers, both male and female, often bypassed me for opportunities, offering them to my male peers, where repeatedly, they were more inclined to offer me more administrative tasks. I wasn't shy about stating my displeasure and demanding that tasks were more evenly distributed. I would often (and do still) battle those that don't realize how quick they are to assign me tasks that require soft skills, but are hesitant to let me perform my share of tasks that are the reason I entered the technical industry- I'm technical. After being assigned tasks that are administrative on a regular basis while a male peer is offered none, I will directly ask why they haven't assigned a share to my male peer. The below responses I've had said to me almost word for word on more than one occasion in response to only receiving administrative task assignments:

> *Tom isn't very good at work like this.* – He won't get any better if he isn't assigned any, either.
>
> *Don't you like to do this type of work?* – This is a job, not about liking or not liking, it needs to be done, but if you have the same title as your male peer, you should be assigned the same variety of work.
>
> *So, you want me to take tasks away from Tom?* – Nope, never said that. I want tasks assigned to me that are technical, too.

The challenge here is that you should expect to have a task or two that you don't like in your job. You need to do the work anyway and share with your peers in these tasks. The bias lies in that there is an assumption that women prefer non-technical tasks. Again, this bias drives many women out of tech. If you don't get to do what you're passionate about and only your male peers are, then why stay there?

Having a wide skill of talents and not enjoying management positions as much as technical ones, I found that I still enjoyed sharing my technical knowledge. Speaking was a natural next step from all the documenting I'd been doing for a couple years as a blogger and it served my career well. Nothing smashes the glass ceiling and impacts pay gap like having your technical knowledge demonstrated in written form, without your gender being presented. As I entered the technical community as a speaker, I received many questions that weren't posed to my male peers:

Do you have children?

Who watches them while you present?

Does your ex-husband babysit while you travel?

I'm always, (equally) amused and annoyed by the last question. Why are men viewed as babysitters instead of parents? We both worship the smallest contributions from them and then remove the value of the role of father, sometimes in the same sentence. I wouldn't have learned the value of risk taking if I hadn't spent as much time as a child with my father and grandfather while my mother worked.

When we do emulate the men around us, most of those around us are incredibly uncomfortable with women's ambition. In one position I'd been hired with a percentage of my time allocated to presenting, I was receiving many speaking opportunities, but I noticed that I was starting to get less approval for speaking engagements with little explanation as to why. My team was under the impression that I'd been hired to speak at events, so they were as confused by some of the side comments being stated in meetings about me presenting. I approached my management to gain some perspective. I was told, (with a straight face...) "For our company, we picture a forty-year old guy, with a Southern accent and we just don't think you should consider yourself our spokesperson." Now I have no doubt that there are some folks reading the statement and cringing; it was a cringe-worthy moment. You have to recognize how bias and the importance of representation have impacted what they pictured as a spokesperson and that who I was, as a female techie from the great North conflicted with this.

This same company was quite comfortable with me leading their DBA group, but I was never granted an official title. Another male peer held the title, the third one during my time there, even though he performed none of the lead duties. These male leads were busy doing cool technical work and I was able to continue working transparently, "under the radar" in the unofficial position, often performing administrative tasks, with less public speaking. This limitation quickly drove me to search out a new opportunity. I wasn't the first woman to hold the unofficial role of managing the team while never being offered the official title and if you speak to many women in tech, it's a common story among them.

As often as we hear that men have been taken credit for women's ideas or work, I don't think it's as often intentional. There's an "invisibility" to women that has nothing to do with how persistent they are about being seen or heard. Almost weekly, another story of a woman tells me about how a manager or lead looks to her male peer for confirmation for multiple scenarios. This is quite discouraging, but not as damaging as what I call "is this thing on?"

Let's start by admitting how quickly we're becoming a digital world. More of us, especially in the technical world, work remote or utilize technology to communicate. There is less one on one, where someone can clearly see the communication, or more importantly, the lack there of, and call out problems when they seem them. Men are raised to be heard, to demand to be heard and when challenged, to stand up to the challenge, as it's their word that's being "attacked". All of us have been in a situation where a man may have stated, in one way or another that they justified a combative tone because they felt their word was being questioned. Taking a man at his word goes back centuries, but women don't have this history and there is a lack of trust of women, but also no inclination to search out a woman's respect like one would a man's. We more often seek out a woman's admiration and, in many cultures,, this has is due to more patriarchal hierarchy. This results in an extensive amount of energy expelled to let men know in our interactions that we hear them, that we want to interact with them and that we wish to collaborate with them- all in a goal to earn their respect. This can often leave women in the room to silence. Little to no interaction, no acknowledgement that they've even spoke, and credit being offered only to a man in the room when he's chosen to pick up on the topic, maybe even stating the same idea as the woman we aren't interacting with.

I perform a lot of sponsorship for those around me. I find positions with companies and promote individuals to write articles, books. I worked for one company where I was either the initial contact for the candidate or the one to convince them to apply for a position. I started to notice in a few instances where other people were credited with bringing the person on board, even when I'd been paid the finders fee. As it happened more frequently, I did some research as to the situation or people involved when the credit was being redirected to a male peer or superior. I found that offering credit for my "find" to a male peer or superior was received with more credibility if they used a person whose name was known to the audience or the speaker had assumed it sounded more credible. One person I referred and recommended to work at the company was the one to say they were placed by someone they thought was more important than they decided I was. I can say, without hesitation, that this not only hurt their standing with me, but as they continued to do it, cost them respect within the community. Karma has a way to come back and haunt those that disrespect the people around them.

Being Fearless

As I wasn't shy about stating what impressed me, I had gained wonderful mentors quite easy and early on. I had started blogging and subsequently speaking at technical events shortly after. My mentors were often fearless individuals in the community and as I'd done for my entire career, I began to emulate their fearlessness. When I received backlash for "daring" to be as much as my male peers or mentors, I first identified it as something I was doing that created the situation. In time I learned through conversations with numerous women who'd left the technical industry, my story is far from unique and I simply had mentors and luck that had kept me here. I hadn't come across a store that would be considered traditional discrimination or harassment, but a more subtle and consistent push. These subtle situations often lead to "pin prick" size wounds to the woman's career that would accumulate and with time, caused them to leave the industry for an industry that didn't have these added challenges.

For those of us that do stay and as our careers mature, how can this impact our ability to receive recognition, move upward into the higher ranks and onward to c-level? The challenge of single path advancement, with little technical opportunities and higher levels of scrutinizing were also of serious concern. Some were leaving because the opportunities that were left just weren't that interesting. Those that did stay, were scrutinized about their lacking technical experience, (remember, they weren't receiving the same technical opportunities as their male peers) and the nit picking over their management skills and other soft skills could be debilitating.

I was fighting the good fight and commonly appear to be winning. My career continued to flourish and my skill at finding the right jobs for me improved. I learned how to strategically negotiate around bias and avoid non-technical positions. I tiptoed around people's egos that I often found were incredibly uncomfortable around my ambition. I didn't have to do anything to trigger this behavior other than be me- I'm comfortable in my own weaknesses, often finding ways to empower myself with them. This will bring out the insecurities in quick fashion in both peers and management. Yes, I bring out the worst in a workplace bully. This results in both a positive and negative situation. Good because the bully may go completely postal and the company finally has a clear opportunity to be rid of them. Bad because if the company is one that wants to avoid conflict with the bully, realize that bully is going to go postal and there are no innocent bystanders when they do.

Workplace bullies are identified as such because they may understand the boundaries of acceptable behavior very well. They're more likely to manipulate and use passive/aggression measures. It costs companies millions of dollars each year in the form of employee turnover, HR payouts and other compensation.

Needless to say, as I progressed through this point in my career, I began to move away from confrontations with workplace bullies and began to deal with even more subtle challenges to success.

As women succeed in the technical industry, there are still significant challenges we face. If they're not addressed head on, very little change will happen over time. Culture is an overwhelming component to the scenario and due to this, cultural changes and especially around bias, needs to be part of the conversation.

One of these biases has to do with how men and women communicate from the time we're children and how it impacts us once we're in the workplace. There's an old saying,

"Men insult each other and don't mean it. Women compliment each other and don't mean it."

I'd like you, as the reader to not skim over the meaning of this statement. As women, we are often expected to speak pleasantries, even when it's not what we are thinking. We also are raised to network with other women by complimenting each other. How often do we approach another woman and compliment what they're wearing or something about their appearance? This is how we connect to other women and begin a conversation.

Research has shown that women are less likely to be:

- Given credit
- Be recognized
- Negotiate positions and salary

Boys are raised insulting, taunting and testing each other with insults. It's common enough for a man to approach another man with an opening comment that few women would ever say to another women. This is how men connect and begin their conversations- this is how they network with each other.

There is a second level connected to the business. Men are prepared for straightforward and blunt talk. They have spent their lifetimes hearing insults and take little personally due to this. They've been raised to take their own opinion over what someone else says. Women, more accustomed to being complimented and having pleasantries in public conversations, are often left less prepared for blunt conversation. Men are also left ill prepared for women who do speak plainly to them and find it as uncomfortable as women find it from other women.

Scrutiny

I was on a social media platform recently where a woman posted a tip with a link on how to keep your dog naturally cool. A male poster responded that this was incorrect and why he thought it was incorrect. The response was stated in an authoritarian way, speaking down to the original poster without any links or confirmed data to back up his response outside of his experience. I did some quick research and there was multiple Vet and animal care sites that backed up what the original poster claimed. The scenario came across to me as a perfect example of "mansplaining" and although I wasn't offended by it, I did find it humorous and responded with, "I think you just mansplained this post…LOL"

The rebuttal from, not just the male poster, but from other posters was decisive and swift. I was told to get over it, to chill, that I was disgusting, I was sexist and that this was why people didn't take feminists seriously. The original poster, who had continued to be told her post was fake news and that she needed to stop posting on the page, left the site. This was a pet site dedicated to dog photos and there were just as many female posters as male that were part of the bullying.

When women are able to speak plainly, then overcome and succeed, especially in a field that is more male dominated, there are subtle challenges and backlash that can impact them from continuing on this path. We often hear women identified different from men when using the same phrases and making the same choices. Where men are viewed as assertive, women are viewed as aggressive. Where men can simply contribute to a meeting, stating their ideas, concerns and feedback, women will receive harsh criticism for doing the same.

Many have also discussed how woman are subject to higher levels of scrutinizing. There are two common responses to these women:

1. Complex silence as the originator attempts to understand the woman and how she's achieved so much outside the expected norm.
2. A second group, who is extremely vocal in their scrutiny, often attempting to understand her, as she doesn't fit within the expected stereotypes of what they expect.

There's been significant research focused on the increased scrutiny that women endure in the workplace. As frustrating as it is for the woman in question, it also has some surprising backlash for the one who's scrutinizing her. In an attempt to justify their previous behaviour, the manager may assign less challenging work, (i.e. administrative work) to the woman who over-achieves or even more troubling, the woman may begin to under perform to avoid the scrutiny. For some managers, this may appear to prove the woman wasn't worthy of their added attention and either situation will often drive the woman to leave the industry due to career dissatisfaction.

Drive for Change

As I've experienced some of these challenges first hand and even more often through my peers in the industry, I began to identify not just the frustrations, but the opportunities to overcome, too. There were some direct and clear options for change. As we built out "mentoring teams" of 3-4 individuals, we found that small changes created large successes and it was worth promoting these changes to the world at large.

Representation

When I first was asked to speak to girls and young women about being a woman in technology, I really didn't get it. I was naturally a loner and wasn't sure why it mattered. I wanted increased exposure to technology to young women, what could they learn from me, talking about my challenges and successes. It wasn't until my 16 yr old, feeling exasperated, said to me, "Mom, you're perfect- you NEVER screw up!" I was incredibly taken aback by this comment and responded, "Sam, I screw up all the time, I just never give up!" I truly believed my imperfections and mistakes were on display for my children 24/7 and to hear this from my oldest child forced me to recognize that even those close to you may view your world as something unattainable and never try. I finally was able to recognize why it was important to share my story, not just my technology with those around me.

Credit Where Credit is Due

No matter where the blame or complexities lie in the frustration, we need to address crediting women when credit is due. Acknowledge women for their contributions and achievements. We need to be aware when we do feel discomfort at women's accomplishments, either in the way of ideas or contributions, due to cultural or bias. For women, we are raised to network and connect with other women by complimenting them on their looks or attire. Its not that there's anything wrong with telling other women that you like their dress, hairstyle or shoes, but with as little credit as women are receiving, take the time to identify what a woman you admire is contributing and reach out to her peers, her manager and the business to recognize what she's accomplishing.

If you note that a woman is remaining unseen when credit is being given, speak up and ensure she is included. There are types of recognition that women are often bypassed that help promote men that is due to our idea what cites credibility, too.

Take Me To Your Mentor

As we just discussed, women in technology have less representation, less opportunities to network and as a result, less mentors. Locating mentors is crucial to an industry where when less than 25% of a team is female; you're often the only woman on the team or even in the department. There is very little women in leadership to offer mentoring and even more importantly, sponsorship opportunities and in turn, women in IT often turn to men as their mentors.

I was one of those women who had nothing but male mentors when I was younger. I quickly emulated them, duplicated their efforts, but was surprised when I received different responses to my ambition. Having women mentors offers us a perspective that men simply aren't able to offer us. Our male peers rarely will have the knowledge of gender bias, personal obligation and challenges that women go through from a personal perspective.

If we have so little opportunity to find these mentors in the workplace, where do we go? Although we do have family obligations and challenging careers, I recommend that women in IT become part of their local technical user groups, join meetup.com and find groups like Women Who Code, Girl Geek Dinners and Girls Develop It. If you have family obligations, you may only have time to offer one group, but the value can be significant to your career.

If you write code, upload it to online repositories, use social media, blog and be part of the online communities. My contributions to a technical forum offered me my first three mentors back in 2007-2010. Written communication can offer some relief from gender bias and an opportunity to publish your work. It also offers you an opportunity to network without leaving your home or office, connecting you to more women in the industry.

Scrutinize in Return

If you think you're being offered less technical tasks than your peers, carefully document your peers and your own workload for a period of time. If you're being scrutinized at a higher level, it will be important to have exact data and information, so take your time and pay attention to every detail about differences in task assignment between you and your peers.

Keep notes of conversations and ask for communication and follow up in writing as often as possible. Remember that this type of bias is subtler than forms of discrimination and you should avoid any discussion on how it makes you feel, but be as objective as possible with the other person. Before meeting with the person, ask yourself questions the following:

1. By limiting your contribution, how does it impact the team's productivity?
2. What tasks could you have performed that would have offered more value, (specifically in project completion and revenue)?
3. What opportunities do team members have access to that you may not due to limited task assignment?

If you do find that you are experiencing unequal task assignment, the next step is to get advice from a trusted confident, (hopefully a mentor.) I recommend approaching both female and male peers/mentors for their feedback on the situation. Men can find this type of situation very foreign and although their advice can be valuable in how to respond to it, the approach may not take gender bias into consideration or have first-hand experience as another woman would.

Consider meeting with HR with the goal to resolve the issue with your manager one-on-one. Ask HR to simply document the challenge and let them know that you appreciate their support.

Now that you've validated there is an issue, the next step is communicating with management and can be done in a few ways:

1. Request a meeting with your manager and ask for an opportunity to have more challenging assignments.
2. Any discussion of bias will have to be focused on education, not persecution and is often not recommended.
3. If there's been a communication breakdown, consider bringing HR in as a mediator to assist. Explain to both HR and your manager that your goal is to improve your working relationship with your manager to make it more productive for you both and that the goal is to increase productivity for the company.

Hopefully your manager will work to create a work plan that will include more meaningful challenges for you as an employee and provide you both with an opportunity to grow and add more value to the company.

Proof of Concepts

If administrative work is offered and for more challenging technical tasks, there is only hesitation without assignment to other team members, you may decide it's an opportunity to step up and create a proof of concept. As this is a task that was discussed, but never officially assigned, its important to ensure its something that has value to the company, will bring recognition not just to you, but even more so to your manager that may have been hesitant to assign it to you and also make sure that you can perform the task spectacularly.

I have significant experience "proving my weight in gold" through projects like this. They can require that you be a bit fearless and is best done by someone who's taken the time to build a strong network in the company. The goal will be to shine the light of accomplishment on your manager more than yourself, hoping that this will provide incentive for the manager to trust you with more challenges in the future.

Getting What You Need

As you gain more credibility, move away from administrative tasks that limit our options for career growth and then bridge out to gain mentors and sponsors, you'll have better opportunities in jobs, too. This leads us to negotiating salaries and getting the right job.

You should be interviewing your possible manager as much as he/she is interviewing you. We rarely have pensions that will keep us at a position for an entire lifetime, but employee turnover is expensive. You're doing both you and the company a favour by making sure the person you report to be the right manager for you. Employees don't leave companies, but they leave managers.

When negotiating a position and/or a salary, inspect your network, (Linked in is excellent for this) and see whom you know at the company. I've never regretted approaching a woman at a company and ask her to support me and for her advice on a position, department or salary. Most data state women are terrible at negotiating salaries, but women are incredibly skilled at negotiating for each other.

Reverse it

Most, if not all of the challenges come back to gender bias. It's an incredibly unconscious culprit in our society that restricts half the population in the world from being fully productive members of society. Often when I've been on the receiving end of it, I'll feel a prickly sensation of discomfort, but it may take a bit for me to realize what was said or why what happened was limiting to me or another woman. Bias can fly under the radar, but when it doesn't and why you recognize it, there are ways to address it.

1. Have honest discussions with a focus on a goal of what you want to achieve, not to retaliate against the person who showed the bias.
2. If someone has said something with clear bias, ask them to repeat the sentence back reversing the gender and see if it still makes sense or sounds acceptable. Many times, that will identify the bias and open the discussion.

With all the complexities that go on with the challenges of wanting to be in the tech industry, there are some opportunities to succeed and avoid the administrative task onslaught that seems to impact so many. As obscure as some of the options may seem, they all have shown to offer success and provide higher success rates of retaining women in the industry.

As we evolve and mature as part of the IT industry, the next generation becomes more familiar with women being standard contributors to technology. As technology becomes more a part of our day-to-day life, we begin to introduce and teach technology like we currently teach the basics, such as reading, writing and arithmetic. Just as we introduce science, history and literature to the next generation, in the hopes that they may decide if it's an opportunity for a career or just a passion they never would have realized on their own, we hope that our education system can do the same with technology.

These changes may seem unrelated to having women take on more similar roles to their male peers vs. being viewed in an administrative one, but it's all related. Just as women doctors are less likely to be assumed to be nurses in today's world, we recognize that exposure to girls in more equal standing, as well as representation once they become adults create vital changes to cultural bias.

CHAPTER 9

Not Your Wife.
Not Your Mother.

By: Angela Tidwell

We have all seen the signs hanging around offices and public spaces (most notably in a break room or kitchen area) "Your Mother Does Not Work Here." It most normally applies to being an adult and picking up after yourself. The signs have always struck me a bit odd...that we have to remind grownups to clean up after themselves.

I am a wife, and I am a mother. I do my fair share of cleaning up after both my husband and my son. And to be fair, they do clean up after themselves more often than not. Having said that, it does seem rather odd that the signs say "Your mother...." instead of "Your parent..." Why is it always just expected that we woman have to be the ones cleaning up everything? Let's stop and think about that for a moment.

Womanly Things

Countless times in my life, at various ages and stages in life, I have been expected to do certain "womanly things." That is, jobs that ONLY women do, and all women are expected to do. As a young girl growing up in small town Texas, it appeared to me that women were not really revered for their strengths. Women were put on this planet to please men, clean and cook, and raise children. I remember hearing my dad complain about how women were trying to take all the jobs away from men. I heard him talk about how women were the weaker of the sexes and how they should just stay at home where they belong....unless they were going to be a school teacher or a nurse. My father was an old-fashioned guy and these statements were the standard fare of the time. As a young girl being raised in Texas in the 80's, that was the common view I would hear.

Something stirred inside my mind, even as a young child. A quiet, sullen, yet raging desire to be 'more' than the future that had seemingly been painted for me. I yearned to be equal. I yearned to make my father see how strong I could be. I wanted him to see how I could be anything I wanted to be.

A voice was growing in me from a small age. I realize now that it was the voice of my mother. I remember her pulling me aside and telling me she was always proud of me, of how I was strong and resilient and could be ANYTHING.

Fast Forward

I am now a very proud wife to a wonderful man and mother to an amazing young son. My goal every day is to be the mother to him that my mom was to me. I tell him every day how brave and strong he is and how it is okay to make mistakes. He hears constantly how we learn and grow more from one failure than we will ever learn from a hundred successes. I am also teaching by example how strong a woman/wife/mother is by taking on new challenges daily and never giving up in the face of fear. My ultimate goal is to raise a man who knows how to respect all women as he respects his mother. That is a very big job that I don't take lightly.

In my teens I was just your average girl who loved hair bands, drama club, and hanging out with my friends. I never really felt like I fit in, but I never felt like an outcast either. It was important to me to befriend everyone instead of just being lumped into one group or another. This sometimes put me in tough situations between groups of people. Nevertheless, I tried to always be the peacemaker. I succeeded at times and failed at other times. Life in small town Texas was not what I wanted for my future and I knew I had a tough climb ahead of me.

Being that strong lady who was never afraid to let rejection stand in her way, I struck out on my own as soon as I could. I decided I would be fearless and strong and I would make sure everyone knew that I could be anything! College was not affordable for my family, but I knew it was a way out, the way I needed to go in order to live the life I wanted. I worked hard to get scholarships, worked many jobs to pay tuition, and eventually had to take out a few student loans. Failure was not an option. I was fully invested in myself and was determined not to fail.

Putting myself through college, a whole new life, direction, and determination opened up for me. Some experiences were amazing and wonderful, others were less so. But there were failures, lots of failures.

While on my way to making a better life for myself, I was struck by the number of people who asked me if I was attending college "just to find a husband." Why would you ever ask a young woman who is out on her own, making a life for herself, facing down fear itself, if she was going through all this trouble JUST to get a man? Was I not a whole person on my own? Was I not worthy of a life without marriage or children?

Entering the Adult Workforce

As stated above, I put myself through college. Times were really hard, but I was determined. After many long years of working every job I could find to make enough money to pay my bills (most months) and get through college, I made it. There I was, Bachelor of Fine Arts in hand and ready to take on the world!

The jobs I held in college were fast food jobs, retail, university library, secretarial… and the list goes on. There were years there that I worked 2 full time and 2 part time jobs along with taking a full semester course of at least 19 hours. These jobs were not career-making jobs. Often the patrons were not the greatest and did not treat me with respect. Somehow that seemed normal. Looking back, I wish I had known it was okay to speak up and expect common decency. Upon my graduation, I felt sure that I had arrived at the point where I was an adult and was on my way to greatness!

Finally, I was there, fully in the adult workforce, at an office…with a real TITLE! However, along with my duties in this position, I was expected to clean up the breakfast, snack, and lunch dishes of the men who worked there. Interestingly enough, it was made clear to the ladies in the office that we were NOT allowed to eat any meals or snacks at the office. We were also expected to wear dresses, stockings, and dress shoes with a heel no less than 2 inches tall. Now, if it dipped below 30 degrees Fahrenheit, we were allowed to wear dress slacks with our stockings and heels. The men wore mostly suits, but in the summer showed up in shorts and polo shirts. There was NO casual Friday afforded to the women. The strange thing about all of these rules regarding the women in the office is that none of them were created by the male partners. The rules were constructed and enforced by the wife of the owner. She did not even work at the office but did come in almost daily to make sure we were taking care of her husband and son! All of these years later I look back and see that perhaps the women in the office were expected to be the substitute wife and mother to her husband and son who owned the company.

I wish I could tell you the experiences cease here at this particular office. They don't. This is not an isolated incident. Being the replacement wife/mother doesn't stop at cleaning kitchens and June Cleaver-like dress codes. Sometimes we are expected to be others' maids just because we're Mom away from the office! In 2009 my loving husband and I were blessed with the most adorable baby boy who ever walked the face of the Earth (don't even try to correct me on that opinion!).

Upon my return from maternity leave, I was approached by a peer. Expecting to hear how excited she was for me and how she and the team missed me, I was instead met by her asking me to clean her office. Perplexed I asked why she thought I should clean HER office. She remarked that since I was a wife and a new mother, she thought I would naturally be better at cleaning her office than she was. Feeling rather strong and cheeky, I replied "Maybe you should call your mother and ask her to come in for you." I am glad I stood my ground with this peer. It was a defining moment in our work relationship.

Women Enjoy Cleaning

Stop right there. Honestly, I do not know any woman nor man who truly enjoys cleaning. Yet it seems no matter where I go, no matter who I speak with on the subject, women are expected to clean. Many times, I have been faced with being seen as the "cleaning crew." Recently, I was in my office space which is shared with employees of other companies. I was at the sink washing my coffee cup when a man who works at another company came in and tried to hand me his dirty dishes. I heard a voice behind me say "Here ya go." I turned to find a man standing there pushing his dishes at me. I gave him one of my oh no you did NOT just do that looks and replied, "I am NOT washing your dishes." I then walked away. I wish I could say that is the ONLY time something like this has happened to me.

What made that person think I was there to wash his dishes? Was it an assumption that I would do it because I am a woman? Perhaps he saw me there cleaning and thought that one more set of dishes would not bother me. Perhaps he saw me there washing my cup and assumed that since I am a woman, it is my job to clean the office dishes. Either way, he was mistaken. My time is just as valuable as his. Taking time away from my clients and projects merely to make more time for him to get his work done is not even a blip on my radar of important tasks. In actuality, I had taken a short break from solving a difficult problem. I had to get up and walk away for a moment to clear my head, so I thought that washing my cup would give my mind a needed break. If I had given in and washed his dishes, and then all the other dishes that had piled up in the sink, it would have impeded my time and threatened my ability to timely solve the problem that had me stumped. Let me say that again: My time is just as valuable as his. I do not get paid to clean dishes. My time is better spent solving problems for clients and working on new projects.

Texts with Mom

Another note-worthy experience of me being treated like someone's mother or wife happened via text message. I was busy working away on a project when I received a text message. The message was telling me to check my boss' calendar and to reply back as to whether he would be able to make an appointment that had been scheduled between the text-sender and me.

Incredulously staring at my phone, questions began to form!

Why didn't he just reach out directly to my boss?

Doesn't he know that I am the primary on this project?

Is this a joke?

Is he trying to go over my head?

Does he not trust that I can do this project?

I have been a secretary in the past. I know that job description well. There is no part of my job title nor description that denotes that I am a secretary, or that I am responsible for the calendars of anyone in my company.

From the beginning of this project this person was told that I would be the one to handle the full project. My boss was no longer going to be working on it. This text message caused me a great deal of frustration. And as we know, frustration often leads to doubt, hurt feelings and sometimes aggression. Perhaps it was simply a miscommunication. Often times miscommunication is at the center of all problems that lend to frustration and discontent.

I chose to take a few moments to cool my jets. A few deep breaths later I responded to his text kindly reminding him that I would be taking the lead on the project and that my boss would not be working on it at this point. After some time, he replied that he had not remembered or did not know that I would be the one running the project. I appreciated his reply. Miscommunication impacts each individual on a team as well as the company's bottom line. Had he reached out directly to my boss, he would have been reminded that I was the lead on the project. This could have saved me not only time, but frustration and aggravation as well.

Standards Throughout Time

In discussing this topic with my mother-in-law, she shared a story of when she was in college. She was hired by the Department Chair of her University to do some work assisting his secretary. Unbeknownst to her, part of the duties including going to his home and packing his bags for trips. We must pause here to answer a few questions I posed. Were any men he employed expected to clean his house or pack his bags and make travel arrangements? (No males were hired by this professor.) Were other females hired for the same thing? (Yes, many other female students shared the same experiences.) Why can't this grown man take care of his own packing? (shrug)

My mother, too, has had many experiences where she was expected to be the mother of the office. Many times she has been put in the position where she was told it was expected of her to keep the office clean, make sure everyone was on top of their tasks, and even was expected to not only remind the boss of his anniversary but also had to buy presents for his wife! Once she was even asked to play chaperone at dinner between her boss and his two girlfriends! And yes, he was married. What an impossible and uncomfortable position to be put in just to provide for your family!

Search any job posting site and you might find a posting that reads "other responsibilities as required." What does this really mean? Does this mean your job title can be one thing, but your manager can assign you work outside your regular duties? Yes, that is exactly what this can mean. This means you may be assigned work that is more personal in nature. For instance, your job title may be "Assistant Director of Finance" but may end up running personal errands, shopping, or picking out gifts for your manager's significant other! While this is highly unethical, the legality of the situation is a blurry mess. Federal and state employment laws don't govern what managers can or cannot do when it comes to making their employees perform personal tasks.

The Nest has a great article "Can Bosses Legally Involve an Employee in Their Personal Business?"[1] in which advice is given on how to spot potential jobs that may involve personal tasks, consequences, and how to deal with the issue if it arises. Clearly this happens all to often. I have been asked numerous times to perform personal tasks for managers. Some of them I just grumbled through because it really WASN'T my responsibility, but I knew I had to do it or be fired. Some of them I was wholly uncomfortable with. Uncomfortable enough that I quit the job on the spot. No notice given, just explained that I could no longer work in the given environment and left. I know, not really the ideal way to leave a job. I read a great article "How to Tell Your Boss 'No' When Asked to Run a Personal Errand"[2] that points out that experts tell young professionals to work hard to demonstrate how dedicated they are to their job and how willing they are to make life easier for their boss. As a woman, I have often felt that good jobs are so hard to come by, that when I did have a good job I had to give my job everything I had just to keep it.

---

[1] "Can Bosses Legally Involve an Employee in Their Personal Business?" Ruth Mayhew - https://woman.thenest.com/can-bosses-legally-involve-employee-personal-business-14414.html

[2] "How to Tell Your Boss No When Asked to Run a Personal Errand" John Boitnott - https://www.entrepreneur.com/article/288151

This is in no way how we should feel. No one should feel they have to sacrifice their very happiness in life just to make their boss happy and their company profitable. Having said that, these personal errands could be prevalent at some point in your career. The aforementioned article demonstrates how to think outside the box to help your boss and not use too much of your precious time doing so.

My mother, mother-in-law, and I have had many years of the same experiences where we were put in a position where each of us were expected to "take care" of our male counterparts and/or "mother" other members of the work team. Why? And why hasn't this standard of gender discrimination changed?

Are You His Wife?

One of my favorite things to do is to talk with people. I love to tell a good story, and I love to listen to other peoples' stories. No doubt, one of the most fun parts of my job is marketing. While working the marketing booth at a tech event a few months back, I was enjoying conversation with tons of people from all walks of life. There is one instance that stuck out to me. I was explaining our services and expertise to a gentleman when a nice lady walked up. She listened to our conversation for a while. The man asked a question I was not familiar with, so I directed him to my boss for the insights he needed. I turned back to the lady expecting to speak with her about her SQL needs when she stopped me in my tracks with one simple question. "Are you his wife?" It was like the whole space-time continuum stopped. In my stunned mind, all motion around us stopped and the room went silent. "Why would she ask this? What would it matter one way or another? Is she expecting something different if I say yes or no?" In all honesty it took me a bit to answer. I told her that he was not my husband and that I was the Marketing DBA for the company. I was an actual employee. Her reply was a simple "Oh", and then she walked away.

Later in the day it dawned on me that perhaps she saw me as not a viable individual who was smart enough to work in this industry. I can't help but wonder why she stood there listening to me for all that time just to ask me if I was his wife. Granted, I look younger than I am, and am very outgoing, something that one does not always equate with those in the tech industry. So perhaps her bias was more toward my appearance than my gender. Either way, that interaction has left me with questions about how I appear to others.

First impressions are strong, and like it or not, we are all judged initially on our appearance. Think about the last person you saw in passing. What did you think of that person? We all have biases. In a 2017 interview with The Guardian, Director James Cameron remarked on the movie Wonder Woman, "All of the self-congratulatory back-patting Hollywood's been doing over Wonder Woman has been so misguided. She's an objectified icon, and it's just male Hollywood doing the same old thing! I'm not saying I didn't like the movie but, to me, it's a step backwards. Sarah Connor was not a beauty icon. She was strong, she was troubled, she was a terrible mother, and she earned the respect of the audience through pure grit. And to me, [the benefit of characters like Sarah] is so obvious. I mean, half the audience is female!"[3]

If you have not seen Wonder Woman yet, it is a story about a strong, fierce, beautiful woman who finds herself, finds her strength, and shares her gift for the love of mankind. Cameron feels that Wonder Woman, played by Gal Gadot, is just too pretty to be strong. His idea of a strong woman character is Sarah Connor from Terminator. She was flawed, and fierce, and strong, and…she had a very masculine appearance. The big picture Mr. Cameron is missing is that a woman's strength or value is not derived from her level of feminine or masculine appearance. Each one of us is unique, and wonderful.

Patty Jenkins, Director of Wonder Woman, responded to Mr. Cameron's assessment of the beauty vs strength of Wonder Woman:

> "If women have to always be hard, tough and troubled to be strong, and we aren't free to be multidimensional or celebrate an icon of women everywhere because she is attractive and loving, then we haven't come very far have we, I believe women can and should be everything, just like male lead characters should be. There is no right and wrong kind of powerful woman."[4]

Think about your biases. Can I be short, wear makeup, curl my hair, wear pretty clothes and still be smart enough to work on the cutting edge of the data industry? Can I be strong and feminine? "There is no right and wrong kind of powerful woman."

How Did YOU Get That Job?

In 2016, I attended PASS Summit in Seattle, Washington. What an amazing time! One of the coolest experiences was attending the Women In Technology luncheon. I was so very excited to not only be there with so many amazing, wonderful, smart, supportive women in the Data Industry, but I was also there to hear Kelly Lockwood Primus[5],

---

[3] " James Cameron: 'The downside of being attracted to independent women is that they don't need you'" The Guardian – Hadley Freeman - https://www.theguardian.com/film/2017/aug/24/james-cameron-well-never-be-able-to-reproduce-the-shock-of-terminator-2

[4] " Patty Jenkins hits back at James Cameron: 'He doesn't understand Wonder Woman'" – The Guardian – Gwilym Mumford - https://www.theguardian.com/film/2017/aug/25/patty-jenkins-hits-back-at-james-cameron-criticism-of-wonder-woman

[5] Kelly Lockwood Primus - https://www.linkedin.com/in/kellylockwood/

SVP, Strategic Client Solutions at Leading Women give the keynote presentation! Her session was called Leadership, The Missing 33% and Career Success for Women.

I found a table and asked to join the ladies there. With warm smiles and gestures, I was welcomed to sit at the table. We began introducing ourselves to each other and discussing our roles, companies, expertise and expectations of the presentation. There was witty chatter about the experiences of Summit, talk of how tasty the lunch was, and general uplifting support.

During our conversations, one of the younger ladies at our table was explaining her new position with a great company and how excited she was to start it. She had just recently been promoted to this position and we were all so very impressed and pleased for her. Except for one woman who scoffed incredulously and asked, "How did YOU get THAT job?!" Silence fell upon the table as if someone had slammed a door shut. With a straight face, the young lady said, "I applied for it." A smile sprung to my face and I said "That is so awesome for you! I know you deserve this and I wish you all the happiness in the world!" The other ladies at the table began their comments of congratulations to her as well.

Why? Why did that comment have to arise? Do we as women have our own biases against each other? Yes, ladies, yes we do. And it is time we take stock of how we view each other, our actions, and ourselves. My mother raised me to be courteous, inoffensive, and polite. This often meant taking jeers from others and turning the other cheek or ignoring them. The jeers still hurt, they still scarred my psyche. I just stuffed them down so as to not make a fuss. This was the common practice of the time. I still hear mothers telling their daughters "he hit you because he likes you." NO MA'AM! Stop saying that right here, right now. This is just telling our daughters it is okay to take abuse! Are these mothers telling their sons "it is okay to hit her, just not too hard"? We as women have to stop and THINK about what we say to each other!

At 16 years old, I got a job in a bakery/deli that was housed inside a grocery store. One of the young men who carried out the groceries for customers insisted on spending his break time leering at me. It made me very uncomfortable. He would try to corner me any time I was away from others. I raised my concerns to my manager. She told me that he was harmless and that she didn't want to get him fired, so sometimes we just have to take it and be uncomfortable with the way they look at us. "After all," she said "you are pretty, and you like that he thinks you are pretty, don't you?" She put me in danger. She did not listen. This lack of action resulted in him doing something to me and I was powerless because an alarm had not been raised beforehand. That still stings.

Ladies, we do not have to "be cool" and accept crass jokes at our expense. We do not have to belittle each other over our looks. I look younger than I am; it doesn't mean I am any less qualified or able. I love makeup and hair styles. I enjoy wearing color on my oval nails. This does not mean I am coming for your man, your job, or your seat at the table. Men, this does not mean I am open game for your jeers, insults, or come-ons. And none of this means I am frigid and don't know how to have a good time. What it all means is that we should no longer allow appearances to guide our perception of others' strengths or weakness.

The truth is that we are all human. Men and women alike, we have our biases. We need to take a look at ourselves and work together to move beyond the gender biases, the jealousy, and negative talk. There is room at the table for all of us. We can always pull up a chair for another!

Exploration Leads to Insight

While exploring the stories I wanted to share, I got the opportunity to really dive into myself. Over and over I came up with instances that left me upset, hurt, frustrated, and determined to find answers. Many questions arose.

Why are woman naturally thrown into positions in the workforce where they are expected to:

- clean
- keep things organized
- make sure the male members of the team do their job
- take care of administrative work
- order lunches or provide snacks and drinks
- take notes in meetings
- deal with trouble clients while receiving little to no support when they raise red flags

Why are women often given all of the responsibility with none of the authority to make necessary changes?

As always when dealing with human nature, there are more questions than answers. I am a firm believer in finding answers and sharing those with others who seek counsel, so let's see if we can find some answers.

Let's discuss this question first: What is the measure of a woman? The simple answer is "the same as the measure of a man." The men in the office who got to enjoy eating in the office clearly were measured higher than the women who had to clean up after them. Not only was this very inconvenient, it was wrong to set us apart because of our gender roles. I have been doing a lot of soul searching the last several months. I realized that I don't even know my own strengths. A friend suggested I take a strengths test to see what my natural strengths are. The interesting thing about this test is that it asks questions that are specifically non-gender related. I understand that the results of my test were not the total measure of who I am, but it did give me a really strong insight into how I work through problems best.

Despite the answers to my strengths test, I am still female. So what is it you see when you look at your female coworker? Do you see her strength? Do you see her brilliance? Be honest with yourself here. Do you see her as equal, or do you see her as not as bright or as qualified as you. Recently a friend told me that she was introduced, "This is Shirley. She can't keep a job." But that is not at all true. Shirley has moved up through many positions and job roles the last few years at a fairly quick rate. Note that I said "moved UP" she has not just flitted from job to job. Despite how awesome Shirley is and how she quickly becomes an expert and moves forward, she is seen as "not able to keep a job."

Adversely, I have a male friend, Mike, who has traversed the career ladder at approximately the same speed. I have heard many people marvel at how brilliant he is and how smart he is for moving up so quickly. Not one person has remarked at how he cannot keep a job. These people admire Mike, as they should because he is dedicated and driven. What is the difference between Shirley and Mike? Shirley is brilliant, dedicated, and driven as well. The difference is perception and gender.

Second: Why is a woman's time not as important as a man's? Well, that is just silly! Is it though? Remember the story I told of the person who texted me to stop what I was doing and check on my boss' calendar for a meeting that he was CLEARLY already not going to attend? He could have just reached out to my boss directly. So why interrupt me to make me run to the calendar to check? At the time, and still right now, I feel that my time was not viewed as important, so he chose to interrupt me instead. I know that I am not the only one who has had this kind of experience.

I am guilty.[6] When I need to ask a question, I normally start by apologizing for the interruption. It frustrates me that I do this. I am taking my time to reach out for help or to include another person. Why am I apologizing for using my time to include them? When I was interrupted, no one apologized to me! Why are we less likely to apologize to a woman for interrupting her? Don H Zimmerman and Candace West conducted a study Sex Roles, Interruptions and Silences in Conversation in which they analyzed 31 two-part conversations (10 were between two men, 10 between two women, and 11 between a man and woman). They found that in the two same-sex conversations interruptions happened only 7 times. So of the 20 conversations, there were only 7 interruptions. Analyzing the 11 conversations between a man and woman

---

[6] "Sex Roles, Interruptions and Silences in Conversation" Don H.Zimmerman and Candace West (1975) - http://web.stanford.edu/~eckert/PDF/zimmermanwest1975.pdf

yielded a whopping 48 total interruptions, 46 of which were instigated by the men in the conversation!

Forbes ran an article in 2017, *Gal Interrupted, Why Men Interrupt Women And How To Avert This In The Workplace*[7] in which they discuss how men and women are taught to communicate differently. Their advice "Men, think twice before you interrupt. Are you interrupting to become the speaker and gain power? How will you look to everyone else in the room? Are you interrupting to get clarity? If so, make sure you ask a clear question and allow the speaker to regain the floor. Are you interrupting because you think you will forget what you want to say? Jot key words on your notepad for use later, instead of interrupting."

Whether you are a man or woman who interrupts, make sure you are interrupting for the right reason and in the best way. Remember that everyone's time is just as valuable. Each one of us have a unique view to share. Their time is worth your time. Stop and listen. Pause before you interrupt. And if you are someone who is constantly being interrupted, bring that to the attention of the person interrupting. Personally, I have had to put my hand out and say "Stop interrupting me. You asked me a question, I am giving you the answer." Don't be afraid to stand your ground.

Third: Is this really a 'Man's World'? No, this is a world that is made greater when men and women work together alongside each other for a common goal. In WWII, women not only raised their children and tended to their homes, they entered the workforce in droves. They picked up axes, hammers and riveters. They were pilots who flew military missions. They kept the country running while the majority of the males in the country were fighting abroad. Upon the end of the war the majority of women reported they wanted to keep their jobs. However, they were forced out by men returning home.[8]

Female veterans were not even able to benefit from the veterans' programs for which they had fought. The nation they rose up to fight for was not ready for social equality. Women were expected to just stop working and go back home to have babies. Despite their strength, drive, and dedication to this country, they were rebuked and sent back home. Without these brave women, this country would have suffered greatly, and production of most items needed to fight the war would have not been manufactured.

Today we are a far cry from where we were in the 1940's, but we stand here on the backs of those who fought before us. And we are the backbones who will support those future men and women yet to come. Together, we are stronger.

---

[7] "Gal Interrupted, Why Men Interrupt Women and How to Avert This In The Workplace" Leslie Shore – Forbes (2017) - https://www.forbes.com/sites/womensmedia/2017/01/03/gal-interrupted-why-men-interrupt-women-and-how-to-avert-this-inthe-workplace/#11c86fcd17c3

[8] "History at a Glance: Women in WW2" The National WWII Museum, New Orleans - https://www.nationalww2museum.org/students-teachers/student-resources/research-starters/women-wwii

Fourth: Isn't this like, a 1940's or a 1970's problem? I was born in the 1970's and still remember the marketing of the day. I remember when I first saw the rise of the feminist movement. I still hold in my head the vitriol I heard spew from adult men as they spoke of "Fem-Nazis" and "Bra-burners." I wonder what those men were thinking when they were shouting these things in front of a small girl. I am sure they did not think they were shaping my views of them as well as strengthening my resolve to be seen as equal!

I have a friend who is in her early 20's. The world has been vastly different for her. She reports to me that she has NEVER been treated the way I have. To which I reply "Good!" But just because she has not yet been met with it, does not mean she will go through life unscathed. And when it does happen, I hope she is able to be the backbone she needs to be for those who come after her. We have come a long way, but there is much still to be done. Do you know what it is going to take? It is going to take men and women standing together to break down the old ideals that women are the lesser beings. And break down the ideals that if someone is different, that person is not worthy.

Moving on: How do we broach this topic of being treated like a wife or a mother by our team, boss, or even clients? This is a superbly tricky and uncomfortable topic. We must be brave and we must set our limits, both men and women. Drawing our lines in the sand and setting our personal expectations will allow us to keep our goals in sight. Staying calm in the face of strife will go further in winning the race against bias and inequality.

I have discussed this topic with my husband ad nauseum. He and I set our boundaries a long time ago. We have agreed to never fight a battle in which the other does not wish to engage. So when I am enraged and upset, I start with "I don't need you to do anything, just please listen to me." He knows this is his cue that I need to verbalize all my thoughts, emotions, feelings, worries, fears, and angers so that I can bounce them off him and back at myself. This is the way I process and find my answers. It is extremely different for each one of us. My method may not work for you. You will need to find your own way to make sense of the situation that faces you, draw your lines, and stand your ground. I will say this: if you are looking for other people to fight your battles for you, the chances of you winning that war is slim. Be strong. Enlist others to help, but always be prepared to fight your own battles.

As a man who is an excellent listener, my husband asks "What can I do to help?" Dear reader, no matter your sex, no matter your station in life, no matter your job title, you CAN assist others who are being mistreated. When you see someone being treated unfairly due to bias, speak up. You can support that person in many ways. Take the person away from the situation and express your concern as well as willingness to help if help is desired.

An Honest Proposal

If there were easy solutions, this problem would have already been solved. As women, it seems that we are put in impossible situations more often than our male counterparts and expected to just handle it with grace and strength. I propose the following solution.

Let's sit down together, set aside the biased thoughts and work to break down the gender role standards. Let's discuss ways in which we can provide support for each other, lift each other up, and set boundaries for both men and women. I propose we have a frank and honest discussion about that which is causing strife and division between so many. History shows that when a group of people sit down and actually listen to each other, they can come up with solutions to problems that are too great to tackle alone.

Women, do not be afraid to draw your lines. Unless it is expressly written in your job duties, you are NOT the office Mom. You do not need to make sure the office is cleaned and stocked. You do not need to wash other people's dishes or clean their offices. Your time is important, just as important as your male counterpart. It is not impolite of you to demand to be treated as equal. That is your right.

Speak up. I have learned from my experiences that as long as I keep quiet, nothing will change. There have been many times in my life that I have just stayed quiet and taken the mistreatment. I was afraid to take a stand. Afraid I would look bad, lose my job, afraid people would no longer like me. Often times I look back at myself and wish I had said something, done something to stand up for myself.

Check your emotions at the door. Trying to fight a battle with pure, raw emotion does not gain any ground. Without being rude, without showing any emotion, I told the man holding his dishes out to me "I am not going to wash your dishes." Simple, plain, easy to understand. He knew where I stood, I showed him my line in the sand. I stated my piece and walked away. No need to engage further. I grew that day.

Final Thoughts on Bravery

I will leave you with one final thought. Being honest can be very uncomfortable at times. Allow yourself to grow in the uncomfortable void between here and there. Find your strength – it is there, and it is shining. We can work together to make a better environment for each other. Bravery is being afraid yet pushing forward despite the fear.

Although wives and mothers deserve your respect in so many ways, I am not your wife. I am not your mother. I am your peer. I am your boss. I am your team. Let's work together in unity.

CHAPTER 10

Invisible Leader

By: Tracy Boggiano

"It is never too late to be what you might have been."
-- George Eliot

Early Years

I was six years old when I played Pac Man on an Atari for the very first time. It was genius. I knew right then that I wanted to become a computer programmer. I must admit, there was a brief period somewhere in the middle where my mother convinced me to become a lawyer because they made more money and she wanted me to grow up and buy her a house and take care of her. I also wanted to right some wrongs in the world and become a District Attorney who made sure good people got justice and criminals got what they deserved. Later I would discover that this was driven out of my own desire for justice for the wrongs that were done to me by my own family. So, I decided to go back to my true self, the thing that brought me joy, and I let myself be a computer geek. You always have to be true to yourself.

I got my first computer in seventh grade from my father, and my uncle sent me two books, one on MS DOS 3.2, and one on QBASIC. It took me all of three days to read those books and remember everything in them. That summer, I went to visit my cousin and it just so happened that he was taking his computer to my uncle for repairs. So we decided to write a program to password protect the computer on boot-up. We had it all set-up so that every key punch would randomly select a different color as it displayed an asterisk. My uncle was far smarter than us kids, you see, he was a computer chip designer, so he knew how to hit Ctrl-Break. I remember that moment fondly and how incredibly fun it was, even if we were outsmarted on the double.

Later that year I got a program called MyDatabases, and with it my first big self-appointed programming project. I had a sports card collection that was my pride and joy, so I wrote a program to meticulously catalogue every single card. When I finished I was incredibly happy with it, and it made me want to figure out what else I could do with computers. It was at this time that I started running our school's bulletin board system between the schools, which would transmit weather reports for our 7th grade science class. And of course, I tried to master Oregon Trail. Looking back, I never once as a child questioned whether I would work on computers as an adult, or whether I could because of my gender.

Fast forward through high school, there was only one computer class, Word Processing, which was lame, but at least it had to do with what I was passionate about. I found it lame because this was something I already knew how to do. I had taught myself programming three years earlier and desired to do more. Yet, I would have to wait until college to get any more exposure to computers, as I was in for a very tough childhood. By age sixteen I was living on my own, or anywhere safe I could find to stay. I had a troubled home-life situation, and the treatment I experienced on a daily basis by my immediate family was sadly cruel and abusive in very traumatic ways. There were many factors in my childhood that impacted my being able to attend a four-year college, but I didn't let that stop me. So when I graduated, I went on to attend a community college. I got a two-year degree in Computer Programming in four years, as well as some additional certifications (MSCE 7.0 and MCDBA SQL Server 7) to bridge the gap between what I was being taught in school and what I was actually doing in my first job. The school was in a manufacturing community that ran on mainframes, so they weren't really using Windows in most business applications, and as a result the school didn't teach that. We were learning RPG and Cobol on an AS400 at school. In contrast, at my job we had Windows NT 4.0 installed, and I was beginning to learn Visual Basic. One instructor I had was curious about me getting certified in Windows and I gave him guidance as to what he would have to do to get certified.

Career Start

I got an early start in my career as a computer operator at the age of 18, and with it came my first pager. I landed the job by chance. My then husband was working at a company that needed a part-time computer operator for an AS400. This company would later transition into the Windows world and I would excel in learning everything I could, which led to getting my MCSE. This is where I experienced some uncomfortable work dynamics for the first time. My boss didn't seem too pleased with me now having more preparation and practical knowledge than he had, nor the fact that I was quickly becoming the go-to person in the company. Later I would learn how to be a developer in ASP and Visual Basic, which gave me my first exposure to SQL Server. From there, I would have several more programming jobs, including one as a manager, before becoming a full time database administrator (DBA). That first company and role would prove to be almost like a testing ground for my spirit as a person and professional. During my time there, behavioral dynamics were rough, and in many instances, I wasn't treated professionally or respectfully by colleagues and managers. Maybe it was because I was young, or a woman, or maybe because I kept developing as a professional and working hard, or maybe all of the above. But one thing I know for sure: I learned a lot and have many stories of endurance and perseverance as a female employee in technology. Again, my first DBA job came by chance, I had been laid off from a job and a friend recommended me for this job, after all I was a MCDBA at the time. I aced the interview and was off to the races as a DBA.

Superheroness

I started getting involved in the SQL Community on a whim three years ago by submitting to SQLSaturday. Admittedly, I did this after some prodding from my boss. He believed in my skills and potential, and so he thought I could be a really strong contributor in that space. At the time I did not even know that he was on the speaker selection committee or that they gave preference to the local community. Since then I've spoken at over 30 SQLSaturdays, as well as local user groups, virtual groups, and PASS Summit 2017. In addition, I provide career mentoring to colleagues and fellow technical experts. It's really humbling to think that I'm recognized within the SQL Community, a community of very talented people that I respect. I find that quite hard to believe.

My journey is quite unique, and not without some difficult and painful experiences, but it has also been incredibly strengthening and filled with hope. I experienced unconscionable abuse at the hands of my stepfather and mother as a young child, which resulted in me still suffering from PTSD as an adult. I have also survived a difficult divorce, worked hard to be able to raise a child as a single mother, and became a Database Superhero while battling bi-polar disorder. In large part, those very struggles have enabled and fueled my dedication to my work and helping others, especially children who are in difficult and painful circumstances themselves. Volunteerism is a big part of my life, I actively advocate for foster children through the court system as a Guardian ad Litem. Computer programming allowed me to pursue many career and personal goals, and gave my over-active mind a powerful outlet, something to really concentrate and focus on.

Over the course of my career I would always become known as the person who would jump in and fix nearly any situation, even technical issues unrelated to the database. In one job where I was solely and exclusively focused on the database server, I was able to figure out an issue on the application server. I have recovered corrupt databases while on vacation multiple times and take on extra on-call shifts if someone needed them covered. I basically jump in any time I can be of help.

In my experience, typically, when walking into new employment, it's commonly expected that others will know more than you. Even though I had the credentials and had been actively working on the software for years it did not seem to matter or change the perception of the teams that I joined. I have been in teams that basically handcuff you and would limit what you can do when you start, and there is an unspoken amount of time that needs to pass before you 'earn your stripes' so to speak. This is something that I want the tech community to challenge. After all, the company took the time to interview and hire someone they felt was qualified for the position, yet they aren't willing to make the most out of the new asset. I find it to be wasteful in terms of time and resources. They were not leveraging the vast experience and knowledge that I could contribute starting on day one, and in a way, were undermining it completely. This can also be highly discouraging to any new employee, regardless of gender. In most of cases, I just deliberately jumped in and would teach the team a few new tricks that they didn't know before. It would get their attention in a positive way and would quickly begin to bring those invisible unspoken walls down.

While it is slowly improving, I do believe that in many instances women in technology tend to be put in a position where they must prove themselves to their professional colleagues or male counterparts in order to be heard and professionally respected, sometimes they have to work harder than men for the same level of recognition or for well-deserved promotions. It is my hope that this will change. I believe that skills, knowledge, experience and hard-work should speak for itself in all cases, regardless of your gender. Credit, opportunities, pay and recognition should be given where it is due.

Women in Tech Issues

When I first started my career, I was genuinely not aware of the gaps between women and men in the technology industry. I was maybe too naive at the young age of 18 to notice, but within a few years it became quite obvious that things were somewhat lopsided. This topic is not an easy topic, it can easily be perceived as off-putting, but it is a reality that we need to be able to discuss openly and honestly in order to drive change. Becoming unafraid to discuss the difficult dynamics for women in the workplace opens the door for true change.

At times, although my jobs titles, responsibilities, and skills were advancing, I was not being treated positively or fairly by some managing leaders. As you now know, abuse is something that negatively marked my early life, and so I've had to learn how to establish healthy boundaries for myself in the workplace. There was one job where the manager would call me the "abused DBA" because of some stories I had shared about my experience as a woman in the technology industry. It would take me a while to open up and make my mark at that job, as I had successfully done in every other job, simply because it felt like an unsafe and unhealthy environment considering my personal experiences. Establishing boundaries in the front-end with colleagues and managers instead of figuring it out as you go is something that I believe really helps, and it's definitely something that empowers me to take off and become a leader in my area.

My first tough challenge came when I found myself having to navigate the whole dynamic of organizational politics. Regardless of your gender, everyone experiences that in some way or another. I think that this is a skillset that gets particularly murky for women. It has been proven by studies that when women are being assertive in certain situations it is perceived as aggressive; on the contrary, the same behavior in male counterparts is perceived as them being confident, driven, or career oriented. In one job I was confronted with a tough political dynamic when I found myself stuck in the middle of a cold war between departments. Accounting and IT were at war, and I was caught in the middle. I was lucky that executive management got involved at just the right time and made the call on what should happen. I felt a huge sense of relief, like being let off the hook, and I was finally allowed to just focus on doing my job. Looking back though, I really wish I would have been bold and courageous, and just stood up for myself and done what I believed was right, instead of being afraid to say anything and hiding from the situation. I've learned a lot since then, and I believe that what defines a true leader is not a title but how they are able to successfully drive, influence and encourage people towards a particular goal. It may not have been a technical goal, or part of my job description, but it was a very important objective, conflict resolution. I saw myself as a middle-man, but I actually had the opportunity to be a positive leader in the situation. I would handle things differently now. Developing those types of soft skills is critical for all professionals in any industry, but I must admit, it is certainly easier said than done.

Over the years I have found myself still not keen on maneuvering the necessary politics it takes to get ahead in an organization sometimes. There have been moments where I have not put myself "out there" enough in front of higher-ups, and I stay too focused within my department. Although I am well-respect by my peers, sister departments, and immediate management, limited visibility inevitably affects career progression, and I have experienced the negative effects of this. I've had jobs where I've made a suggestion to a male counterpart or worked on an idea with them and then seen them get the credit for the work. I've helped former male colleagues with issues at work shortly after leaving the position and heard the story retold by another former colleague where I wasn't mentioned as being of help. I have experienced being overlooked for promotions and other opportunities for being an invisible leader in the eyes of upper management. It's interesting because being an invisible leader, in many ways, seems to be ultimately about outside perception and awareness. This is a tough space to navigate politically. It can feel very personal and biased when you feel like merit, experience, and knowledge are not properly being considered or assessed. I found myself 'invisible' although I was technically successful, making strong contributions and my peers looked up to me. While I was well respected by the developers and my team, one of the male colleagues I had trained was promoted to a senior position before me.

Another time, I was a top contender for a manager position that opened up, but I wasn't given the opportunity to interview, and a male colleague was automatically promoted to the position, even though I had expressed strong interest and had more experience. They didn't meet with me to discuss the position until after the decision had been made. The position was also never internally posted. I was told that I was overlooked because I was too valuable in my current position to promote, and that upper management didn't believe that I was well-known enough within the company. They use certain examples, like me not participating in certain meetings (which I wasn't invited to) and me not being the face of the department (even though I technically was). My male colleague had become very well known for certain strategic projects that he worked on that were used by all of management and the developers. This was how he made a name for himself and got invited to the meetings that I wasn't invited too. They didn't allow for other candidates that could successfully execute many other aspects of the manager job such as mentoring, negotiation, experience. or strong technical skillsets to have the opportunity to compete for the position. It boiled down to his visibility on certain projects in comparison to my projects. While I had worked on the back-end projects, he had the projects that internally showcased him in front of the business, making the business believe he was the obvious choice for the position. When I was spoken to about the position it was more out of concern that I would leave because I wasn't give the opportunity. It was apparent to me at the time that I didn't have a future at this company, so I moved on to a company where I was instantly promoted and well-respected for the skillset I have and the overarching value

I brought to the table. There was another instance in my career where a male colleague was promoted over me, and if they had not been promoted the company was going to look for an external candidate for the position, despite other people in the company wondering why I wasn't considered for the position. Those are key moments where the cracks in the gender dynamic are shown, when upper management fails to take the time to understand and acknowledge the full work a team puts into a project, or your value to the team as whole, as a leader.

At the time it was tough for me, but it revealed something important about managing my career, which helped me grow and enabled me to get to where I am now. This is a situation that many people in technology experience. Sometimes when you are truly passionate about your work, you do anything and everything to ensure a successful and reliable result or operation, perhaps at the cost of participating on some other projects that can offer a different type of exposure and visibility. Being aware of this is important in order to effectively drive your career path. Sometimes you need to make some deliberate decisions regarding work priorities and project opportunities depending on your short, medium, or long-term goals.

There are several unfortunate examples of other moments where I've felt that as a female my contributions are undervalued or undermined, invisible if you will.

This brings up the question: how do you go about getting noticed in a positive light without being seen as being too aggressive or too passive? I think that one powerful way is to have a strongly positioned mentor, boss, or sponsor within the workplace that supports you and promotes your work to executive management. Don't be afraid to reach out and network with good leaders in higher positions. This opens opportunities to build visible professional relationships. Also, don't be afraid to discuss difficult issues with your superior. Make him or her aware of the issues, and if they do not support you, you know it might be time to find a place that will. If you are dedicated, talented and hard-working, the odds are that you have options. Another important thing is to be proactive when you share ideas. If you get the support of your peers in a meeting when you share a good idea, make sure to not fall into the 'just go with the flow' trap and allow others take ownership of your ideas. Get involved! Different ways to get involved include:

- Mentor someone in your workplace.
- Set up a wiki in your workplace to share knowledge and processes.
- Start by presenting at your local user group. If that feels uncomfortable do a lunch and learn at your workplace first. Check out speakingmentors.com and pick out a mentor to help you get started.
- Blog about what you learn. Everyone learns differently, so just because someone else has written about a topic doesn't mean you can't.

- Go to forums and answer questions, you might learn something trying to help someone.
- Join the sqlcommunity.slack.com and go to the sqlhelp channel or go on Twitter and follow #sqlhelp.

Don't wait for others to kick-start your idea for you or come to you to ask you to lead it, just do it! Third, and probably most important, you have to stand up for yourself in a professional and respectable manner.

Gender bias can show itself in many forms. Although it can be predominantly found as a male-vs-female workplace dynamic, women can sometimes be negatively biased towards other women. The same goes for men towards other men. We have to be willing to identify and resolve these types of dynamics at the onset, so we can ensure that we are establishing a professional and healthy work environment, where we treat each other with respect and fairness. We are peers and we are people.

One thing I've always been good at in my career, before I even started public speaking, was mentoring. I technically started mentoring in high school. I used to sleep through pre-calculus and calculus and then, when the teacher was done (sorry, Mrs. Lawson), wake up and help any student that needed help. I've always loved helping people because I like to see when the light bulb goes off and they get it. Seeing people go through challenges when they can be made simpler if someone would just show them the way is what I think a mentor is there for. Why do they have to struggle through a situation if I can help them through the situation? That's why I volunteer with foster kids. I've been through the abuse and neglect they have also experienced or are experiencing, and I can be there to help them through it. I want to show them that someone genuinely cares. I do the same in IT: I care if someone's career progresses, regardless of their gender. When someone finally understands a concept and says "Aha!", it gives me a warm feeling. I have had the opportunity to train a people in the different roles I've had, and I have always considered my knowledge something to share not to hoard. The truth is that not everyone plays by the same rules. I've seen and experienced this over the years, and I believe that this is an invisible skill I have. Regardless of whether it's part of my role's responsibilities or not, it's something that I am personally proactive about and always seem to naturally take the lead on. I've trained people from the most junior levels to senior level experts, in an array of technical topics. One of my trainees went from a junior position at my company, right into a senior level job at another company. I have found this to be a passion of mine, so now I mentor people in the community, in any aspect of their career. I volunteer through http://speakingmentors.com, and it's always great to get more speakers into our community. One mentee turned into more than just a speaking mentee, but a career mentee as well. This soft skillset can often go unnoticed, because it's something that is often done in the background of it all, and there is little visibility, a.k.a. management in your company doesn't know you are doing it. I want to encourage and say to all people, particularly my female peers, that we need to be more vocal to our management about how we spend external career-related time, so they are aware of these relevant and valuable activities and contributions. This could lead to new opportunities and at times to getting much deserved credit. You don't have to boast or yell about your invisible leadership from the rooftops. One way of doing this without seeming entitled or blatant is to just invite people to join you and participate as a collective. Maybe you could arrange a Lunch and Learn for the team about the topics that you can teach or lead, or you could set up a training or a technical deep-dive, or simply present on a subject that is an opportunity for growth and collaboration for your colleagues. You can invite your team, other teams, as well as management to the event, giving you a visible platform. These are just some ways that can positively allow you to let others see some of your strong invisible competencies.

Another interesting trend that I've noticed throughout my career is that I tend to naturally become the go-to person for certain subjects. I think that teaching other teams as much as possible has also helped me better understand things in my own job role. I remember one situation where the developers actively avoided one of my coworkers because they considered the person grumpy and unhelpful. It went as far as having to divide the workload up among teams, and I was told not to help any of the teams unless my coworker was out of the office. I'll admit I'm a little too nice and passionate about my work for that, so I would just help anyone that called or emailed me asking for support. I also remember one company where I provided support to a different location than the one assigned to me and was reprimanded for phone time to that location because it was more than my coworkers. Evidently you were only supposed to communicate via email with the people (shrugs shoulders). You see, despite being the go-to person among developers and end-users, it was a struggle for me to be seen and acknowledged, mostly because I was leading from the background. I was problem-solving, supporting, mentoring, training, and executing, all from behind the curtain. I felt great joy and satisfaction from my dedication and quality work, but to be honest, at the same time I also desired to be recognized. I think this is true for a lot of professionals out there, especially female professionals. Being an invisible leader, although incredibly impactful and truly rewarding in many ways, can also be challenging and discouraging at times. Those are the pivotal moments where you can use those feelings as motivation to take charge of your career. You could reach out for new opportunities within your role, develop yourself through learning opportunities, or explore new horizons. There was a moment in my career where I knew it was in my best interest to seek out new job opportunities, and it took some courage, but it was one of the best decisions I've made.

Although it is improving, in IT, sometimes women aren't welcome or treated very well by all-male teams. I recall a System Operations team leader that, to put it plainly, didn't like me and made it known. I was certified in his area and was very experienced in that particular line of work. I was always respectful of him and his leadership, but judging by his behavior it seemed like he had a chip-on-his-shoulder attitude because he was intimidated by me. This happens very frequently to female professionals in technology. Sometimes women who are great at their job, talented, experienced, competent, well-liked, you name it, can be perceived as threatening to their peers, especially male counterparts or superiors. Our main focus at the workplace is always our work. We could maybe identify opportunities where we can provide them with excellent technical support or collaboration, and let our good work earn their trust. Sometimes earning someone's trust is all it takes; other times, unfortunately, it's more complicated. This can escalate if there is a competitive edge, like a potential promotion or special project up for grabs. Women have to demonstrate a high degree of emotional intelligence in order to manage or neutralize those behaviors in the workplace. Throughout my tenure at that job, he would consistently question what I said and would ignore my requests for pretty much everything. As new people came into his department, he would also talk about my accomplishments in a backhanded way, like for example, if I had successfully fixed an issue he would turn it around and say how I must have broken it to begin with in order to know how to fix it. He did this in order to create rapport with them and set them on the path to be on the same page with him in regard to me. I eventually just had to go through one of my other male coworkers and request things from him when necessary. This was a very challenging situation, and when management became aware of this situation they did not do anything about it. I had to be strong and do my job to the best of my abilities and be resourceful. Creating trustworthy professional relationships with other people within the department was a great way to help overcome some of these obstacles in the short-term. As females, we sometimes have to work harder to make friends with our coworkers. It is also difficult to walk that line because you want to be respected for your work and don't want to give the wrong impression if you ask them to lunch to build rapport and get to know them better on a personal level to break the ice. It is something to be very mindful and wise about. Maybe I could have organized a group lunch and taken that as an opportunity to talk to that person about topics unrelated to work and see if that opened positive dialogue. The truth is that sometimes the behavior is deeply rooted, and it is not up to us to psychoanalyze the situation or try to find answers that explain it.

One common scenario for many women is being questioned about their decisions with more frequency and bluntness than their male colleagues. I have experienced this throughout my whole career. It was particularly noticeable in a company where we had a daily stand-up to go over our change requests. The manager that ran the meeting would look to the boss for confirmation for each one of my tickets. I casually pointed out this behavior to our boss one time and, at first, he didn't believe that happened. He then started to pay attention and noticed that it happened to both of his female employees and not to any of his male employees. He immediately started saying back to the manager "Yes, that is what she said". It was greatly encouraging to have a leader that would promote professional respect within the team, and that made a huge difference to me personally although, even after a year of our boss doing this, the behavior still continued. I do not think the manager in question here was ever even truly aware of what they were doing and how it came across to us as teammates. I didn't speak to him about it because I didn't know what to say at the time and didn't want to not be well-liked or come across as "the offended girl" in the room. Looking back, I wish that I would have said something to him directly in a professional way that did not come across as cross.

A similar situation happened at a previous company. Management would go to the change request meetings and it seemed that every request I sent in was questioned and rejected, to the point where I would have to go to work on weekends that I wasn't on call by the time they were approved. There was a process in place for management to ask their questions ahead of the meeting and my manager did not know SQL Server, so he could not answer any of their questions during the meetings. Neither the management nor my boss would come to me for answers to any questions they had. As a woman, it is my hope that these types of situations become less and less prevalent, and certainly more openly discussed within the workplace and adequately addressed by management.

Promotions have been an area of particular difficulty throughout my career, not only as a young female professional in tech, but as a seasoned female tech expert. It seemed that the more I advanced in my skills, experience, and range of knowledge, the less likely I was to be promoted. It's kind of funny to think about, but it seems like when I knew the least I got promoted more. It was a difficult thing to cope with since it feels like it is completely out of your hands. It was particularly frustrating when I would be promised certain promotions and career progression opportunities upon being hired, to then find that they were flat promises. I also struggled with the fact that I was always being assigned to the high-criticality projects at the company, like upgrades to new versions of SQL Server and setting HA/DR technologies because although it seemed like I was always assigned the most important projects, and executed them successfully, I was consistently overlooked. This happened a few times, and it was hard every single time. However, it led me to understanding that I have to know my value. This was a life-changing lesson for me. Once I understood that I had great professional value in the job market it gave me great confidence to pursue new opportunities and ventures and to reach higher than I ever had before, which I'll touch on later.

I had a decent pager rotation as superhero and so I would gladly take on shifts and be called-in to support situations. I took on the extra shifts mainly because I liked helping others out, it was never out of personal gain. Most of my colleagues had kids and wanted or needed to be at events for them. In my case, my son was an adult so it allowed me to enable them to be present for their kids' big moments. In one job, the situation took a turn. One coworker would intentionally make herself unavailable while developers where doing deploys on Saturday mornings, and I would be out visiting foster kids. The coworker would just simply not answer the pager. They were unavailable so frequently that the computer operator's default policy of calling the manager changed to just calling Tracy because I was the reliable person that could always be reached.

Some may have felt I was being taken advantage of, but in many ways, I encouraged the situation by not taking a stand and by constantly filling the need. Feeling needed for me probably dates back to my childhood experiences, as I needed and wanted to feel loved by parents, and when they asked me to do things that only adults should be doing I would fill in, but for most people, being needed and acknowledged is a fundamental feeling. It makes us feel wanted and sometimes gives us a sense of purpose in the world. I feel like this is something that many women in the workplace experience. Being the person that everyone can count on, and always feeling a sense of responsibility that drives them to always be there and respond, at the cost of their own personal time, lives, wellbeing, and at times health. I have to admit, in many ways I allowed the behavior to continue by not setting clear boundaries. One can be reliable and excellent at their work while enforcing sensible healthy professional boundaries, but this is something that I struggle with to this day. Moreover, as integral as I was considered to the operation, promotions seemed to elude me, and upper management was unaware of the high demand and super delivery. In my last years working for the company I just started to think of the pager as my hero call. When anybody needs help that is what superheroes and friends do for each other. On a side note, I love the hashtag #oncallselfie on Twitter.

Now, while my work and skillset went typically unnoticed and overlooked by upper management in many jobs, there was one job I had where I worked with a team of consultants that were brought in for a project, and they noticed. I worked on a very high-profile project with them involving getting SQL Server to perform with the specific software they were using for the project. I fixed one issue with TempDB for them with trace flags and instantly I was the go-to person for this project, to the point where, when it went to production, I was on-call 24 x 7 although we had two other DBAs. As I was leaving, one consultant took me out to lunch and told me that they had placed bets on how long I was going to stick around in that company because they felt that my skillset was not being fully utilized. Many professionals fall into the same situation, excellent skillset, underutilized but overworked. The demand is high when you are good, and it feels great. I know I thrive in it, but we also have to be aware and deliberate, and make sure we know when it is time to move on from certain situations.

As I have gained some community recognition, i.e. PASS Outstanding Volunteer Award, I've had people chasing me down at PASS to say thanks for a session I did last year, SQL celebrities following me on Twitter, and oddly, being turned into a duck by being made an Idera Superstar. This is all amazing! It's kind of surreal and a really a great sense of achievement, and I couldn't be more grateful to God for all the opportunities. It's really made me wonder: how come the company that I worked for before, and most other jobs I've held, didn't really see or notice my contributions, especially considering how hard I worked every time and all the complex DBA infrastructure projects I delivered successfully? After all my collective experiences, both the good and challenging, I was left wondering what could I do to be more visible? The big common theme across it all seemed to come down to my unknown superpower of invisibility. Was I a pushover, a doormat, a workaholic, too responsible, too passionate, too available, too quiet, too good? It made me wonder, was I truly invisible or were their eyes just closed? I was told I was not visible enough, but I disagree. I worked with dedication, passion, and a heck of a lot of blood, sweat and tears. On call for 20 years, what seems to be like 24/7, and I truly loved my job, every day, every moment, even when it sucked (lol!). So, I've realized that executives, managers, supervisors and leaders need to have their eyes open. Talent is easy to spot if you look intentionally, if you are open-minded, if you want to find it, and if you don't have personal interests that get in the way. Talent can be found in many unconventional forms, styles and places, and it takes a true leader to spot an invisible leader. The one that eludes the masses but is visible in plain sight. The diamond in the rough at times. It comes down to it takes one, to know one. Who carries the load, who shows up, who goes the extra mile, who displays great passion, who lifts those around them up? The answer might shock you and could change everything. Now, I myself am always on the lookout for invisible leaders.

Making Yourself Visible

I think that invisible leaders can definitely shine as visible leaders in their own right. Now I own my own company Database Superheroes LLC., work for a great company and have had many great opportunities come my way because of all my invisible work. For example, writing this book chapter which has always been a dream of mine, and potentially writing a whole book in the near future! Good things come to those who wait and put in the work and dedication. I have personally spent a lot of time in jobs that weren't that great but that continued to develop my skills to make it easy for me to transition to the next opportunity. Always work your hardest, even if the job isn't the dream job you want, because you could be preparing yourself to make the leap to your dream job. I think ultimately, to some degree, we all want people to see us and the things we accomplish, so I have a few things I can highlight for those of us who want to make ourselves visible.

First, if you have the option, be selective of the projects you take on and try to push back if all you get are projects that are exclusive to your area. A lot of times if a project doesn't impact other parts of the business, or the company as a whole, it typically doesn't get visibility with the people that have the power to progress your career. For example, upgrading SQL Server to various versions was a big project, I was the go-to person for that critical task, and it was a big accomplishment, yet it seemed to not garnish much attention from upper management other than the occasional comment thanking me for working late into the night to do it. Also, if there is project that has been chartered by upper management, be bold and ask to be involved in the project and involved in those meetings. That will make strong contributions likely to get noticed.

Next, make sure you promote yourself in your role and take opportunities to share some of your accomplishments with management, even if it's only your immediate supervisor. There is a difference between boasting and showing enthusiasm, between being arrogant and prideful and being confident and bold. I think that in wise measure promoting yourself is a must to have your work be visible. Additionally, most supervisors must submit periodic reports to management, so that information will trickle up. I'd suggest you keep a personal list of your key accomplishments. If you are like me, remembering what you did from day to day is tough, so I keep an Evernote notebook. I have a note for each week, and a list by day with the tasks I completed or worked on that day. It also has the added bonus of being incredibly useful when updating your resume if someone randomly asked you to send them an updated copy for an opportunity, it makes updating it a quick exercise. Sometimes I store code, I write who I interacted with, and even take meeting notes in there. Note that this is also handy for when your work reviews come around or when you are looking to get promoted. During my review, or if given the opportunity to make a case for a promotion, I would be able to bring this up and really showcase and frame my contributions effectively.

Go above and beyond, and professionally shout it from the right rooftops! We work in IT, and I know most of us go above and beyond anyway, case in point if you are reading this book. But the next time you are on medical leave on top of a mountain in West Virginia and the rest of the team has been up for 30+ hours doing maintenance and you get the call to help, don't let them say this was just a SQL bug when you just spent all night recovering a corrupt database from a system table corruption after making good friends with Microsoft support, all with the slowest Wi-Fi on the eastern coast. Make sure that you take action. For example, write a quick incident report framing the issue, the mitigations taken, and lessons learned, and then send it out to everyone in the team and your immediate manager. Also, ask your boss if it would be ok to copy a few people in management and who he would suggest. If you fix an issue that is not your responsibility, don't let that now grow into becoming your responsibility and inadvertently take on the accountability that comes with it. You could very well be taking ownership over it permanently, so make sure that you establish clear and healthy professional boundaries. You can always provide support, but you don't want to end up carrying a heavy burden that is not yours to begin with. This takes away focus from your primary responsibilities and the opportunity to take on new projects. If lines get blurred, from a technical or organization standpoint, you should discuss the situation with management and clarify. The right way to do this is to focus on the facts and the facts alone, no emotions or opinions, no he said-she said, just facts, what exactly happened or is happening, and what you did or are doing to resolve the issue, and then in any case clarify how it is to be handled moving forward. Take the opportunity to correct any miscommunications and tell the technical story (including on your blog if it could benefit others in the community and/or if allowed by company policy).

Lastly, get involved in projects with other departments. To get noticed it is important to participate in cross-functional assignments, where you get exposed to new teams and skillsets. The more aware company managers and coworkers are of your powerful contributions, and the more they trust your execution, the more likely they are to put your name in the running when a promotion or development opportunity come around. Forming and investing in these relationships is important for you and for them, so don't feel shy to ask to work on new out-of-the-box projects within your company, even those that may seem radically outside your spectrum. You'd be surprised at what doors those opportunities will open, so seize those visible opportunities!

CHAPTER 11
Coming to America

By: Brian Carrig

"'So then you're free?'
'Yes, I'm free,' said Karl, and nothing seemed more worthless than his freedom."
*— **Franz Kafka**, **Amerika***

In this chapter I am going to focus on my experience as a foreign immigrant working in the high-tech sector having to navigate the intricacies of the US visa system. Immigration is almost always a controversial topic, particularly so in the current climate, and no country can claim to have a perfect system nor any individual the ideal solution. Countries require borders (even if this is simply a conceptual line on a map) and at least some rules about how to traverse them no matter how wildly people may disagree about what the rules should be or how they should be enforced. What I will be discussing here is simply my own subjective experience and stories I have picked up along the way. I consider myself quite fortunate to be able to live in America, working in an industry which keeps me challenged and sufficiently remunerated. I will outline some suggestions for areas where I feel the visa system may be improved with a particular focus on areas where I believe change would benefit the US economy.

First, perhaps a little background is in order. This is not a tale of woe of an immigrant fleeing some tin pot despot in some far-flung backwater. I am Irish, and Ireland in the eighties was nobody's idea of a paradise (we were frequently referred to at the time as "the sick man of Europe"). At the same time, I grew up in a loving family and enjoyed a fairly comfortable upbringing by the standards of the time. Nobody went hungry, we had the occasional family vacation, my father was employed by a bank and we had a car. Growing up I always had a fascination with America. From Jim Morrison to Jack Kerouac, I loved American art and culture. Even while in college, the spectacle that is American politics held more interest to me than that of Ireland itself with its overtones of what the fabulous Irish author Declan Lynch likes to refer to as "the spectacular eejitry of Irish nationalism". I had no time for that nonsense.

I was introduced to computers by my uncle Sean who worked for the state telecommunications company (called Eircom at the time, which simply means Irish Telecommunications). He was the first person I knew to ever purchase a computer and it opened up a whole new world for me. The computer was a Commodore 64. In my teenage years eventually, I pestered and cajoled my parents enough to get them to purchase me an Amiga. Even if I and my friends mainly used it to play Sensible Soccer, I always recall feeling superior to console game owners. I started to learn Basic and ran the school computing club. Word processing and typing were the only subjects thought in school, but somebody still needed to defragment the hard drives and allow the computers to talk to one another over a now obsolete token ring network. This was my introduction to the wonders of the Internet which was a very innocent place at the time. I still maintain a sense of awe and wonder at the ability to find people willing to discuss the works of Philip K. Dick in depth from halfway across the globe. Now I guess it seems commonplace. The local technical college (something akin to a community college in the US) allowed local high school equivalent level students with an interest in computers to use the modem banks belonging to the college to connect to the Internet for the price of a local call at evenings and weekends. Given that Internet rates were charged at a premium, this time this was a huge boon and I took full advantage. My parents were constantly complaining about how I was tying up the phone line. I was hooked.

In college I studied computer networking. My first choice was actually journalism, but ironically, a computer error meant I missed out when I should have received an offer. In Ireland, your final year high school equivalent exams are scored and based on the number of applicants for any particular course, the number of points needed to get into a particular course are set, subject to certain minimum qualifications. At the time what attracted me to computer networking was the idea that you needed to "learn a little bit of everything" and troubleshoot across a variety of different technological facets. Later I discovered that in reality, this was rarely the case. This might be changing with the advent of Software Defined Networking (SDN), and no doubt there are many challenging and interesting networking related jobs out there, just none that I could find. Graduating with a first class (the US equivalent of 4.0 GPA) bachelor's degree in 2003, during the fallow of the dot com collapse, employment was scarce.

I took a job in a call center, and I had a surprising amount of fun despite it being such a terrible job. I survived by making some excellent friends and trying to "accidentally" reenact scenes from Glengarry Glenross when cold calling potential leads. After a while I grew bored, and a lecturer (in Ireland the use of the word "Professor" is an actual designated title rather than a job description) from the college contacted me to see if I was interested in returning to pursue a master's degree by way of research. I successfully applied for and received funding from the Irish Research Council, this research eventually evolved into the pursuit of a Ph.D. People frequently ask me what I got my Ph.D. "in". Technically, in the EU at least, there are only three types of doctorate degree – a medical doctorate, a very rarely pursued doctorate in engineering (which must be obtained outside of academia) and a doctorate in philosophy (which is what I have). At one time, science was considered to be a branch of philosophy known as "natural philosophy" hence the designation. I find the idea appealing, if somewhat difficult, to explain. I spent my time considering ways to reduce network latency to improve the experience for people who enjoyed playing first person shooter games as opposed to studying the works of Descartes and Kant, fun and all as that might have been.

When I decided to switch to pursuing a Ph.D., I asked a colleague who was close to completion what the process was like. His description was thus "you become the world's foremost expert in some narrow slice of knowledge, but by the time you are finished you never want to think about it again". That is exactly how it was for me.

Academia can be a strange world. Despite or perhaps because of the vast amounts of money sloshing around, politics and absurdist bureaucracy abound. Requisitioning funds for an apple can involve as much paper work as a million-dollar piece of obscure scientific equipment. I rapidly discovered I was having more fun tuning systems to help my colleague's simulations run faster than I was designing my own. I was determined to finish my Ph.D. but had simultaneously decided that once I was finished, I was going to get out of the academic game. Though often derided as if it were close to a hobby rather than a serious job, a career in academia is a very tough and often very lonely pursuit. They use the phrase "publish or perish" for a reason. One of my closest friends who is a full time academic already feels completely burnt out in his early thirties. As a side note, it is worth mentioning that many people have the misconception that it is the business of universities to teach students. This is no truer a statement than saying it is the business of KPMG to teach interns how to become accountants. The business of universities is obtaining funding from research grants.

Another question I find myself frequently asked is to compare American culture to Irish culture, or to wonder if I found anything difficult in terms of adjusting to moving to America from Ireland. I will avoid the rather obvious if not exactly untrue references to attitudes to alcohol (surprisingly Ireland ranks 21st in the world in pure alcohol consumption annually, well ahead of the United States in 48th but behind the sophisticated daily sippers in France, Portugal and um … South Korea). A more interesting difference for me, is the attitude to higher education and the genuine appreciation of it. Some of my colleagues in the Performance Engineering Laboratory (PEL) where I performed a considerable amount of my research actually considered removing their Ph.D. qualification from their resume and saying they spent the years travelling as such was the hostility to the idea of having an advanced degree. There was a Polish colleague who was famed in the lab for his ability to work excruciatingly long hours when approaching a deadline for a conference paper submission. He was told by a British Telecom engineer (at the time certainly not an institution fabled for its work ethic) that he would not be considered for the position because of his Ph.D. "We can't have people who turn up at 11AM, grab a coffee and then head out to lunch" was the prevailing attitude.

As a kind of "half-way house" between academia and private industry, I took a position in the Dublin City Council Roads and Traffic Department, working with the IT systems needed to manage traffic in a modern city that is over one thousand years old. It was a very interesting and very fascinating job. I became a jack of all trades from an IT perspective, exactly the position I wanted to be in. There were no in-house developers and every new project with a budget exceeding approximately $60k had to be contracted out to comply with EU procurement rules. This meant I was managing a hodge-podge of systems, but given that usually the cheapest tender wins since that is the path of least resistance, this meant mostly open source technologies, primarily some kind of LAMP stack. The management at the time had very little understanding of different specialties within IT, so when we were tasked with managing a new real-time bus timing system, they had very little concept of why it might present challenges that the contractor who won the bid had proposed an entirely Windows based system. For me however, my life was about to change.

Our lead developer – I will call him Trevor since that is his actual name and he lives in Melbourne, Australia so he is unlikely to care, and I have only positive things to say about him – needed a SQL Server backend. At the time, I had worked with MySQL and Oracle but not SQL Server. Also, this was going to be an actual OLTP system where people were depending on the information being accurate and timely, something I never had to deal with before. I knew nothing about SQL Server, and the Department proposed bringing in a consultant at what looked to me like exuberant rates to manage the system for me. Naturally, I declined the proposal with my most stringent objections and stated I was sure I could take care of it. I should of course pretend that I took to database administration with SQL Server like a duck to water, but since an important part of this book and indeed this series of books, is about being truthful, I will admit that it was a complete disaster. Log files grew, and I did not know why. I may or may not have corrupted a database unintentionally when testing the "hot-remove" capabilities of an HP SAN in production. Suffice to say, I did not initially cover myself in glory.

Luckily, I had a reasonable lead in time because of project delays, and I started to discover that there was a community of people willing to dedicate their own free time to help people who were trying to learn about SQL Server. Bob Duffy and his wife Carmel need a stand-out mention in this regard, as well as Neil Ferguson (who at the time ran the Dublin SQL User Group). Having spent so much time in academia (where people argued over who was a real academic), followed by a stint in local government (where people argued over who was a real engineer), it was so refreshing to join a community where some of the most fantastically intelligent people you could hope to meet, were so unpretentious and welcoming. These people exist in academia too, trust me, but I believe the system is unfortunately constructed in such a way that it is harder for them to succeed. Thankfully I had already met the woman that was to someday to become my wife because for the second time in my life, I had fallen in love.

Once I decided to dedicate myself to becoming a full-time DBA, I contacted one of the larger recruitment agencies in Dublin, met with a recruiter who specialized in RDBMS recruitment, and gave her an honest appraisal of my skill set (still very junior but holding entry level certificates and second level DBA certificates at the time). I was surprised by the number of job interviews available. In one I was asked to map out a database mirroring solution in AWS in excruciating detail. I later learned this was basically a free consultancy session! For some reason, I had an idea that working in the European Union civil service would be a good idea. I travelled to Cologne, Germany for a job with the European Aviation Safety Authority (EASA), the European equivalent of the FAA. Funnily, there I also spent some time describing how asynchronous mirroring could be used for Disaster Recovery. I was offered a position but ultimately declined as I had interviewed for a remote position with ChannelAdvisor and decided that I wanted the role. The EASA offer had some fun perks: low taxes (handy when living in Germany) and free private school education for my children. But the actual salary on offer was on the low side. ChannelAdvisor were taking a chance on me since they also had a DBA with ten years of experience who wanted the available position (whom the manager of their Irish office would have preferred), but the manager of the DBA team at the time felt I would be a better cultural fit. Much as I frequently came into conflict with the manager of the DBA team at ChannelAdvisor at the time, I will forever owe him a debt of gratitude for his willingness to take that chance. Even if I was not quite willing to admit it to myself, the fact that ChannelAdvisor was a US multinational played a major factor in my decision to choose a role there rather than some of the other positions on offer to me at the time.

The ChannelAdvisor office in Ireland is located in Limerick, and I lived in Dublin, a three-and-a-half-hour drive from Dublin not even accounting for traffic. My wife and I lived in the city center - right within the original walls of Dublin dating back to 800 AD. In the space of a month, we had our first child whom we named Luisne (an Irish word that can be loosely transcribed as "the first blush of light before dawn"), moved out of our one bedroom apartment into a house, and I changed jobs. I swore never again (this was in 2012, little did I know what awaited me in 2013). ChannelAdvisor agreed that I could work remotely and this arrangement, combined with frequent trips to the ChannelAdvisor HQ in Morrisville, North Carolina initially worked well. Over time I found myself less and less satisfied with the position. Although I loved how central our location was in Dublin, we were living in a 700 sq. ft. house with three bedrooms and two bathrooms. There was no driveway and parking was only available on a public street. It almost felt risky to move your car. My wife was pregnant with our second daughter. I had some major decisions to make.

I was covertly looking around for a new job because I felt that working from home was starting to affect my mental health. The feeling of never leaving the office combined with the difference in time zones meant I often felt like I was (and all too often regularly was) working fifteen to sixteen-hour days. I was so anxious that I would wake up in the middle of the night to check my phone and started drinking heavily to compensate. During this period ChannelAdvisor was struggling with attrition on the DBA team on the US side. My manager had a very abrasive personality that a lot of people struggled with. He was an intelligent, if immature individual, but he had some major gaps in his SQL knowledge (he liked to enable auto-shrink, for example). We interviewed a woman who had worked at IBM and decided to make her an offer. It was only at the point of offer that she disclosed that ChannelAdvisor would need to sponsor her for a visa.

Note to immigrants: this is a terrible idea and really sets a bad tone for your future employer. ChannelAdvisor was so desperate that they were wondering if they should pursue this option despite the underhanded nature of how it was presented. I contacted my manager to say that I would be more than willing to move to the US office if a visa could be obtained. My manager was on-board with the idea (at this point I was visiting regularly and being asked to stay as long as three weeks). My wife was pregnant with our second daughter and planning to take a sabbatical from work anyway. If ever we were going to emigrate to the US, this seemed like the ideal time to do it.

A quick note on skilled visas, to get people up to speed: most foreign workers in the IT industry work legally in the US under what is known as a H1B visa. This is a visa designed to accommodate companies hiring immigrant workers with specialist knowledge. Given the furor over immigration, it might surprise many Americans to learn that the limit on H1B visas annually right now is 85,000 (20,000 of whom must hold a master's degree or higher). This limit is typically hit within a week of H1B visas becoming open for application. They are always massively over-subscribed. Although this is not the visa I began working under in America (more on this later in the chapter), there is a personal touch to this over-subscription as a woman on the team of engineers I currently manage has been trying unsuccessfully for two years now to obtain a H1B visa. She is a genuine rock star, supremely talented, and if she fails in her next attempt our best option will be to transfer her back to China for twelve months and then apply for a transfer visa (known as an L1) in a similar manner to how I immigrated to the US, since this particular visa comes with no quota restrictions. My current company, Citrix, would never dream of letting someone of such great talent go if she did not want to, but it always feels hard to make a life for yourself when the threat of having to leave is ever present (even if it is not strictly deportation).

I emigrated to America under what is known as an L1B visa. L1 visas, both L1A and L1B, are intra-company transfer visas designed to facilitate workers transferring from a US foreign subsidiary company to its US parent company. L1A is for executive and management level, L1B is for professionals with specific skills like technical workers. I transferred on an L1B (but later converted to an L1A upon assuming a management role at ChannelAdvisor). Interestingly, or perhaps unsurprisingly, despite performing in a team lead / management capacity for a considerable period of time, I was only officially promoted on my then manager's final day. As soon as I could see my employees' salaries the reason for this became clear (it did not even occur to me to check for a period of several weeks). It turned out I was one of the lowest paid members of the team. I felt this was unfair, primarily because I had accepted a considerable amount of extra duties and worked very hard to keep the team together and had been given very specific assurances that I was the highest paid member of the team. I was flat out lied to. Chalk it down to naivety on my part. I do not recall being particularly upset and was happy that my new manager was willing to work hard to correct the imbalance. I do recall being perturbed upon hearing that my low salary was flagged as a "risk factor" in promoting me to a managerial role. I do not doubt that many a similar conversation happen concerning underpaid women in the workforce as well. I am four years now working in some technical managerial capacity. The day I believe I should deny someone of sufficient ability the chance of promotion so I can continue underpaying them, should be marked as the day I have lost my soul.

It is worth noting at this point the influence a manager (or a company) has on a temporary resident (as visa holders are described). Antonio García Martínez described the US visa process as a period of "indentured servitude" in his excellent book *Chaos Monkeys*. This correlates with a consultation I had with an Irish born US immigration attorney operating out of Florida who described the process thusly - assuming the company will sponsor you for permanent residency and they do not garnish your wages to do so, the etiquette is that you give them five years of service in return. This seems highly counter-productive to the idea of a competitive labor market for jobs and capitalism in general (immigrants on visas cannot start their own company for example). As described in Chaos Monkeys, some of the harshest enforcers of this system are foreign immigrants themselves. Sadly, they often know best how to leverage the advantage they have over foreign workers. What is usually more alarming for temporary residents even more than the strict ties to the sponsoring employer, is the requirement to immediately depart the US if employment is terminated for any reason. Given many of us (including me) work in an "at-will" state, this is an alarming concept and makes it very difficult to feel truly grounded in the country in which you want to make your new home. With the best will in the world, you may not be able to prevent your employer having a round of layoffs, getting bought out, or going bankrupt. I understand anecdotally that USCIS are generally sympathetic to the idea that you might not be able to pack your bags and be out of the country before midnight on the day your employment is terminated but nevertheless those are the rules and may cause implication for future visa applications. For anyone wondering what to do in such a situation, the smart play is to take the cheapest flight out of the country immediately and return legally on a travel visa as soon as possible to arrange your affairs and contemplate your options.

I was told that applying for a work visa in the US would be a lot of work, but nothing really prepares you for the fact that applying for a work visa in the US is actually a lot of work. Ever committed genocide? Been a member of the Nazi party? Think Mike Pence has a tiny head? You may well be asked some of these questions. When I was being sponsored for a green card by ChannelAdvisor, I remember the surreal experience at the Application Support Center (ASC) where several staff members stood around me looking intensely into my eyes and spent a considerable amount of time debating whether my eyes were blue or blue/green.

Once my L1B visa was accepted (it was rejected initially because my manager at the time was hesitant to provide salary information for other employees on the team for the aforementioned reason), I had to be scheduled for an interview at the US embassy in Dublin along with my wife and two-year-old daughter. Spending several hours waiting around in a crowded room sitting on hard plastic chairs, trying to keep a two-year-old entertained was no easy task. No bags or electronics are admitted into the embassy for security purposes. Once the queuing was complete, the interview process was trivial. I was asked a few basic questions about my job title and job function, and we were done.

After I was promoted to a managerial role, I converted my visa to an L1A. There were a few reasons for doing this. Obtaining permanent residency is typically faster when holding an L1A rather than an L1B or a H1B. Obviously, the United States Citizen and Immigration Services (USCIS) understand the need for America to do what it can to address the crippling lack of middle managers in the country. Having an L1A would also lengthen the total amount of time I could spend as a temporary resident to seven rather than six years (renewing every year). Most states, of which North Carolina is most definitely one, require that legal presence documents be shown when renewing your license and the license will only be renewed until visa expiry. Anyone who has experienced the North Carolina DMV will fully understand my joy upon receiving a green card and being able to receive a ten year driving license instead of having to renew every single year!

I was once sent home to fetch my i-797c form, a form which explicitly states it may not be used to denote legal presence and is merely an indication that your application has been approved and the proper legal presence documentation will follow. I have no experience of living in other states besides North Carolina, but it always seemed highly dysfunctional to me that a state motor vehicles agency could be so distrustful of documentation provided by the federal agency responsible for ensuring immigrants were who they said they were. Meanwhile I was legally driving around the state on a foreign driving license provided by a country that decided at one point in the nineteen eighties that the backlog for "fully provisioned" (aka qualified) driving licenses was so great and the failure rate so high, that all provisional (i.e., non-qualified) drivers on the waiting list were given an amnesty and allowed to become fully provisioned drivers without even passing a driving test. Finally, because an L1A visa is the visa most typically used by C-level executives in large multinationals, it is looked upon more favorably by mortgage lenders than an L1B or a H1B visa. At this point, I had decided I wanted to live permanently in the US and was looking to buy a house to accommodate my wife and (now) two daughters.

At this point I will digress slightly to talk about the H1B visa system in particular. This is one of the most commonly used (and abused) temporary work visas in the US tech sector. The visa is not exclusive to tech workers, rather it is designed for what may be loosely referred to as "speciality occupations", with the intention of plugging critical skills gaps in the American labor market. This covers everything from nurses and dentists to fashion models, with most speciality occupations requiring an advanced degree (with the exemption of said fashion models). What may surprise readers is how low the annual quota is for H1B visas, currently standing at 65,000 a year (down from a peak of 195,000 in 2003). There are an additional 20,000 visas available for applicants with a master's degree, over and above the 65,000 quota for those with bachelor's degrees. The quota does not apply to those renewing a H1B visa within term limits (six years total with annual renewal required after the first three years), universities, government agencies and non-profit organizations. This is why, for example, in 2017 there were 365,682 H1B visas awarded (257,581 visa renewals and 108,101 net new H1B visas).

I have already mentioned the unfairness of being strictly tied to the sponsoring employer for both H1 and L1 visas. Consider how much more difficult this is for the H1B holder, who may be negotiating with an employer he or she has never worked for before to work in a country they are unfamiliar with. At least in the case of the L1 visa holder, it is an intra-company transfer and the person will have a better sense of company culture and established working conditions. Spouses and eligible immediate family members have no entitlement to work under a H1B visa, further complicating matters. An unusual quirk of the L1 system is that spouses (who are awarded what is known as an L2 visa) are eligible to apply for work authorization, with no restrictions placed on either the profession in which they can engage or the company for whom they may work. In the case where a married couple may both be considered to have a "speciality occupation", it would likely be more advantageous monetarily and certainly less restrictive for only one individual to obtain an L1 visa rather than both.

I touched on the widespread belief that fraud and abuse of H1B visas in particular is considered relatively common place. This ties in with a belief among many that the visa program can be counterproductive, or at least not solving the problem they were intended to solve. Certainly, in my years in IT I have heard many credible cases where US workers were told certain clients had a preference for H1B visa holders to be assigned to particular projects to keep costs lower. There are a number of facets to these arguments that merit considering. Of the top ten employers who obtained the most H1B visas between 2006 and 2015, all ten were either primarily in the business of providing IT services or ran a large IT services division (e.g. Deloitte). Six of the ten, including the top two (Infosys and Tata Consultancy Services) are headquartered in India, only four of the ten have their headquarters in the US, with only Accenture being headquartered in Dublin, Ireland.

A 2014 report by the Center for Investigative Reporting (CIR), found that many high-tech workers were indeed abused by so-called "jobs brokers" who lured primarily Indian workers to the US without actually having a job arranged for them (a violation of visa rules), housed them in substandard accommodation and encouraged them to send out exaggerated resumes in a bid to secure employment (and subsequently obtain a H1B visa). Companies such as Cisco, Verizon, eBay, Google and Apple, even branches of the federal government, were found to avail of these brokers (with no suggestion they were complicit or aware of the unethical practices being engaged in). Anecdotally, many people working in the IT industry have heard of the concept of a "ringer", where an experienced IT worker performs a technical phone screen or virtual call for a remote contract position, and the work is then performed by a considerably less experienced individual, often to the bafflement of the engineers who were involved in the original technical assessment (who may be afraid to speak out lest it call their own technical judgement into question).

In 2008, the number of IT workers prosecuted for H1B fraud (such as false statements, fraudulent documentation, etc.) was almost triple that of any other profession at the admittedly very low rate of 104 cases. The arguments that an influx of foreign workers can lead to wage depression, the loss of jobs for American workers (perhaps even humiliatingly being forced to train their replacements) are well known and definitely not without merit. While the visa rules state H1B visa holders must be paid the prevailing market rate, this is in practice very difficult to enforce and a Department of Homeland Security (DHS) report in 2014 found that software developers on H1B visas earn a mean salary of $75k, almost $25k below the mean for the profession overall. Numerous other studies support similar findings. If this points merely to less proficiency or greater inexperience on the part of H1B visa holders, it would still seem to go against the stated ethos of the program.

There is a rather more intriguing argument and one that is naturally in line with the idea that the visa program, no matter how well intentioned, is being used as a source of cheap labor. This argument entails that there is no strong evidence of a major skills shortage in IT. I am aware of one large international hotel chain who suffered a major outage during a Storage Area Network (SAN) upgrade that went badly. Their IT services were provided by a large global IT services provider. Upon reviewing the incident report in detail, it was noted that there were several deviations from the change request proposal and most crucially a failure to rollback at a critical juncture when it should have been obvious that the team needed to do so. The length of the outage was measured in days and the potential for near fatal data loss to the company was so high that the chain decided to no longer outsource their IT. They held a large jobs fair in the US Midwest and were able to recruit sufficient people with the skills they required at a cost not much different than what they had been paying the services provider who claimed there was an extreme shortage of IT skills in the US.

Famed economist Milton Friedman was noted by some as having described the H1B program as yet another government subsidy for corporations. Many critics point to the lack of empirical evidence for a serious skills shortage in the technology industry, and numerous studies, including ones carried out by the US Department of

Education, Office of Educational Research and Improvement have demonstrated that only 30% to 50% of newly qualified STEM (Science, Technology, Engineering and Math) graduates are able to find work in STEM related fields. The IEEE (Institute of Electrical and Electronics Engineers), an international STEM organization boasting over 400k members for whom I was a proud author of several papers during my academic years, announced in a 2012 study that they backed the 50% after immediate graduation number and stated that ten years after graduation as few as 8% of US graduates remained in the STEM field.

I am very sympathetic to these arguments, but I have come to believe (and perhaps conveniently) that dissatisfaction with STEM related careers is not due to the influx of foreign workers (although it may be a contributing factor) as I believe the numbers involved on the foreign worker scale are simply not large enough. There were approximately 8.6M people working in STEM related careers in 2015 according to the Bureau of Labor and Statistics, representing a whopping 6.2% of the US labor force. The vast majority of these roles are computer related. IT, as we know from the existence of this book, has its problems with imbalances when it comes to gender, race and sexual orientation. Many people avoid the field for this reason, and no doubt many leave for similar reasons. I would be surprised if many of these people do not make significant contributions in other areas of endeavor to the detriment of STEM and the tech industry in particular. Anyone who is Irish is very familiar with the concept of "brain drain" through decades of emigration of young people.

America has always been considered a primary emigration destination for Irish people due to overlap in language and culture and a prolonged shared history dating back hundreds of years. However, with cultural shifts and tides, young people emigrating from Ireland (of which there were 65,000 last year (1.5% of our population and this not in a time of strife!) appear to favor Canada, Australia and the UK. Certainly, to the extent that my immigration attorney was happy to note, there was "no queue" from Irish applicants and my green card application would be fast tracked. The process is organized in such a way that countries get a certain quota of green cards processed per year. Applicants from India or China may need to wait a decade or more due to demand. This was fantastic for me of course for very selfish reasons, but I am saddened so many young Irish people now see America as a less favorable destination to migrate to. I, of course, cannot speak with any authority on behalf of my fellow countrymen and women but certainly all of my friends, some of whom have remained in Ireland and many of whom have emigrated, retain a fondness for America.

One question that arises with surprising regularity when discussing immigration with Americans, is a distinct confusion between permanent residency (known as a "green card") which entitles the holder to live permanently in the United States, and citizenship. Permanent residency is the no-brainer for the emigrant. With very few exceptions, you can now work in almost any position and enjoy a life almost no different from a naturalized citizen. Deciding to become a citizen involves some element of considerable personal preference in my opinion. Not all countries support the concept of "dual" citizenship, so becoming a citizen of the US may require renouncing citizenship of your country of birth. This is rare in western countries and countries that are allies of the US, but it can be a factor. Some people have personal reservations about the concept of dual-citizenship, particularly when it comes to pledging an oath of allegiance to another country. This can be an issue for some Irish people in Commonwealth countries like Canada, where the oath of allegiance must still be pledged to the Queen of England. I am firmly in the "if you don't like the rules …" camp, but I can at least have some understanding of why some people might have some difficulty with this. Another factor almost exclusively peculiar to America is the concept of global taxation. If you are an American citizen, you are subject to income tax, no matter where in the world you reside and where you derive your income. It should be noted that this global taxation policy also applies to green card holders but is usually less of an issue, as a condition of maintaining a green card involves employment and residency in the US. For most people reading this book, who likely derive the bulk of their income from labor, working in another country that has a tax treaty with the US, the main impact is going to be simply the additional hassle of filing a tax return in your country of residency and in the US. However, it is certainly a point of consideration, and it is not for no reason that USCIS has details on how to renounce your citizenship for tax purposes on the front page of its website.

Having given it a great deal of consideration, I for one intend to try and naturalize as an American citizen when I am eligible. The British-born and naturalized (in 2007), sadly deceased author Christopher Hitchens gives a great account of his reasons for becoming an American citizen in Hitch-22. I share the same opinions with the great man. I can only somewhat hope forlornly that the answers to the questions he described in the citizenship test are nowhere near as emphatically taught in public school education. From a citizenship test perspective, it is entirely understandable to have to answer that the Proclamation of Emancipation *actually* freed the slaves, in the same way some Irish people might insist the birth of the Irish republic occurred after the 1916 rebellion. I, of course, completely understand the need for a lack of nuance in something like a citizenship test. In my experience, Americans take very seriously their politics and the identity of their politicians, and perhaps internalize it too much. I will never forget being told by an American during the second term of George Bush Jr. that she was so ashamed to be American, she liked to be called a Manhattanite. Debates about Bush Jr's presidency aside, no country should define themselves by the quality of the people they occasionally elect, but perhaps it is the rest of the world that should be grateful that Americans truly do so.

> *"Patriotism is supporting your country all the time,*
> *and your government when it deserves it."*

> **Mark Twain, The Czar's Soliloquy (abridged)**

CHAPTER 12

The Color of I.T.

By: Leighton and Kerrine Nelson

Introduction

Working in tech can present its own set of challenges. From the increasingly complex and evolving technology to balancing work and family. However, being an immigrant black couple in tech can present some interesting experiences - both negative and positive. In this chapter, we will share our individual and collective journey and experiences. This will hopefully help others in a similar position to navigate the world of tech and life in general.

Leighton's Career Development

As someone who considers himself a lifelong learner, I've always strived to learn more about all aspects of the technology and the technical environment in which I work. That has always been how I approached things. Call it aptitude or willingness to learn. I've never limited myself to what can be achieved as a minority or "person of color."

My very first job in tech was a Systems/Database/Network Administrator for a mutual funds company in Jamaica. You know, the type of job where you are the IT department. Handling everything from fixing computers to the CEO's complaints about his email not working. Perhaps this is where that instinct of learning everything stemmed from.

Working in the US

I started as a "consultant" for a company that does "head hunting" from countries such as India, Jamaica, and other Caribbean nations. You're actually brought in with the promise of getting a job, working for a well-established company and making enough money to support your family back home. At least, that's the theory.

After a couple of weeks doing interviews along the east coast, I was subcontracted to represent another consulting firm to work on a project at a corrections facility in New Jersey. Having never been to one before, I didn't know what to expect. Who knew they had databases in prison?

It turns out that one of the systems administrators that was working at the facility was a gentleman of color. He looked a bit puzzled at first when I told him that I was there to work on their database project. While he was their main "IT guy", he wasn't very skilled in databases. He told me how happy and impressed he was by having someone like me (I assumed he meant black) to have the skills and expertise that I did. Of course, I still had to prove that I knew what I was doing. Or who knows, I could've spent much longer than I had to there.

My second project in the US landed me in my current city, St. Louis. I was asked to lead the database team, where I was the second person of color on my team. Due to some construction in the workplace, we were asked to share cubicles. I thought cubicles were very personal spaces. Spaces where you could kick your shoes off and leave papers strewn all over your desk without caring what others think. Anyway, I was asked to share cubicles with the other person of color. I've never really thought about it before. But I wonder if that was done intentionally, or if there was any reasoning behind it. Hey, let's put the two black guys in the same cube. I'm sure they'll get along.

Fortunately, we did get along. But not because we were both black. He was a great guy, a seasoned DBA and open to suggestions and ideas.

Community Involvement

One of the most significant contributions to my career has been the involvement in the tech community, primarily the Oracle community. Early on in my career, I found that the tech community in particular offered the benefit of collaboration, whether through blogs, whitepapers, meetups and community events, or even Twitter. I recall attending an Oracle user group meeting in Jamaica, with the now defunct Eastern Caribbean Oracle Users group. While this was a small regional group comprised mostly of Oracle database administrators, I began to realize the potential that such a group could have on both a professional and personal level.

In fact, my very first blog post, published in 2007, was a result of collaboration and communication between me and several others in the Oracle community. The problem was that we encountered numerous issues while trying to build out an Oracle

RAC cluster. So I decided to try and build a sandbox environment on VMware. Yes, you heard me, kids - Oracle RAC 10g on VMware ESX 3! I've been doing virtualized Oracle way before it was "cool" or practical for that matter.

Since arriving in the US several years ago, I started getting involved in a number of Oracle community events. Due to my interest in databases and Oracle RAC, I got involved with the Independent Oracle Users Group (IOUG) Oracle RAC SIG. After a couple years, I held the post of IOUG Liaison and Website officer for the SIG. This led me to broaden my professional network. And not long after, I was invited to be an Oracle ACE. Oracle ACEs are usually nominated by peers in the community, to recognize one's contribution to the Oracle community. Fortunately for me, I met some lovely people, including my colleague Tim Gorman and wife Kellyn Pot'vin-Gorman. Kellyn later invited me to contribute to a book, Oracle Enterprise Cloud Control 12c, along with her and several other brilliant and renowned individuals in the Oracle community. Several years later both Tim, Kellyn, and I became co-workers, which was entirely not planned.

I was fortunate enough to work for leaders who encouraged me and provided me with the time and finances to participate in community events, including Oracle OpenWorld and IOUG Collaborate. On a personal level, my wife would always encourage me to pursue my ambitions, even if it meant leaving her alone at home for days with four boys to look after. I think that was a much more difficult job than any job that I've done. And now that I spend most of my time at home with the kids, I can understand how tough that was for her.

While attending or speaking at these community events, it was quite noticeable to me that there very were few people of color attending and especially few speaking at these events. The ones I've been lucky enough to meet are as brilliant and intelligent as any others. At one Oracle OpenWorld event that I attended, I met a few attendees from Ghana. They expressed to me how elated and excited they were to see someone of color that was speaking at these events. We talked, and I told them about my career in IT and how I got to where I was. Coming from a country that is 92% black in population to one that is slightly less than 13% black does take some getting used to. I get it.

Work/Life Balance

This is where things get very complicated. Trying to excel in your career can undoubtedly affect the quality of life where the family is concerned. Having a wife and three kids at the time indeed demanded a lot of quality time, energy, and focus. This is where having a spouse that is not just understanding, but supportive of your career is so vital.

I can't talk enough about how fortunate I've been to have a wife who put up with me staying up countless nights while trying to figure out solutions or reading blog posts on how Oracle RAC really works and why it even exists in the first place.

She would listen to me ramble on about high availability and why the developers coded their applications poorly, without having a clue what I was talking about (or so I thought). I'd like to believe that this is what sparked her interest in tech, but she may differ on that.

Fast forward to seven years later. Kerrine has transitioned to tech, and I've also done some transitioning, from a Database Administrator to a technical manager role.

Kerrine's Transition to Tech

Before moving to the US, I honed my skills and expertise in the hospitality industry in hotel, restaurant and event management. However, after playing the role of a stay-at-home mom for years, I started researching some of the things that would keep my husband up at nights in an attempt to help. Not long after, I was having conversations with him about how databases should work from an end user standpoint and he would explain things from his technical lens. I started connecting the dots and became hungry for more knowledge about how systems should work and the different ways that they could be impacted.

While in one of my 'digging for more' rabbit holes, I stumbled upon MIT's Scratch website for beginners. It was easy, fun and my goodness, it was logical! I was exposed for the first time to conditional statements and loops. Of course, at the time, I was just fascinated by the object doing something based on an action block that I dragged on the canvas. I'll be the first to admit that this was my introduction to coding. There was a certain sense of fulfillment that I was learning and understanding something that was very foreign to me. So I pursued it formally.

Back to School for This Adult Newbie

Going back to school as an adult, wife, and mom of four boys meant that these roles and the corresponding responsibilities did not stop. I had to quickly figure out how I would make it work while continuing to support Leighton in his career. If that wasn't challenging enough, I was entering an academic program that I was entirely new to. But I showed up every day and became the master of observing the knowledge and skill levels of the students and professors to start building my network. It was pretty straightforward. Most of the students were relatively new to the technical concepts that were being taught, and most of the professors taught concepts based on how they are applied in the 'real world.' I was fortunate to have great professors that I could be very open with about my 'newness' and my desire to excel in the technical space. I also worked very hard learning the requisite skills and application of those skills to solve business problems, which helped me gain tremendous support from my fellow students and professors alike.

The sky was the limit, and I had charted my path to academic excellence with the hope that it would propel me into a successful career. After attending several networking events at my school, I noticed a pattern in the student population that showed up as well as the speakers who would share at these events.

It was the same students - mostly white students, even though the school had a relatively diverse population. It was also mostly male students. All the speakers were white males.

I struggled with being the odd one out at these events initially. I wondered how many females were in the program and if they were getting the same event notifications that I received. I took note and sought out the organizers for the events that were happening on campus. I also signed up to become an officer for the Programming Club and used the platform to begin marketing events to everyone, and especially to females and people of color. Surprisingly, more people started showing up. More diversity was showing up, and for me, that was a win.

It was during one of these events that I met one of my mentors, and yes, he was a middle-to-upper-age white man. I approached him, introduced myself, and started a conversation about what kind of gaps he was seeing in his company concerning skills and business value. He was very interested in sharing, and to my surprise he went straight to the 'D' word. Yes, of all the responses that he could have given, he called out "lack of diversity," specifically about female representation in the tech landscape. After our hour-long conversation, he requested my resume and a follow-up conversation. I walked away with the feeling that I could make an impact to help fill the diversity gap and help other women and people of color do the same.

The Start of a New Career

Mike became one of my mentors as well as one of my most prominent advocates. After sending him my resume, I got a call from his company to do an interview for a summer internship role in the IT division. I got the role, and at the end of the internship, I got to stay on part-time while I finished my academic program.

Having Mike as a mentor opened up many other opportunities for me. I gained additional mentors and advocates, who helped to fast track my success over a short period. These people defended me, included me for consideration for essential projects, shared their experiences with me, and even acted as my sounding board for my wild ideas in preparation for important presentations. For the most part, it is fair to say that I was surrounded by great people.

However, as I continued to grow, I was coming into contact with the few who would do try to stifle my growth and success. I would often read blogs and articles describing some of these challenges but didn't think that I would experience it so soon. After all, I had just gotten started, and the challengers were complacent in their roles at this company for many years.

Some of the challenges that I began dealing with every day included things like sharing an idea with a leader and that person running off with it and representing it as their own, or presenting an idea in a meeting only to be ignored while the guy that I hardly know sitting next to me echoes the same exact idea and the earth stops turning to acknowledge his brilliance. It was a lesson I had to learn from quickly if I was going to keep adding value in a space that was dominated by males who openly asked, "What are you doing in Infrastructure anyway?" I had to start socializing my ideas at every level before presenting it formally.

After talking to a couple of my female colleagues in the tech space, I realized that we all face similar challenges. Darla, my co-worker, shared her experience with me about an interaction between her team and a client. She said "I remember about two weeks into the project I was in a conference room with two male coworkers. Another male from the client team came into the conference room, pointed at the two males in the room, and said: "I have a question for you two." It was a technical question that I knew the answer to so I started to reply. The male from the client team almost immediately interrupted me and said, "That's not what I'm asking." He proceeded to ask the exact same question, but now focusing his attention on only one of my coworkers. My coworker replied with the same answer that I was attempting to give. The client then said, "That makes perfect sense. Thank you!", and left the room." While Darla, like me, has learned to overcome many of these challenges, each day presents a unique twist, and we have to figure out how to move forward.

My Best Friend and Coach

Thankfully, at the end of the day, I come home to my best friend, who completely understands the challenges that I encounter and must overcome. He has walked the path for a long time and is usually able to help me determine the best course of action. This is definitely one of the advantages of being a couple of color in tech. We understand the layering challenges that come with being of color, and for me, being a woman and of color, trying to succeed in a male-dominated industry.

We get to pass on our experiences and lessons learned as first-hand guidance to our four boys, who aspire to become leaders like us. Unfortunately, we are not able to protect them from the many challenges that they will face, but at least they'll know that we can relate and provide our best advice.

I am grateful for my husband's support throughout this journey. He was one of the key reasons why I transitioned to tech and continue to excel in every area. We make one very high performing team, and I look forward to writing many more success stories with him.

About the Authors

Melody Zacharias – MVP: Data Platform

Melody wears so many hats it is a wonder how she finds time for it all. In addition to finding a little quiet time for her morning coffee, she is an insightful mentor, a sought-after speaker for technology events, a Microsoft MVP, a PASS chapter leader for the Southern Interior of British Columbia, the Regional Mentor for PASS Canada, a PASS Outstanding Volunteer a very successful entrepreneur, and a highly talented IT professional with an international reputation for completing both large and small projects on time.   She is able to do all of these things because she loves what she does. She brings enthusiasm to all that she does, and it shows. You can follow her infrequent Twitter posts at: @SQLMelody. You can follow her blog at: SQLMelody.com

You can learn more about the IT services she provides at ClearsightSolutions.ca

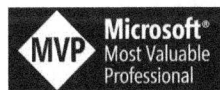

Kellyn Pot'vin-Gorman

Kellyn Pot'Vin-Gorman is a Technical Solutions Professional in Power BI and AI for Microsoft. She is an Idera **ACE** alumnus in the Microsoft community and an Oracle ACE Director alumnus, having joined the ranks of alumni after joining each company to immerse myself in their technology. She is proud to be a member and one of only six women who are part of the **Oak Table Network**. Kellyn has a long history focused on environment optimization tuning, automation and designing robust environments for longevity. She has extensive experience in multi-terabyte Very Large Database, (VLDB) management of OLAP/DSS systems. She presents internationally at Microsoft, Oracle, DevOps and Big Data conferences and her blog, dbakevlar.com is known for it's insight and technical content. She and her husband recently sent off their youngest child of five and with this, sold their home and are now embracing the full-time RV life, blogged on danceswithwinnebagos.com.

Rie Irish – MVP: Data Platform

Rie Irish is a single Mom raising her beautiful, strong-willed daughter in North Georgia. She is currently the Director of Database Management for a payment security firm in Atlanta. Over the last 20 years, she has been a SQL Server DBA in many industries including the non-profit sector, big pharma, federal contracting, eDiscovery and payment processing. She is very involved with the Atlanta MDF User Group, helps plan SQL Saturday Atlanta and is co-leader of the PASS Women in Technology Virtual Group. She is a frequent speaker at SQL Saturdays, tech events and women's conferences. She is a Microsoft MVP in the Data Platform , an Idera Ace and a PASS Outstanding Volunteer.

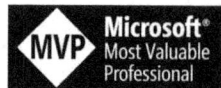

Randolph West – MVP: Data Platform

Randolph West was issued to startled parents in the mid-1970s along with a large bottle of scotch, and has been surprising audiences all over the world ever since. An actor, singer, and filmmaker, Randolph has worked on stage and screen and sung at Carnegie Hall. TV and film credits include Fargo S3: *Aporia* (2017, dir. Keith Gordon); *Night of the Shadow People* (2017, dir. Blaise Kolodychuk); *Joy to the World* (2016, dir. Morgan Ermter); *The Winner* (2015, dir. Jury Rodionov). Theatre credits include *Run for your Wife* (2016); *Move Over, Mrs. Markham* (2014); *Hands Across the Sea* (2011); *See How They Run* (2010). Choir credits include *Unison Festival* (2018, 2014); *GALA Choruses* (2016); *Distinguished Concerts International* (2012). Randolph moonlights as an IT consultant and speaker, co-authored *SQL Server 2017 Administration Inside Out* (2018, Microsoft Press) and was recognized as a Microsoft MVP in 2017. For more information, contact Jay Fox at Ten48, Inc. or read Randolph's blog at bornsql.ca/blog.

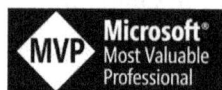

Sage Franch

Sage Franch is a technologist and writer based in Toronto, Canada. Known as "the Trendy Techie" for her blog of the same name, Sage is also a public speaker and mentor to young technologists around the world. At the time of her contribution to this book, Sage was a Technical Evangelist at Microsoft, where she worked with emerging cloud technologies including cognitive computing, mixed reality, and blockchain as a service. Prior to this, she was a technical educator on Microsoft's global online learning team. In January 2018, Sage left Microsoft to co-found *Crescendo - Inclusive Workplaces*, where she now builds AI-powered training tools for diversity and inclusion.

Lori Lalonde

Lori Lalonde has been developing software for over 20 years and is still going strong. She is a Tech Evangelist, an Apress author, blogger, community leader, and international conference speaker. Although her career began in 1997, her love of technology dates back to her early childhood. Lori spent countless hours teaching herself how to program in BASIC on a Commodore 64 and playing video games on an Atari 2600. She was a gamer girl before there was a name for it. In her spare time, Lori enjoys being involved in her community, serving as the lead organizer for Canada's Technology Triangle .NET User Group, mentoring up-and-coming software developers, and participating in local Women in Technology groups.

You can find her on Twitter at @loriblalonde.

Susan Ibach

Susan is a technical evangelist for Microsoft working with developers. Specifically I help faculty and students at universities keep up with and adopt current Microsoft technologies.

I have always enjoyed sharing technical knowledge with others. Before I joined Microsoft, I spent over 10 years working as a Trainer. I delivered courses, presented at conferences, and wrote course content.

I always insisted I wanted to be the instructor who knew more than what you saw on the slide. My time at Andersen Consulting/Accenture and my work supporting both Learnix and CTE Solutions IT systems behind the scenes allowed me to keep my knowledge relevant and practical.

Elizabeth Hosang

Elizabeth Hosang is a Senior Software Engineer by day, currently working for CAE Canada where she has been the Project Engineer on projects both large and small. She has done Object Oriented design, development, and testing her entire career. Her areas of expertise include data correlation and fusion (including some SQL/database design work), multi-tiered architectures, Command and Control protocols, and process improvement. For the last three years, she has been involved in the Professional Women's Network at CAE, supporting skills development.

By night, she likes to plan murders and mayhem. Her short fiction in the mystery, science fiction and fantasy genres has been published in over a dozen anthologies. Her short story, "Where There's a Will", in the collection *The Whole She-Bang 3*, was a finalist for the 2017 Arthur Ellis award for Excellence in Canadian Crime Writing.

Depending on your area of interest, you can contact her at Elizabeth.Hosang@cae. com, or find her list of fiction on her Facebook Author's Page, facebook.com\eahosang.

Angela Tidwell

Angela Tidwell is a fun-loving lady whose story telling is inspired by a long line of interesting family characters. She is a loving wife to a wonderful, supportive man and a proud, doting mom to a handsome, fun, strong-willed, fearless boy. Angela loves telling stories and helping people find the beauty in every day. Her favorite days are rainy ones and her drink of choice is hot coffee. As a graduate with a degree in theater, she has a unique outlook on life and is not the one you will find standing in a corner waiting for introductions.

Angela serves as the Marketing DBA for Procure SQL, LLC with a specialty for database performance monitoring and tuning. She's worked for clients with various architectures and volume, presenting various types of issues to be resolved in order to keep their business thriving. When she's not helping her clients resolve their biggest problems, Angela supports SQL Saturdays across the country and blogs about her experience in order to help other data professionals grow. Armed with a zest for life and quick wit; her experiences and unique views on the world provide the backdrop for a plethora of great stories. She blogs at TidwellTidbits.com and tweets @AngelaTidwell

Tracy Boggiano

Tracy is a Database Superhero. She has spent over 20 years in IT and has used SQL Server since 1999. She is also the owner of Database Superheroes LLC, a company that specializes in all aspects of administration and deals heavily with performance tuning, high availability and disaster recovery. Tracy is also a co-organizer of a Special Interest Group (SIG) dedicated to advanced DBA topics in our local user group TriPass in Raleigh, NC. In addition, she is also the founder of WeSpeakLinux.com. Before she worked full-time as a DBA, she was formally a developer and network administrator. She also tinkered with databases in middle/high school to keep her sports card collection organized. She is a member of SpeakingMentors.com which helps get others involved in presenting. She has presented at over 30 SQLSaturdays, various virtual and local groups, and PASS Summit 2017. She has been awarded the PASS Outstanding Volunteer Award for work in getting SQL on Linux content available via the virtual means to the SQL Community.

Tracy also volunteers through the NC Guardian ad Litem program for over 15 years advocating for abused and neglected foster children in court. This is her life's passion computers and her favorite job. More information about this program in North Carolina can be found at volunteerforgal.org or the national organization CASA at casaforchildren.org

Brian Carrig

Brian Carrig is a Microsoft Certified Master of SQL Server and is currently working as a Site Reliability Engineering (SRE) Manager on the DevOps team at Citrix ShareFile. In a previous life, Brian spent some time as an academic and holds a Ph.D. in Computer Science. He is a native of Dublin, Ireland but now lives with his wife and two daughters in Cary, North Carolina. If he is not talking about, thinking about or working with technology you will usually find him watching Chelsea FC.

Leighton Nelson

Leighton Nelson is an Education Technology Manager at Delphix, providing EdTech solutions to customers for Delphix Virtualization and Masking products. He is a lifelong learner and knowledge enthusiast, data practitioner and educator with a focus on data platforms and databases. Leighton shares his knowledge through blogs, presentations at conferences and lectures on topics ranging from big data and database administration to programming. He is also a co-author on Expert Oracle Enterprise Manager 12c published by Apress.

Leighton has over a decade of experience working in various data roles including database administrator, developer, and consultant with Oracle, MS SQL Server, and MySQL among others.

He holds a Bachelor of Science degree in Computer Science, Oracle 11g RAC Expert, Oracle Database 12c and VMware VCA-DCV certifications as well as Oracle ACE recognition.

Leighton hails from the island of Jamaica and is happily married to Kerrine Nelson. They live in Missouri with their four sons – CJ, Brandon, Justin, and Matthew.

Kerrine Nelson

Kerrine Nelson is a consultant at Slalom Consulting, providing data and delivery leadership solutions to its customers. She currently leads the inclusion, diversity and equity initiatives at Slalom, St. Louis and is passionate about all things women in tech.

Kerrine has over a decade of experience in delivery leadership and most recently entered the data scene where she uses various data tools and techniques or develop data strategies to solve business problems or drive value.

Kerrine holds a Bachelor of Science degree in Information Systems and is currently pursuing her Masters Degrees in Data Science and Business Administration. She is a certified Project Manager and Scrum Master.

Kerrine is from Jamaica and is happily married to Leighton Nelson. They live in Missouri with their four sons – CJ, Brandon, Justin, and Matthew.

Sponsor

IDERA

IDERA understands that IT doesn't run on the network – it runs on the data and databases that power your business. That's why we design our products with the database as the nucleus of your IT universe. Our database lifecycle management solutions allow database and IT professionals to design, monitor and manage data systems with complete confidence, whether in the cloud or on-premises. We offer a diverse portfolio of free tools and educational resources to help you do more with less while giving you the knowledge to deliver even more than you did yesterday. Whatever your need, IDERA has a solution.

The End

I hope you enjoyed this book and learned something new. If you have any comments or would like to be considered as an author for Book 3 in the series, please contact me at SQLMelody@gmail.com. The theme of book 3 has not been chosen yet, so don't disqualify yourself.

If you enjoy tech, please join me on my blog at SQLMelody.com. You can also follow my infrequent tweets at #SQLMelody.

Thank you for your support!

www.ingramcontent.com/pod-product-compliance
Lightning Source LLC
Chambersburg PA
CBHW051212200326
41519CB00025B/7090